HUNTING WHITEY

Also by the Authors

CASEY SHERMAN

The Finest Hours (coauthored by Michael J. Tougias)

Above & Beyond (coauthored by Michael J. Tougias)

12: The Inside Story of Tom Brady's Fight for Redemption (coauthored by Dave Wedge)

The Ice Bucket Challenge (coauthored by Dave Wedge)

Boston Strong (coauthored by Dave Wedge)

Animal: The Bloody Rise and Fall of the Mob's Most Feared Assassin

Bad Blood: Freedom and Death in the White Mountains

Black Dragon

Black Irish

A Rose for Mary: The Hunt for the Real Boston Strangler

DAVE WEDGE

12: The Inside Story of Tom Brady's Fight for Redemption (coauthored by Casey Sherman)

The Ice Bucket Challenge (coauthored by Casey Sherman)

Boston Strong (coauthored by Casey Sherman)

HUNTING WHITEY

THE INSIDE STORY

OF THE **CAPTURE & KILLING** OF

AMERICA'S MOST WANTED

CRIME BOSS

CASEY SHERMAN AND **DAVE WEDGE**

WILLIAM MORROW

An Imprint of HarperCollins Publishers

HarperCollins books may be purchased for educational, business, or sales promotional use. For information, please email the Special Markets Department at SPsales@harper collins.com.

FIRST EDITION

Library of Congress Cataloging-in-Publication Data has been applied for.

ISBN 978-0-06-297254-5

20 21 22 23 24   DIX/LSC   10 9 8 7 6 5 4 3 2 1

For my darling Kristin, thank you for embarking on life's journey with me, for Bella and Mia, and in memory of my beloved stepfather, Kenneth Dodd, a trusted editor of my work and a kind and gentle soul.
—Casey Sherman

For Jessica, thank you for the love, support, and daily conversations about writing, news, and life that inspire me to do what I do. And to my amazing children, Danielle and Jackson, you guys are everything to me and I love you both.
—Dave Wedge

Perseverance, secret of all triumphs.

—Victor Hugo

James J. "Whitey" Bulger's Hit List

March & April 1973—Michael Milano, Al Plummer, William O'Brien, James Leary, and Joseph Notorangeli

December 1973—James O'Toole

February 1974—Al Notorangeli

October 1974—James Sousa

November 1974—Paul McGonagle

June 1975—Edward Connors

November 1975—Tommy King, Francis "Buddy" Leonard

December 1976—Roger Wheeler

December 1976—Richard Castucci

Late 1981—Debra Davis

May 1982—Brian Halloran, Michael Donahue

August 1982—John B. Callahan

July 1983—Arthur "Bucky" Barrett

November 1984—John McIntyre

Early 1985—Deborah Hussey

HUNTING WHITEY

Prologue

SANTA MONICA, CALIFORNIA, 2010

It's dusk in Santa Monica and a gentle breeze blows off the Pacific Ocean near the famed Santa Monica Pier. One hundred and thirty feet above the platform, a giant Ferris wheel turns slowly while nearby a steel roller coaster rumbles along at thirty-five miles per hour to the delight of screaming passengers.

On the beach nearby, Whitey Bulger is strolling hand in hand with his longtime girlfriend Catherine Greig just beyond Pacific Park. Both are dressed in white and are illuminated against the pinkish hue of the setting sun. They look like any other retired couple enjoying a warm evening outside. They also look vulnerable.

Whitey savors these nightly walks, as they give him a sense of freedom that he lacks while being cooped up most days inside their two-bedroom apartment at the Princess Eugenia less than a mile away. But Bulger senses that something is wrong—that they are being followed. He notices a vagrant walking a few paces behind them, studying their every move.

Is it an FBI agent working undercover? Bulger thinks to himself. *Is it finally the end of the line?* The living on edge, always prepared for someone to recognize him, these were realities that Bulger had grown comfortable living with ever since he fled Boston just before Christmas in 1994. His vigilance was constant—it was how he'd survived on the run for so long—it didn't matter whether he was sleeping in his Santa Monica apartment or strolling on the beach.

After a few more steps, a homeless man senses an opportunity and rushes the couple.

But instead of pulling out a badge, he shows them a knife.

"Give me your fucking money, old man," the robber shouts while holding up the long, steel blade.

Bulger smiles, rubs the white whiskers of his neatly trimmed beard, and lifts his arm slowly. He's holding a gun close to his body.

"Kid, never bring a knife to a gunfight," Whitey snarls.

Bulger, the avid movie buff, has no doubt lifted the line from the Brian De Palma film *The Untouchables* about the most legendary mobster of all—Al Capone.

The threat works.

The vagrant puts his blade away and disappears into the night.

And Whitey continues on his way.

PART I

THE HUNT

1

NOREEN GLEASON CARRIED A CARDBOARD box bulging with personal and professional mementos up the elevator and into the Boston office of the FBI. It was February 3, 2008, her first day on the job as assistant special agent in charge of the criminal division (ASAC), and as she stepped off the lift, she walked past a bullpen of agents who were glued to their computer screens or reviewing stacks of files dedicated to the one case that had haunted the office and the city for decades. The agents kept their heads down, going about their work without passion or energy. The New England Patriots had just lost the Super Bowl the night before to the New York Giants, ending their bid for a perfect season. There was reason to be glum. But the feeling here was different.

Gleason studied their mannerisms and recognized the problem immediately.

These agents look haggard and beat down, she said to herself.

Gleason placed the box on her desk, sat down, and took a deep breath. Gazing around her office, she realized how far she'd come from her strict, military-style upbringing in her sleepy hometown of Hawthorne, New Jersey, and the seven long years she'd toiled as a trooper in the state police there.

Her desk phone rang.

"Mr. Bamford will see you now," the secretary informed her.

Mr. Bamford was Gleason's new boss, Warren T. Bamford, the special agent in charge (SAC) of the Boston field office. Gleason walked confidently into Bamford's office, where he stood by the window with arms folded, staring out at Government Center and City Hall. He didn't waste time.

"I have one job for you, Agent Gleason," he said. "My top priority is capturing James Bulger and bringing him to justice."

Gleason didn't respond right away. She needed to process the statement for a moment. By this point, James "Whitey" Bulger had been on the run from the FBI for more than thirteen years. In that time, he'd become something of a ghost story, a larger-than-life criminal who'd been written about in books and mythologized on the big screen, whose exploits had become crazier than fiction. His ability to evade capture had grown his legacy into infamy—instead of being a mob murderer and henchman, he'd become a folk hero.

Bamford's decree was nothing new. Every SAC of the Boston field office had made similar pledges before. His predecessor, Kenneth Kaiser, had pumped out his chest after taking the job in 2003 and promised that he'd do everything in his power to arrest the fugitive crime boss on his watch.

"I will do whatever it takes to get this guy," Kaiser told reporters then. "I don't care who catches him; I just want it over and done with. My goal is to have him caught and move on."

That didn't happen.

But Bamford was a quiet leader, and more methodical than the bombastic Kaiser. As a kid, Bamford watched the Efram Zimbalist Jr. television drama *The FBI*, and knew that's what he wanted to be when he grew up. A native of Lowell, Massachusetts, and a former US Marine, Bamford had served on the FBI's Hostage Rescue Team and was sent as a sniper to the deadly standoff at Ruby Ridge and the siege at David Koresh's Branch Davidian compound in Waco, Texas. Tellingly, Bamford did not fire a single shot at either tragic event.

Bamford understood that cooperation between all the agencies—the FBI, state police, US Marshals, and US Attorney's office—was imperative in ending the now thirteen-year-old manhunt for America's most wanted mob boss. Bamford also needed someone who was smart and action oriented to lead the effort. He believed that he'd found the perfect candidate in Noreen Gleason.

"You were a state trooper in New Jersey and I think you'll have a good rapport with our counterparts. They'll respect you. We need everyone rowing in the same direction if we're going to pull this off."

"If catching Bulger is the priority of the office, that's what I'm gonna do," she told her boss.

Like Bamford, Gleason had always dreamed of a career in law enforcement. She entered the New Jersey State Police Academy in 1985 and served as a road trooper for the next seven years, eventually becoming an instructor teaching state police cadets defensive tactics, physical training, and water safety.

But Gleason wasn't satisfied with her career working for the New Jersey State Police.

"I felt it wasn't a truly professional organization and it didn't respect women," Gleason says. "The FBI offered me more."

She entered the FBI Academy at Quantico in 1991 and was schooled in an advanced level of academics, firearms, and physical training. She took these skills to New York City, where she worked as a field agent investigating Dominican and Jamaican gangs. Gleason was driving into Manhattan to rendezvous with her squad for an undercover drug buy when the Twin Towers came down on 9/11. She was immediately dispatched into the toxic smoke and debris at Ground Zero to join the bucket brigade on top of the smoldering pile of twisted metal and ash.

Like everyone in New York that fateful day, the attacks affected Gleason personally. She immediately moved from monitoring drug dealers to counterterrorism, where she interviewed and vetted terror suspects for imprisonment and deportation.

After a year on that job, Gleason moved to FBI headquarters in

Washington, DC, for leadership training. She has always felt that she had the organizational and interpersonal skills to be a good boss.

She eventually returned to Manhattan, where she supervised eleven agents and six New York City police officers on the Metro Gang Task Force, a unit whose mission it was to penetrate murderous organizations like the Crips, Bloods, Latin Kings, and the ultraviolent MS-13, an international gang originating in El Salvador and known to dispatch death squads to eradicate perceived enemies.

Gleason was not only committed to putting street killers behind bars, she also felt the added responsibility of protecting innocent people from getting caught up in gang life.

"It's the underbelly of America. It's the most impoverished segment of society," she says. "I always felt very comfortable in that environment helping people live a better life there."

One person she could not protect was a valuable female informant who was executed in cold blood by a gang member in front of her two children.

"It bothers me to this day, the sheer brutality of it all. To murder a woman purposely with her two kids watching. I feel a responsibility for what happened to her to this day."

When she saw a posting for the Boston office, she jumped at the chance despite its sullied reputation following revelations that a former agent, John Connolly, had conspired to help Bulger.

"John Connolly had left a terrible black mark on the entire Bureau," she says. "It bothered me personally about what he did with Whitey Bulger."

Indeed, Gleason was not alone in feeling this way—many others shared her disgust about the mark Connolly had left on the Bureau. The fallout at the Boston office after details of Connolly's corruption spread had been extreme—even now all these years later in 2008, the office still had not recovered its reputation.

What Connolly had done during his career as an FBI agent was to protect Whitey Bulger at all costs while working with the gangster to eliminate his rivals. After Bulger disappeared in late 1994, no one believed that the Bureau was serious in its effort to bring him to justice. When Gleason moved to the seaside town of Scituate, Massachusetts, and told new friends that she was an FBI agent, they immediately presumed she was corrupt.

"Are you like John Connolly?" one neighbor asked her.

"They were so mistrusting of the FBI," Gleason recalls today. "I'd never experienced that before in New York City or DC. People were respectful of the work we do, but not in Massachusetts."

Gleason wasn't alone. As she stared into the eyes of each agent now working on the Bulger case, she saw men and women who were going through the motions and had all but given up the ghost.

"They were so ingrained in that Boston downtrodden, woe-is-me head space that I knew we had to shake things up," she said.

Gleason brought the team in for a huddle and gave them the cold reality.

"You guys simply aren't getting it done," she told them. "We're gonna bring in some fresh eyes and see what we can do."

In Gleason's mind, it was time to bring in the heavy hitters.

She was the newest agent working in the Boston FBI office and she was already the least popular. Agents who had been working the Bulger case for months and years were both stunned and offended by her decision to shake things up and bring in so-called ringers from the outside, but she forged ahead, undaunted.

"What have you guys been doing?" she asked the team.

Gleason already knew the case agents had aggressively investigated a potential sighting of Bulger and Catherine Greig in Sicily in the spring of 2007. The Bureau had secured a photo and video of an elderly couple fitting their description walking the cobblestoned streets of Taormina, a hilltop village near Mount Etna.

The man in question looked similar to Whitey, with snowflake-white hair and sunglasses, and the woman appeared to be roughly Greig's age. But the FBI's facial recognition analysis on both was inconclusive. The images were later used in an episode of Germany's equivalent of *America's Most Wanted*. A German couple immediately recognized themselves on TV from their vacation to Italy and called the hotline to report the bizarre case of mistaken identity.

It was typical of the way the probe had unfolded for years. To Gleason, the Bulger investigation seemed to be a never-ending series of missed calls and dead ends.

The case agents even told her they believed that Whitey was now traveling with someone else, that he'd killed Catherine Greig and had found another girlfriend.

Gleason didn't buy it. She believed deep down that the couple was still together and that was something she could work with. "The investigation had always been about Whitey," she recalls. "I hate to say it, but for most male criminals, their downfall is their women. That's often been the case for our male fugitives—their wives and girlfriends are their weak links."

She demanded that the agents shift their focus in a big way.

"Let's look at the women in his life," she told the team. "Let's look at Catherine and her twin sister."

By now, Gleason was spending much of her time dismantling and then rebuilding the investigative team—the so-called Bulger Task Force.

One agent she thought would be perfect for this case was a man she had worked with in New York City named Tommy Mac-Donald.

"Tommy Mac was one of the most tenacious agents I'd ever seen," she says. "He was especially good at old stale cases."

The hunt for Whitey Bulger had become just that—an old stale case.

MacDonald was a member of the FBI's Joint Bank Robbery Task Force with the NYPD. The unit was created in the late 1970s at the beginning of the crack epidemic, when violent addicts were starting to pull bank jobs. It was a great assignment for MacDonald, who'd always dreamed of a job in the FBI. The youngest of seven kids, Tommy was raised in Ridgefield, Connecticut. His father had a corporate job in New York while his mother worked part time as a secretary. A natural athlete and star basketball player, Tommy Mac earned an athletic scholarship to the University of New Hampshire, where he was selected captain during his senior year, in 1994. The six-foot-two guard averaged nearly ten points a game during his college career. He was good, but not good enough to play professionally, so he doubled his efforts to gain acceptance into the Bureau. He worked days and went to law school at Fordham University at night. Once he'd earned his law degree, he was selected to go to Quantico.

Like Gleason, Tommy Mac was assigned to the New York office right out of the gate. It was a dizzying time for the FBI rookie, as he fought to keep up with the thousand other field agents working cases in Manhattan and beyond. One agent he particularly looked up to was Lenny Hatton Jr., a seasoned FBI specialist in evidence recovery and a father of four. Lenny was also a volunteer firefighter. On September 11, 2001, Hatton was on his way to work when he saw the black plume of smoke shoot out of the North Tower of the World Trade Center. He rushed to the scene to help and then witnessed the second plane crash into the South Tower. When Hatton reached Ground Zero, he hooked up with one of the rescue companies from the New York City Fire Department (FDNY) and entered the South Tower, where he and countless others disappeared forever.

"I went to the hospitals looking for Lenny," MacDonald remembers. "It was so eerie. The hospitals in Manhattan were virtually empty of patients. There were doctors and nurses just waiting to help but there was no one to treat."

Lenny Hatton's remains, like those of so many other Ground Zero victims, would never be found.

In the mid-2000s, Tommy Mac inherited a notorious and truly

disturbing case from another agent who'd been reassigned elsewhere. MacDonald was asked to investigate the disappearance of five-year-old Etan Patz. The little boy vanished on his way to catch a school bus in SoHo in May 1979. The case generated headlines around the world, and Etan's smiling face was the first to appear on the back of a milk carton under the banner MISSING.

Investigators had a prime suspect in the case, a junk collector and convicted pedophile named José Ramos. The man dated a woman who was hired to walk Etan and other neighborhood children. He'd even admitted to being with Etan that morning. It all made perfect sense.

Or did it?

Tommy Mac was skeptical. Some pieces to the puzzle just didn't fit. So he pulled the puzzle apart and started again from the beginning. He went back and interviewed witnesses and worked diligently in his reexamination of the case. MacDonald revealed promising leads that he'd continue to pursue for years until he and other agents identified Etan's true killer, Pedro Hernandez, and locked him up for twenty-five years to life in prison. Etan Patz's body has never been found. The date of his disappearance, May 25, is designated as National Missing Children's Day.

The case of Etan Patz had been old and stale until it wasn't. For Noreen Gleason, MacDonald was the ideal agent for the Bulger case, which had cast a dark shadow over Boston—and the FBI—for nearly two decades.

Tommy Mac got the call from Gleason while he was sitting on the back porch of his Danbury, Connecticut, home enjoying a cold beer with his wife, Susie. After exchanging the usual pleasantries, the newly appointed ASAC got right to the point.

"I want you to come up here to Boston and find Whitey Bulger."

MacDonald knew the name. He'd played college basketball in New England and his brother was a schoolteacher in Boston.

Tommy had also chased down Bulger leads in Manhattan that had gone nowhere.

Holy crap, he thought to himself.

The Whitey Bulger case was the proverbial white whale of the FBI. Gleason might as well have said that she wanted his help finding Bigfoot.

Gleason asked her old friend to sleep on it. Tommy had a lot of thinking to do. He'd been fighting in the FBI trenches for nine years and it was time for a change. But his young sons were now playing travel baseball. How could he just leave his family? He wrestled with the question for a couple of days.

Finally, one day after one of his kids' baseball games, the entire family was grabbing chicken wings at a local restaurant. Tommy Mac was sitting at the table across from his father. The son revealed his dilemma. MacDonald's dad listened and then leaned across the restaurant table.

"It's Whitey Bulger, son, you gotta go to Boston. You gotta go."

2

AFTER AGREEING TO JOIN GLEASON'S team in Boston, Tommy Mac spent the next two months immersed in the Bulger case as his temporary duty assignment was getting finalized. While sitting on a beach along the Connecticut shoreline, MacDonald familiarized himself with the case file and read every news report and book about the near mythical mobster.

MacDonald could hardly believe there were still some people, especially in Southie, who glamorized and even idolized Whitey.

"This guy's committed nineteen murders," MacDonald told himself. "Why are there still people out there defending him and working against those of us who are trying to catch him?"

To find the answers, he had to go back to December 23, 1994—and everything that came after it.

IT WAS JUST TWO DAYS before Christmas, and the city of Boston was in full sparkle in anticipation of the holidays. A gigantic Norway spruce stood tall on Boston Common, its decorations illuminating the park, while in South Boston, less than two miles away, neighbors adorned their stoops, doors, and windows with strings of multicolored lights and festive yuletide wreaths.

Whitey Bulger, leader of the Winter Hill Gang, Boston's violent Irish mafia, was planning to take his longtime girlfriend Teresa Stanley downtown to Copley Plaza for some last-minute shopping at the fashionable clothing store Neiman Marcus. The city was a hive of holiday activity as folks were flowing in and out of shops, picking up their last-minute gifts. Forecasters were tracking a powerful winter nor'easter that was expected to slam New England and much of the east coast on Christmas Eve.

But Whitey was more concerned about another storm, one that was churning inside the US Attorney's office, where prosecutors were getting ready to pounce on Bulger and his longtime partner in crime, Stevie "The Rifleman" Flemmi.

Whitey had Stanley in the car when his beeper buzzed with a message from Kevin Weeks, his thick-necked protégé and right-hand man. Bulger drove over to the Rotary Variety store and adjacent South Boston Liquor Mart, which served as the gang's headquarters. Weeks worked a day job there behind the cash register.

Weeks climbed in the backseat of Whitey's blue Ford LTD and the three of them drove north into downtown Boston. Weeks kept his mouth shut in the car. He was worried that the vehicle was bugged. Whitey had taught him well.

Born in Southie in 1956, Kevin Weeks was the fifth of six children of John and Margaret Weeks. John was a World War II vet and boxer who worked for the city of Boston's housing authority. The family lived in the same Old Colony housing project in Southie where Bulger and Connolly grew up. Weeks and his brothers learned to box from their dad and Kevin showed skills with his hands at a young age, accepting all challengers in the rough Southie projects.

He first met Whitey while working at a Commonwealth Avenue bar called Flicks. He later became a bouncer at Triple O's, where Whitey noticed his talent for handing out beat-downs and recruited him to be his personal bodyguard and driver. He worked for a time for Boston's public transit system, the MBTA, doing rail maintenance. He moonlighted collecting from bookies with

Whitey and soon ditched the day job. Weeks escalated to loan-sharking, strong-arming, and cracking heads for the Irish mob boss, and eventually, helping commit murders.

Now, shortly before Christmas 1994, Bulger and Weeks parked near Boylston Street, which was crowded with holiday shoppers passing by with gift bags bulging under their arms. There was a sense of merriment in the air even with a potentially killer blizzard on the horizon.

Whitey stuffed a wad of cash in Teresa's hand and sent her ahead. He then motioned Weeks to join him near the trunk of his car, which was illegally parked. The young, burly gangster told his boss that he'd just been visited by retired FBI agent John Connolly, Whitey's longtime man on the inside at the Bureau. Connolly had left the FBI in 1990 and now had a high-paying job as security chief for Boston Edison. Retired or not, Connolly still maintained relationships and shared secrets with many of his former colleagues.

During that earlier conversation in the walk-in beer cooler of the liquor mart, away from prying eyes and presumably prying ears, an anxious Connolly told Weeks that Whitey and Stevie Flemmi would soon be arrested on extortion and racketeering charges involving the shakedowns of two local bookies named Chico Krantz and Jimmy Katz, and that the indictments were imminent.

In hushed tones, Weeks repeated the information to Whitey verbatim, just as Connolly had ordered him to. Bulger showed no emotion. He knew the feds would be coming sooner or later.

In fact, he had planned for it.

Whitey then whistled to Stanley and ordered her back in the car. The holiday shopping excursion was abruptly canceled. They would be going on a long trip instead.

Whitey then called Flemmi.

"The indictments are coming down," Bulger warned his partner. "There's a memo in Washington that the indictments are there and they'll be coming down in a week."

Bulger told Flemmi that he'd learned of the impending crackdown from another corrupt FBI agent named John Morris and not Connolly, perhaps in an attempt to shield his longtime friend from trouble. Whitey had lived his life stacking lies on top of lies, keeping the truth from even his closest friends and business partners.

Bulger dropped Weeks off back at the liquor store at 4:30 p.m. The sky was dark, cold, and windy and the waves were crashing to shore along nearby Carson Beach. Whitey took one last look at the patch of land that he'd controlled for decades. He'd raped and murdered here in Southie. He'd created his own mythology as a gentleman gangster here, a Robin Hood–like figure who was respected and even revered, all the while preying on his neighbors, stealing their innocence and money, and destroying their dreams.

He turned the car around and headed south on Interstate 95 with Teresa Stanley by his side. There was a storm ahead, but Whitey Bulger was prepared.

THE COUPLE ARRIVED IN NEW York City sometime later and holed up in a hotel, where they spent Christmas Eve watching the snow pile up on the streets below. Stanley wished that she were spending Christmas back home with her children and grandkids, but this was the life she had chosen. She knew that her man might be forced one day to go on the run and completely detach himself from his past. Shortly before, Whitey had taken her on a trip to Europe, visiting romantic cities like Venice and Rome. They also flew to London and Dublin. Bulger had tried to convince Stanley that the sole purpose of the vacation was to strengthen their relationship after Teresa had caught him cheating with another woman. Once again, Whitey was stacking lies upon lies. In truth, he was preparing for his life as a fugitive.

While the two were marveling at historic sites, Whitey was also scouting banks for a safe deposit box to hide some cash. In London, while treating Teresa to the elegant accommodations of Le Meridien Piccadilly in the city's West End, he stopped into a nearby Barclays bank, where he'd opened another safe deposit box two years prior under both his name and Stanley's. He accessed the deposit box and stuffed it with $50,000 in cash along with his Irish passport, should he be forced to go underground in the land of his ancestors. Bulger's Irish temper exploded on that trip while riding a packed train through London's Underground. He bumped into another rider and said sorry. The guy called Whitey a "bloody Yank" and Bulger unleashed on him, hitting him with several punches as fellow riders looked on in shock.

After their stay in New York City, Whitey and Teresa continued their journey down the east coast. Bulger listened to the car radio, trying to pick up intelligence about what the cops knew. He switched from news station to news station as they crossed state line after state line. As they drove from one motel to the next, Bulger was bleeding stress. They'd argue and he would lunge at her with fists clenched. To escape another beating, a terrified Teresa would run and hide in the bathroom.

They arrived in New Orleans just in time for New Year's Eve. They stayed at Le Richelieu, a small yet stately hotel in the heart of the French Quarter. That night, another tourist from Boston named Amy Silberman was killed by a stray bullet fired while revelers stood on New Orleans' promenade watching holiday fireworks.

Local police and the FBI were called in to investigate the stray bullet death, which meant Bulger would have to be especially cautious. Making things even worse for him was that reporters from Boston also came to New Orleans to investigate the startling death of Silberman, a thirty-one-year-old executive assistant. Suddenly, the Crescent City was too risky for Whitey, so he and Teresa left and drove to Florida. Bulger owned a condominium in Clearwater, as he once planned to retire there like some aging insurance salesman. He didn't go near the place this time, though, because he'd purchased the condo a year before in his own name. Instead, he emptied another safe deposit box, grabbing cash and a fake ID.

He'd been on the run unofficially since December 23, but it was now almost two weeks later and there was still no word on the indictments. Had Whitey received bad intelligence from his former FBI handlers?

Teresa Stanley was homesick and wanted to go back to Boston. She told Whitey that she wasn't cut out for life as a fugitive. He agreed and set course for the colder climate up north. What he didn't know was that the atmosphere had grown white hot back home.

On the night of January 5, 1995, DEA agents and detectives from the Massachusetts State Police swept in and arrested Stevie Flemmi outside Schooners, a restaurant owned by his son in Boston's Financial District. Flemmi was squiring around a new Chinese girlfriend and the pair was about to leave in her white Honda Accord when law enforcement closed in. State troopers driving an unmarked car thrust the vehicle forward, slammed on the brakes, and blocked the Honda, preventing any escape. Flemmi scrunched down in the passenger seat. He thought it was an assassination attempt by rival gangsters but made no effort to shield his girlfriend.

DEA agent Dan Doherty ripped open the car door and shoved his pistol against Flemmi's skull.

"Put your hands where I can see them, Stevie!"

The agent frisked Flemmi and found a hunting knife and mace in his pocket. They whisked the gangster over to the FBI office close by at One Center Plaza, where he'd be held overnight until his first appearance in federal court the following day.

Whitey and Teresa were driving through Connecticut when they learned of Flemmi's arrest in a radio news flash. Authorities had made a run at Bulger too but had no luck. They showed up in force at Teresa's home on Silver Street in Southie and also at another home in nearby Quincy, where Whitey's longtime mistress lived.

Her name was Catherine Greig.

3

WHITEY PHONED KEVIN WEEKS AND told him about the situation with Teresa. She had too many attachments, most importantly her family, which kept her tethered to her old life in Southie. There was no way that she could cut it as a fugitive because Bulger had no plans to return to Boston. Still, Whitey felt that he couldn't run alone. He was fifty-five years old now and had a bad heart. Similar to his criminal enterprises, Bulger didn't live in the moment, but instead had his head far into the future. He had enough money stashed away to live comfortably for the next thirty years. But he knew that his body would eventually turn on him as he got older and he would need someone to take care of him. Whitey was also acutely aware that it would be easier to blend in and disappear with a woman by his side instead of going it alone.

"Nobody looks twice at an older couple," he told himself. "It's the single guy that stands out."

Bulger ordered Weeks to get in touch with Catherine Greig, have her pack a bag, and tell her to be ready to go at a moment's notice. Greig didn't need to know where they were going. She didn't care. What mattered to her was that he had finally chosen her over her romantic rival, Teresa Stanley. Life with Whitey on the run would force Catherine to remain in the shadows, but she no longer had to pretend that she didn't exist in Whitey's world.

Bulger was hers now and hers alone.

Teresa was kept in the dark about Whitey's plan to flee with

Greig, although she probably suspected it. In the beginning, Teresa believed that she and Bulger would grow old together. Although she didn't have a wedding band on her finger, they had treated each other like husband and wife. Whitey and Teresa began living together in 1976 when Bulger purchased a two-story, eight-room colonial on Silver Street near South Boston High School and the monument at Dorchester Heights, a historic tourist spot where General George Washington's forces successfully repelled the British army without firing a shot in 1776.

Whitey moved Teresa, a divorcee, and her four children out of the Old Colony housing project and into his home. At first, Bulger lied and told Teresa that he worked in the construction trade, but she learned soon enough what he did and the nighttime hours he kept. Whitey, however, made sure that he was home just about every night for dinner with Teresa and the kids, Karen, Joan, Nancy, and Billy.

He was the father figure they'd never had. He took them on trips and even lectured them about the importance of homework. Teresa's children didn't call him "Dad"; instead they called him Charlie, a name he would become quite fond of in the years to come.

Whitey had strong paternal instincts and was still devastated by the death of his own child years before. Prior to dating Teresa, Bulger had spent twelve years with another woman named Lindsey Cyr, who gave birth to their son, Douglas Glen Cyr, in 1967. The child bore a striking resemblance to his father, with a head of blond hair that was almost white and piercing blue eyes. Photographs of the boy as a toddler give the appearance of a happy childhood, with the young lad grinning from ear to ear. Whitey was a doting dad in private. He kept the child's existence a secret from his friends and associates for fear they would target the boy for kidnapping or worse if they knew he was the son of Whitey Bulger.

When Douglas was six years old, he was suddenly overcome by extreme nausea and a high fever as a result of a severe reaction to taking aspirin. The boy suffered from Reye's syndrome, a rare disease that causes swelling to the liver and brain.

His mother rushed him to Massachusetts General Hospital, where doctors fought desperately to save him. Bulger held vigil at the boy's bedside until he died.

"When he died, Jimmy [Whitey] was out of his mind," Lindsey Cyr later recalled. "Tears were streaming down Jimmy's face."

Bulger blamed himself for the boy's death and Lindsey proved to be a constant reminder of the tragic loss. Whitey ended the relationship, but continued to see her occasionally after he'd taken up with Teresa Stanley.

Although Whitey enjoyed playing Ozzie to Teresa's Harriet, the day-to-day demands of a domestic lifestyle ran counter to his true self. He was a criminal first and foremost and he prided himself on that. He got frustrated with her easily and beat her on occasion.

Once, in the early 1990s, Bulger assaulted Stanley in a summer cabana hangout in South Boston. The attack was sudden and vicious. Whitey curled his fist and punched her out like a thug he'd beat up on the street.

Whitey eventually moved out of the home but still supported Teresa and her kids and kept her believing that she was his one and only. She was dependable and Bulger liked that, but she was no longer exciting to him, so he looked elsewhere and soon found an attractive and seductive mistress who was much younger than Teresa.

Bulger was old enough to be Catherine Greig's father. Twenty-two years separated the pair, but they had much in common, especially a mutual love for animals.

Catherine, or Cathy as she was called, grew up in Southie in a three-family home on East Fourth Street. Her father worked for Raytheon as a machinist, while her mother worked part-time as an usher at the Colonial Theatre downtown. Greig had a younger sister, Jean, and brother, David, but she was closest to her sister Margaret—her identical twin.

"We ran with different crowds but we were close," Margaret (Greig) McCusker remembers. "[We] had a wonderful childhood despite the fact that our father was an alcoholic."

The twin sisters took ballet lessons together as youngsters and both later attended South Boston High School, where Catherine was voted prettiest girl in her senior class. Upon graduation, she enrolled in a two-year program at the Forsyth School for Dental Hygienists and quickly married her first boyfriend when she was just twenty years old. His name was Bobby McGonagle, and he was a Boston firefighter whose brother Paulie happened to be the leader of a local gang.

Catherine was a homebody, while her new husband liked to go out and party. He had an affair and that ended the marriage in its infancy. As Catherine was going through the throes of her divorce, she met and fell in love with Whitey Bulger.

Some believe that it wasn't fate that brought them together. Instead, the thought is that Catherine had pursued Whitey at his local haunts like Triple O's lounge in a vendetta against her soon-to-be ex-husband.

Whitey had killed two of her husband's brothers in cold blood.

Margaret McCusker, who was no stranger to betrayal herself, blessed the relationship.

"He seemed very nice," McCusker recalls. "I didn't know exactly what he [Whitey] did but I knew who he was. Everybody knows who he is around here."

McCusker liked her sister's new boyfriend, whom she described as very charismatic and easy to get along with. Whitey had a reputation as a gangster, but that didn't raise any eyebrows in the Greig family.

This was Southie after all.

WHITEY TOOK CARE OF CATHERINE much like he did Teresa and tried to keep both worlds from colliding. Stanley didn't know about Greig, but Catherine sure knew about her, and she seethed with jealousy.

In the autumn of 1994, things came to a head and one of Bulger's great lies was finally exposed.

Catherine called Teresa's home on Silver Street looking for Whitey. When Stanley told her that Bulger was out, Greig asked for a private talk.

"Something bad is going on," she said.

Catherine picked Teresa up at home in her green Ford Explorer and together they drove to Greig's house in nearby Quincy. The home, a four-bedroom split-level ranch, had been a gift from Whitey.

The two women in Bulger's life entered the living room and lit cigarettes. Catherine took a deep drag, exhaled, and then went into her story. She confessed to Teresa that she had been having an affair with Whitey for nearly two decades.

Her role as Bulger's mistress was no longer enough for Catherine. She wanted more. She wanted Whitey to make a choice between Teresa and her. This was quite a gamble for Greig, but she felt that it was time to place her chips on the table and go all in.

The revelation startled Teresa, who had been living in a state of ignorant bliss with Bulger. Stanley had kept blinders on for decades. She didn't even know that Whitey had fathered a child who died.

Instead of getting hysterical, Teresa thanked Catherine for her honesty. There was a sense of calm in the room, but it lasted just a few short moments before a red-hot Whitey arrived and pounded on the front door. Catherine let him inside and Bulger pushed past her, followed by Kevin Weeks, and headed toward Stanley, ordering her to get up on her feet and go.

He grabbed Teresa forcefully by the arm while she informed him that his mistress had just revealed everything to her. Catherine interrupted and demanded that Whitey choose between them right then and there.

Bulger exploded, grabbing Greig by the neck, choking her. Catherine's eyes went wide with panic. Fearing that Whitey was going to kill her, Weeks pulled his boss away and tried to get him out the door.

Stanley left also and during a heated car ride back to Southie, Whitey withstood her barbs and pledged his love for her. He promised his girlfriend of thirty years that he'd never see Catherine's face again.

It was just another of Whitey Bulger's lies.

Months later, as Catherine prepared herself to join Whitey on the run, she and her sister Margaret walked close together, huddled against the winter chill on the steep hill of Dorchester Heights.

"We're going on a trip," Catherine told her twin. "I'm leaving with Jimmy and I'll be in touch when I can."

Catherine didn't say where they were going, but Margaret wasn't overly concerned as Whitey, or "Jimmy," as he was called by friends, often took her sister on lavish getaways. Money was never an object for them. At her home in Quincy, Whitey had a globe in the middle of their dining room that opened up to store liquor. But Bulger used it to store cash—$20, $50, and $100 bills. When Catherine needed something, she'd just reach into the globe.

"Oh, my God, do you know how much you're spending?" Margaret would ask her twin. "Do you even know?"

Catherine would shrug and smile.

THERE WAS NOTHING LAVISH OR romantic about Bulger's final moments with Teresa Stanley. They slipped back into Massachusetts and Whitey dropped her off in front of a Chili's restaurant in Hingham, a suburb just a few miles south of Boston. One of Stanley's daughters lived nearby and had offered to fetch her mother.

Whitey said, "See ya." Teresa replied the same.

He turned the car around and never looked back. Bulger was out of her life for good, but Teresa Stanley would have the last laugh one day soon.

Catherine waited alone near the bottom steps of the Dorchester Heights Monument. Margaret had helped her pack and had even handed over her driver's license to her twin in case the couple got pulled over and questioned by police. Margaret also promised to look after Catherine's two beloved dogs, French poodles named Nikki and Gigi.

Suddenly a pair of headlights flashed in Catherine's eyes as a black Pontiac Bonneville pulled slowly to the curb. She opened the passenger door and got in. She was dressed smartly and her platinum-blond hair was freshly done. The interior of the vehicle was soon filled with the aroma of Catherine's perfume. She'd chosen Whitey's favorite for the occasion. Kevin Weeks was behind the steering wheel, his eyes focused on the rearview mirror. He'd circled the location for more than an hour to make sure he wasn't being followed. It was part of the tradecraft for both spies and sinners like him. He lived in a world where one slip-up could get you captured or killed.

Weeks drove in a winding path through Southie, taking random turns down lonely streets while constantly searching for a tail. Once convinced they weren't under the watch of the FBI or state police, Weeks drove Greig to a quiet spot in Dorchester called Malibu Beach. The place was popular with sunbathers in the summertime but was silent on a bitter winter night like this one.

Weeks pulled the car over and he and Catherine stepped out. At that moment, Whitey emerged from the darkness. He was dressed all in black and wearing a matching cowboy hat.

Catherine could no longer hide her excitement. She draped her

arms around Whitey's neck and pulled him close for a long em-
brace. It reminded Weeks of a scene between Bogart and Bergman
from *Casablanca*.

This was the moment she'd been dreaming of for years. They
were finally together.

Whitey led her to his Mercury Grand Marquis and helped her
inside. Weeks got into the backseat and they drove around Southie
for about an hour. Bulger soaked in the atmosphere, taking mental
pictures of the street corners and neighborhood taverns where he
had consolidated his power. He also voiced his concern about Stevie Flemmi. Whitey didn't think he could last long behind bars and
might commit suicide as a way out.

Bulger then drove his protégé back to his car and said good-bye.
They shook hands and Weeks slipped him a new phone number
where he could be reached.

Seconds later, Whitey and Catherine were gone.

4

STEVIE FLEMMI WAS NOW BEHIND bars at the Plymouth House of Correction awaiting trial, but Kevin Weeks was still a free man. He would visit Flemmi often. At first, Flemmi had laughed off the charges against him, but now he doubted whether he'd ever see the outside of a prison again. With a glass partition between them and a phone to their ears, Weeks listened as Flemmi complained about the jailhouse conditions and especially the food. When the topic of conversation got around to Whitey, Flemmi just shrugged.

"It's better for my case that the other guy is out there," he told Weeks. "Tell him to stay free."

In May 1995, Bulger called Weeks and said, "Meet me at the Lions."

Kevin understood what this meant, so he hopped on an Amtrak train to New York City. He met his boss in front of the main branch of the New York City Public Library, where the statues of two marble lions named Lady Astor and Lord Lenox sat proudly guarding the entryway.

Bulger was with Catherine, who was her typical cheery self. Whitey wore sunglasses and a baseball cap. Surveillance photos of Whitey taken sometime before showed him in similar dress. These photos were now plastered inside every FBI office and police station in America. The aging crime boss had done nothing to alter his appearance while on the run.

Catherine stepped out of earshot so Whitey and Weeks could talk privately.

Surprisingly, Bulger was hopeful about the future. He'd heard there was bad blood between the FBI and Massachusetts State Police, and that the case against him was crumbling because one key witness was now dead of natural causes and another was ill and not expected to make it to trial.

Whitey and Catherine were now traveling under the names Thomas F. Baxter and Helen Marshall. They masqueraded as a married couple, which fulfilled Greig's long-held fantasy.

Bulger had been using the alias for years. He'd obtained a Massachusetts driver's license with Baxter's name, Social Security number, and birth date and renewed it every four years as required by the state. The real Tom Baxter died in 1979. In 1990, Whitey got another license from the state of New York. Like the last one, it featured Baxter's information alongside Bulger's photograph. The address he gave on this one was from Selden, Long Island, where Kevin Weeks's cousin lived.

Other members of the gang had not planned their escape as meticulously as Whitey had and were not so lucky. Following the capture of Stevie Flemmi, more dominoes began to fall. In January 1995, Massachusetts State Police detective Steve Johnson learned that Bulger's attack dog John Martorano might be hiding out in Florida. Martorano was a prized catch, as he'd been the poisoned tip to Whitey's spear. Martorano was heavyset with curly black hair and looked like the late comedic actor John Belushi. But he was no funnyman. John Martorano was suspected to have committed several murders, including the brazen daytime slaying of a Tulsa, Oklahoma, businessman on Bulger's orders.

At the time, Johnson had been hunting a bookie turned fugitive who just happened to be close friends with Martorano. After tracing the bookie's phone, the detective noticed a number that he suspected was Martorano's in Boca Raton, Florida. Johnson and a partner flew to Boca Raton and followed Martorano for three days, waiting for the perfect opportunity to strike. He'd been living with his girlfriend under the name Vincent Rancourt.

The detective knew that his prey was a stone-cold killer and that if he didn't handle the situation carefully, it was likely that someone would get killed, possibly even an innocent bystander.

He needed to take Martorano down when he was most vulnerable. Johnson seized the opportunity one early evening when the hit man visited a local ice cream shop with his nine-year-old son and the boy's friend.

Johnson approached Martorano and called him by his real name.

"You've got the wrong man," the mob killer protested quietly.

The detective ordered Martorano to roll up his shirtsleeves. The gangster did so, revealing two tattoos on each forearm. On the right was a drawing of a blue jay with the name *Nancy* written underneath. On the left was the inking of a cross accompanied by the initials *IHS* (*in hoc signo*), Latin for "In this sign thou shalt conquer." To Johnson, the tattoos represented the marks of the beast, and right there he knew he had his man. The Winter Hill Gang's most notorious killer surrendered with less than a whimper.

In August 1995, investigators lured another infamous Boston gangster into their net. Francis "Cadillac Frank" Salemme was the reigning godfather of Boston's *La Cosa Nostra*. He wasn't part of the Winter Hill Gang, but he was especially close to Stevie Flemmi and had been named in the same sweeping thirty-five-count racketeering and extortion indictment handed down earlier that year. Like Martorano, Salemme had fled New England for the warmer climate of Florida.

He was living in West Palm Beach with his longtime girlfriend Donna Wolf, who'd recently traveled back to Massachusetts to attend the funeral for Salemme's son and namesake who had died of lymphoma. Investigators trailed Wolf back to the tiny $600-per-month condo she rented at Sandalwood Lake Village, which was a far cry from the nearby Mar-a-Lago club owned by Donald J. Trump.

Salemme had been featured on the Fox television program *America's Most Wanted*, which resulted in twenty-seven tips, including two from Florida.

The Boston Mafia boss had spent most of his time on the run sunbathing in his backyard, working out, and feeding ducks. His lack of elusiveness was surprising given that Salemme had gone on the run once before in the late 1960s after blowing up the car owned by mob rat Joe "The Animal" Barboza. Salemme remained free for three years until he was arrested in New York City by a young FBI agent named John Connolly, Whitey's man on the inside of the Bureau. What Salemme didn't know until decades later was that Connolly had been tipped off to Salemme's whereabouts by the mobster's close friend Stevie Flemmi.

Like Martorano, Salemme was caught off guard by investigators. FBI agents and local police approached the condo in West Palm Beach just before midnight on Friday, August 13, 1995, and arrested Cadillac Frank while he was relaxing in his pajamas.

AFTER LEAVING KEVIN WEEKS IN New York City, Whitey and Catherine drove out to Long Island and stayed for eight days at a Best Western hotel in the town of Holtsville, just ten minutes from Selden. He booked room 335 under the alias Thomas Baxter and paid cash for the accommodations, $535.29 in total.

The purpose of Whitey's visit was most likely to dip into a steel safe held at the home of Kevin Weeks's relatives, where Bulger had stuffed wads of cash over time.

From there, Whitey drove west with Catherine by his side. A history buff, Bulger visited the site of Custer's last stand at the Battle of Little Big Horn and also the Little Big Horn casino at the crossroads of Highways 212 and 90 on the Crow Native American reservation in Montana.

Bulger was there to gamble and wash his money, replacing old bills with new ones. The casino was drab and dysfunctional, and according to Whitey, not up to par with the Indian casinos back home in New England. The casino floor was virtually empty, which should have been a welcome sight for a fugitive on the run, but not for Bulger.

Instead of staying quiet and in the shadows, he demanded to speak to a manager.

"You can make some real money here if you add some things and change some other things around," Bulger told the casino boss. "This could be a really nice thing for you guys if you put some money in it."

The manager didn't want to take any advice and paid little attention to the white-haired stranger. This indifference frustrated the South Boston crime boss to no end.

Why would Bulger jeopardize his cover to help strangers at an Indian casino? In truth, Whitey had a genuine love for Native American culture dating back to the nearly three years he spent serving time for bank robbery at the world's most infamous prison—Alcatraz—from 1959 to 1962.

As prisoner number 1428 AZ, Whitey befriended and remained very close to a Native American inmate named Clarence "Joe" Carnes, aka "The Choctaw Kid."

Carnes was only eighteen years old when he arrived on the Rock in 1945, making him the youngest man ever incarcerated there. He was an Oklahoma native who was first sent to prison for killing a garage attendant during a holdup. In 1946, he was involved in what became known as "the Battle of Alcatraz" when he and five other inmates attempted a daring escape. Two prisoners were killed, along with two prison officers. Carnes didn't participate in the murders of the officers, so he wasn't sentenced to death. He remained on the Rock until it closed in 1963 and was paroled in 1973. He was sent back to prison for parole violations and corresponded regularly with Whitey from behind bars.

In a letter written by Bulger and obtained exclusively for this book, Whitey described one of their conversations.

> *He told me on the phone in 1988 how he wanted to be free . . . after a life time since 17 yrs of age behind bars so he took off with [some] money and had a period of wine women + song, thought it would never end but it did and back to prison—he was due to be released Oct 15 1988. When I heard where he was . . . [I] told him "Stay Strong" . . . I'll be out in time to pick you up on Oct 15th and you will be all set in life—told him to pick out car he'd like will get it upon release Etc.*

> *Jim Bulger*

Carnes never made it out of prison. He died while incarcerated in Springfield, Missouri, in October 1988. "The Choctaw Kid" was buried unceremoniously nearby with no family members present to say good-bye. Whitey learned of this final, ultimate insult to his friend sometime later and paid $10,000 to have Carnes's body exhumed and reburied on sacred Choctaw soil in Carnes's hometown of Daisy, Oklahoma.

Despite not being able to help his friend, Bulger would look back fondly on his time locked up at Alcatraz, referring to the notorious island jail as his alma mater—a Harvard University for criminals.

While traveling with Catherine across the American West, Bulger wore a reminder of his past life and his friend "The Choctaw Kid" around his trim waist—a brass belt buckle decorated with an Alcatraz insignia. Whitey put 65,000 miles on his Mercury Grand Marquis during his first months on the run.

Eventually he made his way back to the southern coast of the

United States. In September 1995, a cop in Long Beach, Mississippi, spotted a green car with New York plates that was stopped at a red light. The driver looked in his rearview mirror and saw the cop. The officer ran the plate and it too came back to Thomas Baxter of Selden, New York. But Baxter's record was clean, so the officer let him go.

Bulger stayed clear of Clearwater, Florida, on this trip south and instead opted for a small barrier island off the coast of Louisiana called Grand Isle. But there was nothing grand about the island except for its name.

Although more than six thousand vacationers invaded the tiny island during the summertime, the place was virtually dead in early fall. Just over one thousand people lived there year round, most working in the shrimp business or on oil rigs in the Gulf of Mexico.

Bulger pulled his Grand Marquis off Louisiana Highway 1 and traveled across a drawbridge toward the seaside community known as the "Cajun Bahamas." He and Catherine had already cased out the town once before and found it to be the perfect hiding spot. They rented a seasonal camp that was built on stilts for a cheap price. No one there looked twice at the aging couple, and Whitey strongly considered staying in Grand Isle for good.

5

As TOMMY MAC READ THROUGH the files trying to understand facts of the Bulger case, the documentation wasn't just about Bulger's known travels since fleeing from Boston. By 2008, there had been a lot of ink spilled about the work of various agents. The paperwork told the stories of false leads and near misses the FBI had with the fugitive since he'd gone missing, while also detailing the hard work of a handful of agents who, contrary to popular belief, had labored tirelessly during the early years of Bulger's fugitive case to bring him to justice.

By the time Whitey went on the run, Boston FBI agent John Gamel had been on the Bulger beat for the first four years, slowly building a case against the mobster for extortion, gambling, and most importantly, murder. In an office later smeared by corruption involving Bulger, Gamel was a straight arrow who'd been diligently trying to apprehend the mobster. Indeed, even before Gamel knew about John Connolly's role in Bulger's crimes, there was something about Connolly that didn't sit right with him.

"People would talk about him in a way that he was supposed to be famous, a larger-than-life character," Gamel says. "He had an ego the size of Alaska and he was impressed with himself and wanted to impress us. I really felt that I never wanted anything to do with him."

Gamel was in this to apprehend his suspect, so once Bulger disappeared, he was determined to pull him out of hiding and lock him up.

"I'm just a simple guy from Springfield, Massachusetts," he said years later.

Gamel's journey to the FBI was not a straight line and was anything but simple. Instead, he took many divergent paths before ultimately being tasked with bringing down Boston's most notorious gangster. He was the son of a high school principal who died when Gamel was just thirteen years old. Fearing that young John would lose focus in the wake of his father's death, his mother sent him off to prep school at nearby Northfield Mount Hermon, where Gamel eventually boosted his grades and was accepted into Colgate University to study English. After college, he joined the US Navy in hopes of flying fighter missions in faraway Vietnam. With great vision and decision-making skills, Gamel aced his aptitude tests. But nothing went smoothly once he got into the cockpit. John and his instructors soon realized that he was a lousy pilot. Gamel was discharged early from the Navy and then enrolled at Boston University, where he earned a master's degree in journalism. He worked in local television and radio for several years, until his life changed forever in 1975 while covering the shocking murder of a rookie cop in Shrewsbury, Massachusetts.

Officer James Lonchiadis was shot through the heart after pleading for his life during a bungled car theft. His killer later used the officer's gun in a robbery to steal a getaway car. The crime shocked the relatively quiet town of Shrewsbury and it was a major story for Gamel to cover as a young journalist. The case took twenty months to crack and during that time, Gamel spent hours speaking with the FBI agents assigned to the case. Gamel was fascinated by their work and one of the agents told him, "Ya know, this FBI job is pretty good and you might want to think about it."

Gamel researched the idea and liked what he saw. He then told his wife, Beth, that he wanted to join the Bureau and she went along with this new adventure. But there was one major problem. Gamel was thirty-four years old at the time and almost considered too old to apply. Most new agents were in their early twenties, and Gamel was a virtual dinosaur despite being one of the top-ranked recruits in the country.

He began new agents training at Quantico, Virginia, with more than thirty fellow recruits and spent eight hundred hours learning self-defense, defensive driving, how to manage and run criminal investigations, interview and interrogation tactics, and, of equal importance, how to shoot. A reporter's notepad and a reliable pen were once the tools of Gamel's trade, but now the journalist-turned-FBI recruit was spending his days firing off more than five thousand rounds of ammunition as he learned how to handle pistols, shotguns, and submachine guns.

After completing his training, Gamel was assigned to the Boston field office, where he worked on the fugitive squad and investigated the corruption of public officials including the case against Massachusetts congressman Nick Mavroules, who later spent more than a year in prison for bribery, extortion, and racketeering. He learned early in his FBI career that there was often a blurred line between politicians and gangsters in Massachusetts.

Gamel was then recruited to join the FBI's SWAT team and also worked on the counterterrorism squad, where he investigated a plot by the Red Army Faction to blow up a branch of Sun Myung Moon's Unification Church in Gloucester, Massachusetts. The would-be bomber, a Japanese terrorist named Yu Kikumura, had visited the rugged New England fishing town just before he was arrested following a police chase in New Jersey. A search of the vehicle uncovered canisters loaded with gunpowder and attached to wires, flashbulbs, and nine-volt batteries.

Gamel was also the Boston office's top tracker of skinheads and neo-Nazis.

"As a group, they were somewhat dangerous because they could feed off each other," Gamel recalls. "But individually, they were scared shitless and the first ones to run away if you attempted to confront them."

But the Whitey Bulger investigation was different. For four years, Gamel had dealt with a criminal who was bold and dangerous.

John Gamel had faced gangsters associated with Bulger as a member of the FBI SWAT team. During an ambush of armored car robbers outside a bank in Abington, Massachusetts, in 1991, Gamel had encountered an Irishman named Pat Nee, a former rival-turned-associate of Bulger and a man suspected of helping Bulger pull off one of his most shockingly brazen crimes, the murders of Brian Halloran and his friend Michael Donahue in May 1982.

Brian Halloran was a thug who made his living collecting unpaid mob debts through threats or worse. He hated Bulger and the feeling was mutual. Halloran had information that could put Whitey away, so he took it to the FBI. John Connolly, Bulger's man on the inside, heard the news and told Whitey that Halloran had turned snitch.

Connolly had signed Brian Halloran's death warrant.

Bulger got a tip that Halloran was drinking at the Pier restaurant, a bar on the edge of Southie popular with fishermen and dockworkers. Whitey rendezvoused with Kevin Weeks, handed him a walkie-talkie, and ordered him to keep an eye on the tavern from a lookout point across the street. The front door to the bar had a large window, and that offered Weeks a near perfect view inside.

"When Balloonhead gets up, lemme know," Bulger told his protégé. Halloran was known as Balloonhead on the streets because he had a massive skull, which made him look like he was constantly suffering from some kind of allergic reaction.

The gangster had asked his buddy Michael Donahue for a ride home to Dorchester. Donahue was about to open a bakery with his wife and had no ties to Whitey Bulger or organized crime, for that matter. His only crime, it seemed, was being friends with Brian Halloran.

Michael Donahue had no idea that Halloran was using him as a human shield, as one of the unwritten rules of the mob jungle was that noncombatants were strictly off-limits. Halloran knew that he was being targeted by Bulger and a host of other underworld figures that he'd double-crossed over the years.

Donahue left the bar first to pull around his car, a blue Datsun that he'd borrowed from his father for the day. Halloran finished his drink, paid the tab, and followed.

"The balloon is rising," Weeks told Bulger over the two-way radio.

As Halloran pushed open the front door and stepped outside, Weeks pressed the talk button once again.

"The balloon is in the air."

Whitey swung into action and drove his Chevy Malibu alongside Donahue's car.

"Hey Brian!" he yelled as he peered out the driver's-side window. Halloran and Donahue looked in Bulger's direction and saw the carbine rifle in his hand. They had zero time to react as Whitey opened fire while another man, later identified in court by Stevie Flemmi as Pat Nee wearing a mask, began shooting from the backseat of Bulger's Malibu. Donahue was cut down instantly by a hail of bullets as the Datsun rolled slowly across the street. Halloran managed to stumble out of the car before falling to the pavement. Whitey pulled a quick U-turn and lowered the carbine toward Halloran's position. More bullets flew, each one striking Whitey's target with such force that Halloran's blood-soaked body bounced off the ground.

Brian Halloran was shot twenty-two times in all.

After making his getaway, Whitey sent a voice message to his partner Stevie Flemmi's pager: "The balloon has burst."

The story of the Halloran–Donahue murders was fresh in Gamel's mind when he left the FBI office at One Center Plaza one winter evening in the early 1990s and decided to check on Bulger's whereabouts in Southie. This was in the years before Bulger became a fugitive when the FBI was actively investigating him. Driving a rental car, a gray Ford Crown Victoria, Gamel made his way to Rotary Variety, the convenience store where Whitey and his gang ran much of their business, but the place was quiet except for a few folks buying their weekly lottery tickets. He then took a turn past Teresa Stanley's home on Silver Street, but again there was no sign of the Irish crime boss.

"He must be at Catherine's place," Gamel surmised.

The agent weaved his way through South Boston and onto the expressway toward Quincy.

It was just past 8 p.m. when Gamel spotted Bulger driving with Greig along Quincy Shore Drive heading toward Squantum, another small barrier island, where Catherine lived at the time.

Gamel followed two to three car lengths behind, using the surveillance skills he'd learned and mastered during his years with the Bureau. Whitey had no clue that he was being followed.

As Bulger turned right toward Catherine's split-level ranch house on Hillcrest Drive, Gamel continued on over a large hill, passing several small, well-kept homes in the quiet bedroom community.

When the agent came back down the hill, he saw the headlights of Whitey's car approaching in the distance. Gamel's rental car was similar to a vehicle driven by one of Bulger's gang members, so Whitey waved as the two cars passed each other.

When Bulger got a closer look at Gamel, he made a quick U-turn in the middle of the street and began following the FBI man.

"Okay, this may not end well," Gamel told himself as Whitey continued his pursuit. "Let's see how far he'll follow me. He's crazy but he's not stupid."

But Gamel came dangerously close to losing that bet with himself. When the two men approached a stoplight, the agent was stunned to see Bulger getting out of his car. Gamel placed his hand on his .40-caliber Glock and waited.

He's well known for coming up with a knife, so let's see what he does, Gamel thought as he watched Whitey approach slowly.

Suddenly, the dead quiet was broken by the sound of laughter and Bulger looked to his right, where he saw five uniformed policemen standing outside a Dunkin' Donuts sharing stories and sipping their nightly coffees.

Bulger got back in his car, followed Gamel for a couple more miles, and soon disappeared into the night.

With run-ins like this, Gamel knew Bulger and the case as well as anyone, so once his criminal investigation of Bulger turned into a fugitive case, the agent devoted himself to shaking the trees. He believed it would only be a matter of time before Whitey and Catherine were captured and brought home to face charges.

One sensitive pressure point for the gangster had always been his family—most importantly his brother Billy Bulger, the Senate president of Massachusetts and the most powerful politician in the state.

One day early on in the investigation, Gamel walked from his office up the hill to the golden-domed Massachusetts Statehouse and asked to talk to the lawmaker face-to-face.

"I'd like to speak with the Senate president," Gamel told Bulger's secretary as he handed her his card. "I need to see him now or make an appointment."

Billy Bulger's gatekeeper sized up the FBI agent and offered a fake smile.

"The Senate president is very busy," the secretary told him.

"Please ask him to give me a call so that we can discuss his brother's status," Gamel said before leaving.

Less than two hours later, as Gamel was working in his office cubicle, Bulger's secretary called his office line.

"Please hold for the Senate president," she advised.

Gamel rolled his eyes as he waited for the emperor-like Billy Bulger to come on the line. The agent spoke to Billy, explaining the purpose of his recent visit, and asked the lawmaker for a formal interview.

"I'm not interested at all in helping you," Billy Bulger said deliberately before slamming the phone in Gamel's ear.

GAMEL'S ATTEMPT WOULD BE REPEATED throughout the years of Whitey's run from the law, but Billy Bulger would remain elusive, beyond the FBI's grasp and protected by a powerful attorney along with his own reputation as one of the most influential men in the history of Massachusetts politics. While there were always suspicions about what Billy and other members of the Bulger family knew about their brother's whereabouts, he was never forced to address them directly. But in 2019, Billy Bulger sat down with the authors of this book to share for the first time his deep thoughts about his killer brother.

"He at different times of his life became wayward," Billy Bulger said, looking back. "But that's part of the mystery of why people do what they do, our own motivations and our own purposes. He was his own person and did his own thinking and he insisted on charting his own course."

That course was set early on in Whitey's life. His father, James Joseph Bulger, was born in Newfoundland and came to Boston in 1894 when he was eleven years old. Small in stature but powerful nonetheless, the elder Bulger rode freight trains looking for work as a teenager at the turn of the twentieth century and was almost killed when he attempted to jump a train but fell beneath its wheels. His left arm was nearly severed in the accident and couldn't be saved, so doctors were forced to amputate the badly injured limb.

James Bulger was fitted with a crude wooden hand that he kept hidden in his pocket for the rest of his life. He had two wives. The first was a woman named Ruth Pearce, whom he was married to briefly beginning in 1916. A decade later, he married a Charlestown girl twenty-two years his junior named Jane "Jean" McCarthy—Whitey's mother.

"They were both faithful to their task—their family," Billy Bulger says. "My father had a job as a night watchman over at the docks because no one else wanted the job. He was a good provider and even worked holidays when no one else would do it."

Whitey, the couple's second child, was given the name James Joseph after his father. He was welcomed into the Bulger family on September 3, 1929, just as the world was plunging into the Great Depression.

The growing family moved from Everett, Massachusetts, just north of Boston, to the neighborhood of Dorchester on the city's southern shoulder. Younger brother Billy came along five years later, just before the Bulgers made their final move to a housing project in Southie with its neighborhood parish of St. Monica's, the patron saint of difficult children.

"He [Whitey] kept comic books under his mattress, not Batman & Robin and Superman and such," Billy Bulger recalls. "He had true crime comic books and I would always be seeking them out to read them. Maybe he thought that that was the way to go."

Billy spoke softly in his thick Boston accent, tinged with a hint of Irish brogue, while reminiscing about his brother. A true academic with a vast and impressive vocabulary, he's rarely spoken about Whitey and had not made any public comments about his brother for more than a decade when he broke his silence with the authors. He sat at the wooden kitchen table in the same modest home where he has lived for decades, right in the heart of the very neighborhood where his brother's actions made countless mothers, wives, and girlfriends cry. The townhouse-style home is located directly across the courtyard from the longtime home of Mary Flemmi—Stephen Flemmi's mother—where cops once found a cache of weapons Whitey and his gang used to commit all sorts of atrocities. During the conversation, Billy was guarded, but he opened up about their childhood. With his wife, Mary, sitting by his side, he recalled how as a child, Whitey was particularly fascinated by a pair of killers from Texas—Clyde Barrow and his lover, Bonnie Parker. This attraction eerily foreshadowed his future on the run with Catherine Greig. In a letter written to a friend decades later in 2014, Bulger presented a photograph of the murderous bandits with this description.

> *2 of my favorite out laws*
> *"BONNIE + CLYDE"*
> *Died together, shot down*
> *from ambush by Frank*
> *Hamer Texas Ranger*
> *Tombstone for Clyde*
> *Barrow Read;*
> *"Gone But Not Forgotten"*
> *James Bulger 1428 AKA "Whitey"*

But South Boston wasn't a crime-ridden place back then and it isn't now. Southie residents went to work, attended Catholic church, and had pride in their neighborhood. Trouble existed, but one had to find it and Whitey found plenty of it, which caused great pain to his father, James Joseph.

The elder Bulger and his wife, Jean, had six children—three boys and three girls. When young Whitey got out of line, his father beat him severely. He once ran away with the Ringling Bros. and Barnum & Bailey Circus just to escape his father's wrath.

While the other Bulger children maintained good grades in school and kept away from trouble, Whitey struggled in the classroom and felt inferior—weak. On the streets, he was strong. He lifted weights and marched through the neighborhood with a distinctive swagger that he would maintain his whole life.

At sixteen, Whitey began his life of crime when he stole merchandise off delivery trucks and fenced them for a good price. It was called "tailgating," and it had a long and rich history in Southie dating back before World War I. That's when the Gustin Gang, which took its name from a street just a block long in the heart of their own territory in South Boston, targeted delivery trucks at city intersections. By handing down a serious beating to the driver, or simply by the mere threat of one, the gang terrorized Southie and then spread fear to other city neighborhoods. Known originally to police as the Tailboard Thieves, the Gustin Gang grew and diversified during Prohibition to the point that they controlled much of the illegal booze coming into New England. What shipments they didn't control became theirs through other means. Armed with fake badges of the kind used by government agents, the Gustin Gang confiscated cases of liquor from rival bootleggers and then sold them through their distribution network in Southie.

The Gustin Gang also owned and operated more rum-running boats than most of their rivals combined. Their vessels would steam out of Boston Harbor several times a week to rendezvous with liquor ships stationed three miles offshore in international waters. The bootleggers would stock up along "Rum Row" and head back to Boston, where eager patrons were happy to plunk down twenty-five cents for a watered-down beer that would have cost only a nickel before Prohibition.

Those early gangsters were legends to young Whitey, pulled right out of the true crime comics he kept stuffed under his bed. But what the comics failed to show was the price often paid for committing even the most minor crime. Once Whitey's name became known to police, they pulled him in at every opportunity and roughed him up for information.

"He talked often about police beatings and abusive police officers," Billy Bulger remembers. "I thought it was a bit of an exaggeration at first."

Whitey would later reveal that a cop had once stuffed a pistol in his mouth while another beat him so bad that he thought his arm was broken. In detailing Whitey's early life, Billy Bulger chooses his words carefully, and speaks pointedly and deliberately, as if to exonerate himself from responsibility while explaining his brother's life of crime.

"I'm not sure how one persuades or dissuades someone who's made up his own mind," he says. "At times he became impatient with me as I urged him into a different behavior . . . I wished it all could have been different."

When Whitey was eighteen years old, he was charged with assault with intent to rape. The victim was a young woman who claimed that she'd been mauled in a car by Bulger and two friends. Bulger wound up pleading guilty to a reduced charge—assault and battery—and paid a $50 fine. His family urged him to leave Southie, so he enlisted in the US Air Force.

While in the service, he earned his high school diploma and learned how to fix airplanes. He was arrested in Oklahoma City for going AWOL in 1950. He received an honorable discharge two years later despite more scrapes with the law, which included a charge of rape while stationed at a base in Montana.

Once back home in Southie, Whitey slipped right back into his previous life of crime, stealing, and eventually graduating to robbing banks.

His first big score came in 1955 when he and a small group of bandits robbed a bank in Pawtucket, Rhode Island. The heist took only four minutes and the robbers walked away with more than $42,000.

Two more bank robberies followed, including one in Hammond, Indiana. Waving a pistol at the terrified tellers, Bulger said, "We're not here to hurt anyone, but we have to make a living. Dillinger did."

Later, one of his bank-robbing buddies snitched to police and a warrant was issued for Whitey's arrest. This prompted Bulger to go on the lam for the first time, driving to Chicago, Utah, Reno, and San Francisco. He returned to Boston once he felt the heat had cleared but walked around Southie in disguise, wearing horn-rimmed glasses and dyeing his fair hair jet black.

A tip came into the Boston FBI office that a wanted bank robber was in town, so a young, flamboyant federal agent named Paul Rico followed the lead to a bar in Revere, just north of Boston, and arrested Bulger without incident. Neither man knew it at the time, but their meeting proved to be prophetic, as Rico and Bulger would join forces decades later to commit murder and mayhem on a grand scale.

Whitey was sentenced to twenty years in prison and was taken off the streets just before a mob war exploded in Boston between two Irish gangs that would leave fifty-six men dead in a span of just three years. There's little doubt that Bulger would have gotten caught up in the neighborhood combat, but instead, he sat in a prison cell where he read Machiavelli and waited patiently for the time that he could return to Boston and take over the city.

During his interview with the authors, Billy Bulger painted a romantic picture of Whitey's early years while also trying to distance himself from his brother's emerging criminal behavior. But Billy was no innocent bystander. During his career in Massachusetts politics, he benefited from his brother's reputation, which struck fear into his opponents. In the 1970s, Billy battled Boston mayor Kevin White over forced busing in Southie, which Billy vigorously opposed. The mayor strongly believed that he'd be set up for assassination by Whitey.

"I was never more scared in my life," Kevin White later admitted in an interview. "Whitey would be crazy enough to do it. And if they shoot me, they win all the marbles."

Throughout his storied political career, Billy Bulger was simultaneously haunted and elevated by his brother's reign of terror. He was guilty by association in the court of public opinion and always wore the scarlet letter of corruption due to Whitey's infamy. Every action he took on Beacon Hill throughout his career was met by hallway whispers about him being Teflon because of his crime lord brother. Tucking line items into budgets to cut state police funding, horse-trading government jobs, or working back channels to strong-arm political rivals frequently raised eyebrows and fueled speculation that he was in cahoots with Whitey, despite no hard evidence. Whitey was always an albatross around Billy's neck that he could never lift, and he certainly did nothing to remove it during the sit-down with the authors. In fact, he shrugged his shoulders and sighed when asked about his brother's life on the lam and what he knew about it. He was straightforward in his answers about why his brother chose the path he did, but was evasive about what he knew about his brother's fugitive escapades, just as he was throughout his entire career.

6

MUCH LIKE BILLY BULGER, WHITEY'S other siblings weren't talking about their fugitive brother's whereabouts in the months after he fled Boston. But just because they weren't talking didn't mean that they were immune from scrutiny.

Gamel figured that if he couldn't find Bulger, he could at least inflict pain on him from afar. Gamel huddled with then–US Attorney Donald K. Stern on an idea to seize Whitey's portion of a $14.3 million lottery jackpot he'd claimed back in 1991.

The lottery win had been another one of Bulger's brilliant schemes to launder his drug, extortion, and loan-sharking money. Back in the summer of 1991, a winning Mass Millions lottery ticket had been purchased at the South Boston Liquor Mart by Michael Linskey, who was the brother of a Bulger underling named Patrick Linskey. The FBI had learned that once Whitey heard about the jackpot, he ordered the real winner to sign the ticket over, with Whitey and two associates paying $2.3 million cash for 50 percent of the winnings. Bulger himself paid Michael Linskey $700,000. Although Linskey lost money in the deal, he really had no choice. It came down to selling the ticket or risking his life. Kevin Weeks, whose name also appeared on the winning ticket, later claimed that Linskey had purchased a large batch of tickets to hand out as Christmas gifts and promised to split any winnings with Bulger and Weeks. But Weeks's story makes little sense; the so-called Christmas gifts were purchased during the dog days of summer.

The gang took the winning ticket over to the South Boston Savings Bank, where they received a lottery check split four ways among the Linskey brothers, Bulger, and Weeks. The scam set up a twenty-year legitimate income stream for Whitey, where he earned $119,000 each year.

When news first broke about Whitey's lottery winnings in 1991, many in South Boston rose to his defense.

"God bless him, his number came up," said one local resident.

"He had the same chance to lose, right?" said another. "I think he ought to pay his taxes and keep the winnings."

Lottery officials took some heat, but they too called Whitey's lotto win legitimate.

"The only person that probably would have caused more trouble is if my mother had won," Massachusetts treasurer Joe Malone said at the time.

There was still $1.6 million left for Bulger to claim in 1995, so John Gamel won approval from the US attorney to serve the Massachusetts State Lottery with a federal seizure warrant to confiscate the remainder of his winnings. The forfeiture suit would require Whitey Bulger to appear in court in thirty days or give up any rights to his lottery prize, which was scheduled to be paid out until 2010.

There was a lot of money on the table, and Gamel relished the fact that he'd just scored one for the good guys and might possibly smoke Whitey out from hiding. The runaway mobster didn't show up to court the next month, but his older sister did. Jean Holland came forward and demanded that she be made receiver of her brother's estate in his absence.

When Gamel first heard that Whitey's sister wanted to lay claim to his lottery money, he drove to her house and tried to interview her on the front porch.

"I want you to understand what it means to harbor a fugitive," he told her. "If you are knowingly harboring your brother in any way, we can lock you up for a full year."

Holland looked at the agent with utter contempt. She said nothing and disappeared through her front door. Soon after, her attorney called Gamel in his office and berated him for "intimidating" his client.

Gamel locked eyes with Whitey's sister once again when she arrived at the Norfolk Superior Courthouse in Dedham, Massachusetts. Cameras packed the courthouse as Holland filed her claim to Whitey's winnings, stating that her brother had disappeared and that she had no idea where he was. Holland was treating her brother as if he were a missing person instead of the fugitive from justice that he truly was.

The fight between Whitey Bulger's sister and the US government would be tied up in court for the next several years. Ultimately, the Bulger family wouldn't receive a penny from the lottery winnings.

7

ALTHOUGH WHITEY WAS LONG GONE, Teresa Stanley still
lived in fear of her former mate. After all, he'd killed women
before. She was never out of Bulger's reach, as Kevin Weeks
kept close tabs on her during the months that his boss was crisscrossing the country with Catherine Greig. Teresa had a treasure
trove of information about Whitey's meticulous planning for his
possible life on the run, but she remained elusive to the FBI and
had refused to sit down for an interview. Stanley was now dating
another alleged hoodlum from South Boston named Alan Thistle.
Word on the street was that Thistle was an FBI informant working
directly for Gamel, earning $1,500 each month. How much infor-
mation about Bulger Thistle may have learned through pillow talk
with Stanley and shared with Gamel is not known. But the Bureau's
lack of results during this time spoke volumes.

To get to Stanley, John Gamel needed some solid backup. Enter
FBI agent Charlie Gianturco.

Gianturco was a classic street cop, having worked for years chasing New York's most powerful Mafia bosses, including Gambino
family godfather Paul "Big Paul" Castellano and the man who'd
seized power from him through the barrel of a gun, John Gotti. On
Gotti's orders, Castellano and his driver were assassinated in 1985,
gunned down in spectacular fashion in front of Sparks Steak House
in midtown Manhattan.

Gianturco, who had been schooled on mob life by none other

than legendary FBI agent Joe Pistone, aka Donnie Brasco, maintained wiretaps on Castellano's home and then on Gotti's headquarters in New York's Little Italy. The wiretaps on the Ravenite Social Club provided federal agents with countless hours of tapes incriminating Gotti in five murders, along with loan-sharking and a slew of other mob-related crimes. The "Dapper Don" was convicted on all charges in 1992 and sentenced to life in prison, where he died of throat cancer a decade later.

"The difference between Gotti and Bulger is that John Gotti was a thug and a hijacker of trucks out of the airport in Queens, New York. That's where he made his bones. He had a big fucking mouth and that's what got him into trouble," Gianturco says. "Whitey Bulger was a user of people. He used people and spit them out. But he was very smart."

The Bureau wanted a set of fresh eyes on the hunt for Whitey Bulger. John Gamel briefed Gianturco and two other agents on the case and set them loose.

Gianturco reviewed the file and tried to put the manhunt in its simplest terms.

"It's a guy from Southie versus a guy from Chelsea," he said, staring at a surveillance photo of Bulger. "Let's see how smart you are, Whitey."

For Gianturco, everything was about competition. Like Gamel, Gianturco came from Massachusetts, but Charlie was a Boston boy born and raised. He grew up playing football, basketball, and baseball in the predominantly Italian neighborhood of Chelsea, which had always been controlled by local wise guys. "In my neighborhood, you got two educations, one on the streets and one in school," he says. The son of a local doctor, Charlie went to private school at St. John's Prep in nearby Danvers, Massachusetts, and then the University of Dayton (Ohio).

His street smarts served him well out of the gate on the Bulger case. Gianturco understood that the key was Teresa Stanley, Whitey's longtime companion. But how do you engage her? Browbeating her into talking wouldn't work. Instead, Stanley had to be wooed and comforted. She was an abused and now scorned woman. The financial support Whitey had offered her for decades had dried up. She had no job; she had no savings. Teresa was also angry about the fact that he'd taken up with Greig again so quickly and easily, which is why she started dating Alan Thistle. Stanley hoped it would drive Bulger crazy with jealousy.

These feelings of financial desperation and personal rejection were tools that Gianturco could use to the Bureau's advantage. He visited Teresa at her home and asked her to lunch. Scanning Teresa's living room, it appeared that all evidence of her previous life with Bulger, photographs and such, was now gone, save for a replica sports magazine cover with a picture of Teresa and Whitey dressed as hockey players from the Montreal Canadiens on it. It was most likely a gift from Stanley's son-in-law Chris Nilan, a former NHL player who'd earned the nickname "Knuckles" as a longtime enforcer for the storied Montreal hockey club and later the Boston Bruins.

Gianturco's lunch with Stanley proved successful. They continued to talk for several more days. On the second day of long talks, Teresa served up some major bombshells. First, Stanley told Gianturco and his FBI partner Bob Walther about Whitey's safety deposit box in London.

"He's also using an alias," she confided. "He's going by the name Thomas Baxter."

Bingo, Gianturco thought.

Within an hour, the agents ran the Baxter alias through the Massachusetts Department of Motor Vehicles database and immediately got a hit. The name Thomas Baxter came up as a Massachusetts driver's license, but the identification card had Whitey Bulger's photo on it. The license was then transferred to New York.

"Baxter was a small-time guy from Woburn and Charlestown

who died back in the '70s," Gianturco says. "Bulger found out that he died and got his hands on the license and brought it in to get his own photo on it."

The agents knew that Bulger must have had someone working for him on the inside at the Registry of Motor Vehicles, but they couldn't get anyone there to cooperate with the investigation.

"We couldn't puncture the registry," Gianturco recalls. "Everybody said, 'This is Billy Bulger's registry' and we got no support."

Gianturco believes that Whitey's all-powerful brother stymied this critical part of their investigation. But the agents finally got the information they needed about the fake Massachusetts and New York licenses and then wondered, exactly how many licenses had Whitey made in how many states?

Gianturco then conducted an off-line search across the National Crime Information Center (NCIC) to see if Thomas Baxter's plates had been run by any member of law enforcement anywhere in the country. That's when he first learned about Bulger's visit to Mississippi, and another near miss in Sheridan, Wyoming, where a security guard at a veterans' hospital ran the out-of-state plates, and a third sighting of a Grand Marquis registered to Tom Baxter of Selden, New York, down in Louisiana.

"It looks like he's not crossing the borders into Canada or Mexico, or even fleeing to Europe," Gianturco said to himself. He thought the mad dash to Europe by investigators after the London safe deposit box was exposed by Stanley would be fruitless.

"It was all bullshit," the agent recalls. "Why put a safety deposit box in your own name like he did in London? He wasn't going back there. He'd changed his identity by then. He was someone else."

8

WHITEY BULGER AND CATHERINE GREIG did their best to fit in with the slower-paced crowd in Grand Isle, Louisiana. Bulger was still using the Tom Baxter alias, while Greig kept the name Helen Marshall. They did most of their shopping at a massive Walmart in nearby Galliano, Louisiana, where Catherine also purchased a pair of prescription eyeglasses.

She told the clerk that she was from New York and was visiting friends on the island. The Walmart employee remembered her as being very talkative. Bulger didn't say much, but his accent suggested that he was from somewhere up north.

The couple befriended a local family, mostly because of their mutual love for dogs. Catherine was missing her poodles Nikki and Gigi terribly and struck up a conversation with a town worker named Penny Gautreaux and her son Glenn Jr., known as "Bruiser," who owned two black Labrador retrievers.

"I was seventeen years old at the time I met him," Glenn Jr. said in a recent interview. "He was awesome. We called him Uncle Tom and her Aunt Helen."

The Gautreauxs invited the couple to their home for dinner, where they met Penny's husband, Glenn Sr., and the couple's other children. Penny served up fried fish and French fries, satisfying Whitey's appetite and also his love for family dinners.

Just as Catherine had missed her beloved dogs, Whitey longed for the good old days of sitting down with Teresa Stanley and her kids around the dinner table.

"He loved how tight our family was, the way we all took care of each other," Glenn Jr. recalls. "And we treated both of them as family also."

Whitey showed up at each meal with cartons of orange juice.

"You all need to drink your O.J.," he'd tell them. "You gotta stay healthy."

Like those family suppers with Teresa, Bulger insisted that the Gautreaux children sit at the table and not over on the couch, and even lectured them about the importance of a solid education and staying out of trouble.

Glenn Jr. got the nickname "Bruiser" because he got into a lot of fights in school. One day, his uncle Tom aka Whitey pulled him aside and stressed to the teen that there was a better way.

"I used to get into fights all the time too," Whitey told him. "You gotta cut out all that bullshit. It'll only lead to problems."

When one of the teenager's dogs got pregnant, Whitey offered him money to build a proper pen for the puppies. When one of the puppies got sick, Bulger paid the veterinarian bill.

"The vet couldn't help her, so I had to put the puppy down," Glenn Jr. remembers. "I dug a ditch while [Whitey] held the dog in his arms. He was crying real hard. He made me put down a bowl of food and water by the hole so the puppy could have a last meal while I dug."

Glenn Jr. retrieved his rifle and Whitey reluctantly handed over the sick dog.

"Do what you gotta to, but don't shoot her until after I walk away," he told the teenager. "I just can't bear to see it."

Bulger turned his back and began to walk. After about a hundred yards he heard the gunshot. Whitey didn't look back. Instead, he put his face in his hands and wept.

But it wasn't just household pets that had such an emotional effect on Whitey. When he'd take Glenn Jr. fishing, Bulger also had to look away as the boy retrieved his catch.

"It's just a fish," Glenn Jr. would tell him. "We eat 'em every night."

"Yeah, but they don't hurt anybody," Bulger replied. "I don't like seeing any kind of animal or even a fish in any kind of pain."

The comments were representative of Whitey's sociopathic behavior. The man had no fear or hesitation when it came to pumping bullets into the body of Brian Halloran. But he couldn't stomach any violence against a defenseless animal, or even a fish.

Whitey and Catherine became surrogate grandparents to the Gautreaux kids, and that meant bringing groceries to their house for home-cooked meals and taking the children out on spending sprees at the local Walmart.

"I'd walk in front of him and every time I'd pass and look at something like a new fishing rod or shotgun shells, he'd follow me and put it in the shopping cart and buy it for me," Glenn Jr. says. "We had no money, so they really took good care of us."

They also took on the responsibility of paying for an eye exam and glasses for Glenn Jr. In all, Whitey would later claim that he'd spent about $40,000 on the family. When asked by the clerk about her relationship to the teenager, Greig told her that he was her nephew. While there, Catherine ordered four boxes of contact lenses, a year's supply, for herself. "We travel and I want to make sure I have enough contacts," she told the clerk.

The clerk found it a bit odd but did not ask Greig aka Helen Marshall where they planned to travel next. There was a good chance that Catherine did not know herself.

The Gautreauxs grew to love "Uncle Tom," but they were also exposed to his dark side and were disturbed by the way "Tom" treated "Helen." He'd clap his hands or snap his finger as a signal to her that he needed something and she would always come running. He treated her much like a servant—not a wife.

When she needed time to herself, Catherine would take quiet walks on the beach or strolls through town, no doubt grappling with her decision to embark on this new and secret life. But she loved him. There was no doubt about that. Whitey was set in his ways, and she'd have to adapt to his lifestyle if she wanted to stay with him.

WITH ALL THE MILES THAT Whitey and Catherine were putting on the car, it was only a matter of time before Bulger swapped out the Grand Marquis for a new car. A reliable vehicle was critical to the aging gangster's freedom.

When Teresa Stanley gave up the Selden, New York, address of Kevin Weeks's cousin to Gianturco, the FBI sent an agent from its resident agency in Garden City by the home every day for four months, but there was no sign of the fugitive Bulger. Then, on a Friday night in 1996, an agent making his rounds by the Selden address spotted the Grand Marquis. The car Whitey Bulger had been driving for months had suddenly appeared in a Long Island driveway.

Gianturco was in Boston enjoying a retirement party for a friend when he got the call.

"I got an eye on the car. It's in the driveway," the agent told him.

Gianturco recalled what it felt like when he first learned the news. "You almost shit your pants when you hear something like that," he says.

He immediately reached out to his partner Bob Walther, and the two drove down to see for themselves. The resident agency in Garden City had only six agents working in the office and they were pulling night shifts watching the Selden address. They didn't have the manpower to handle surveillance of the vehicle. The case could break at any time, so it was paramount that Gianturco take control quickly.

When he and Walther arrived in Selden, they noticed that the home was in a quiet neighborhood at the end of a cul-de-sac.

"That posed a major problem," Gianturco remembers. "We needed a good surveillance position, but there was no rental property on the street that we could slip into unnoticed. There wasn't any way to keep watch on the house."

Gianturco drove through the neighborhood and spotted a home on another street whose backyard faced the driveway. He watched the place for a few hours before approaching the homeowner.

"I believed he was an Italian guy, so I spoke to him as one Italian to another," he recalls.

It was less than a month after the tragedy of TWA Flight 800, which mysteriously crashed into the Atlantic Ocean off East Moriches, New York, killing all 230 people on board. Long Island was crawling with federal agents at the time, which gave Gianturco an idea.

He knocked on the neighbor's door and introduced himself.

"We're in a sensitive situation. This has to do with Flight 800," Gianturco lied. "We need to be in this area to get some information."

"My brother's NYPD, I'll give you whatever you guys need," the neighbor said. "What can I do to help?"

The neighbor allowed Gianturco to park a van in his wooded backyard, where he and three other agents conducted surveillance on the Grand Marquis working in eight-hour shifts over the next forty days.

The car did not move and there was no sign of Bulger.

Each day, the owner of the Selden home, a man married to Kevin Weeks's cousin, started the car and ran it for a few minutes before switching off the ignition and going back inside. The surveillance job was tedious work as the agents sat huddled in the tin can, watching and waiting.

Finally on the forty-first day, the homeowner got into the Grand

Marquis and drove it to his work. Gianturco had previously run background checks on everyone inside the home. Although the wife was Weeks's cousin, there did not seem to be anything nefarious about the family. The husband was a straight guy who ran an honest business, and they had a daughter attending the US Naval Academy.

"How do we approach this guy?" Gianturco asked Walther. They didn't want to embarrass him at his house or his business. They needed to wait until the man was on the move.

The agents watched the man's store until closing time, which was after dusk. That's when he locked up his business and walked across a parking lot toward the Grand Marquis. Gianturco stepped out of the shadows and made the approach.

"Excuse me, sir, can I talk to you a second?"

Gianturco pulled out his badge and a small wanted poster with Bulger's face plastered on it.

"This guy's no good," Gianturco said, pointing at the photo.

"Oh, Tom?" the man replied.

"No, take a good look. Look who it is. It's not Tom Baxter. His name is Whitey Bulger and he's a murderer and a drug dealer, and you don't want him around your children."

The man was stunned. To him, the aging gentleman was Tom Baxter, a longshoreman who just needed an address for his mail and paid the family money to store his car and a safe at their home.

"Bulger co-opted these people," Gianturco says. "They were naive, yes, but they weren't criminals."

The man handed over the car without argument and swore total secrecy to Gianturco and Walther.

Gianturco had the car brought to a bay at the Nassau County Police Department. He drove back to Boston to pick up a forensic analyst and a mechanic he trusted.

"This is on the QT, so just tell your wives that you'll see them tomorrow," Gianturco told them.

He drove them down to New York and watched as they went to work.

"Now, Whitey, let's see where you've been," Gianturco said aloud as the lab technician and mechanic disassembled the Grand Marquis piece by piece.

They removed the vehicle's tires and took samples of the soil stuck in the grooves, as that might tell them what part of the country Bulger was traveling in. They ripped open the cushions and pulled up the rugs inside the vehicle.

"He was very involved in keeping his car in good shape," Gianturco recalls. "He'd been driving about two hundred miles per day, so he had new tires, new oil filters and everything."

The interior rug was attached to rails and when they pulled it up, the forensic analyst spotted a crumpled-up piece of paper underneath. Using a pair of gloves, he lifted the paper and handed it over to Gianturco.

"What's this?" the veteran agent said to himself as he eyeballed the evidence.

It was a receipt for coat hangers, milk, hair dye, and two other items from a Walmart Supercenter in Galliano, Louisiana.

Bingo.

Gianturco also found a Jiffy Lube in Galliano and learned that the Grand Marquis had been serviced there.

"You make your own luck," Gianturco says. "If you work hard enough, you're gonna catch a break."

He called an agent friend named Don Dixon, who worked for the FBI in Lake Charles, Louisiana.

"Don, what's down in the Bayou?" Gianturco asked. "I'm going down there on a case."

"Charlie, there's nothing fucking down there," Dixon told him. "The only place is Grand Isle. It's a summer resort with a hotel and a big marina, but that's it."

Gianturco and Walther caught a plane to New Orleans, grabbed a rental car, and headed for Galliano, driving along a four-mile-wide road with swamps on both sides dotted by run-down fishing huts and shrimp boats in the distance.

"This place is funky," Gianturco told Walther, who nodded in agreement.

When they arrived in Galliano, the agents canvassed the Walmart Supercenter and the local Jiffy Lube. There wasn't much else to see. The heat was stifling and the humidity caused Gianturco to sweat through his dress shirt. He and Walther walked around a bit, hearing the occasional conversation in Cajun French spoken by residents there.

"This doesn't make sense," Gianturco said. "There's no beaches to walk here. It's a pretty desperate place. Whitey's not here. He only shops here."

Then he recalled what his friend Don Dixon told him about nearby Grand Isle.

"Let's get back in the car," he told Walther.

They drove fifty-two minutes farther south and crossed the bridge onto the barrier island. Gianturco swung the rental car by the police station, where they asked to speak to the chief.

Gianturco offered the police chief the same photo of Bulger he'd shown Weeks's relative back in Selden. The chief recognized him immediately. He'd gotten to know "Tom Baxter" a little bit and would even wave hello each time they passed one another in town.

"Yeah, he walks the beach here every winter with a woman. They're supposed to be coming back here pretty soon."

Bingo.

Neighbors who knew Bulger as Tom Baxter said that he'd feed stray dogs biscuits from the back of his Grand Marquis.

Gianturco spent the next several months living quietly in Grand Isle, waiting for Bulger and Catherine to reappear. He stayed at the Sand Dollar Motel, the only motel there. The Bureau allowed only one agent at a time to conduct surveillance on the island, and

Gianturco swapped out with Walther every two weeks. He couldn't believe that the FBI wasn't committing more resources in covering this valuable lead. To Gianturco, this was a cheap way to conduct FBI business and it was also dangerous.

"The guy's probably got fourteen fucking guns on him," he said to himself. "And they [the FBI] assign only one agent to catch this guy?"

He was also concerned that Bulger would fight back if he was ever stopped by a patrolman while using the Tom Baxter identification. He pushed his superiors to include the words "armed and dangerous" to Baxter's (Bulger's) driver's license description in the National Crime Information Center (NCIC) database. In a sense, this was perpetuating Bulger's fraud, as the FBI was reluctant to declare that it was Bulger who was using the phony Baxter ID. A major concern was that Bulger himself might have access to the NCIC database and could be checking to see if his cover had been blown.

"What if some local cop pulls him over?" Gianturco argued to his FBI bosses. "They'll have no idea the danger Tom Baxter truly poses. We gotta protect that patrol officer. We'll be responsible if they get killed."

Finally, the FBI granted the okay. It was a small but important victory as Gianturco watched and waited for Bulger to return, praying each day that the stakeout had not been compromised.

9

TERESA STANLEY FELT GUILTY. SHE'D betrayed Southie's code of silence in her attempt to hurt her longtime lover. Stanley could not keep this secret for long. When Kevin Weeks paid another visit to her Silver Street home, he realized immediately that she was hiding something. Teresa was nervous and fidgety, lighting up one cigarette after another. First, Weeks peppered her with questions about her new beau, Alan Thistle.

"He's with Cathy; I have to live my life," Teresa told Weeks.

"There's plenty of guys out there to go out with. Why him?"

Weeks told Teresa that Thistle was an informant who was only sleeping with her to get information about Whitey.

"Well it's too late," Stanley finally admitted. She told Weeks that she'd already spilled her guts to the FBI. "Where Jimmy [Whitey] and I were in New York, the name Tom Baxter he was using, everything," she said.

Stanley clenched her teeth and braced for a beating. She probably thought Weeks would kill her right there in her own kitchen. Instead, he told her that he'd get back to her and he walked out the door.

Weeks immediately drove to Plymouth, where Stevie Flemmi was still locked up awaiting trial. He wrote a note on a piece of paper and pressed it to the glass partition between them. Flemmi read what Stanley had done and wrote his own note back ordering Weeks to contact Whitey. Until now, that had not been part of their arrangement. Whitey would reach out to Weeks when he needed something, not the other way around.

Kevin finally called Bulger and told him about Teresa. Whitey remained calm.

"Thank God, at least I know," Bulger said. "I'll call you back."

Whitey had a plan. He always had a plan.

When he got back in touch with Weeks, Whitey told him to find his younger brother Jackie Bulger, who looked enough like him with a head of fair hair brushed back atop a broad forehead, and take some photos that he could use for new identification.

"I've grown a mustache now," Bulger told Weeks. "Make sure Jackie's wearing a mustache."

Weeks then suggested killing Teresa's new boyfriend Alan Thistle, but Whitey refused to sanction the hit. He felt that going out with a low-level creep like Thistle was enough punishment for his former mate.

Jackie Bulger worked as the clerk magistrate of Boston Juvenile Court, and that made him, like his brother Billy, a sworn officer of the court. But blood always trumped the law in Southie. Not only was Jackie game to help his fugitive brother, he'd been paying the rent on Whitey's safe deposit box in Clearwater, Florida. Weeks drove to Jackie Bulger's house in Southie and performed a makeshift photo shoot, complete with a blue cotton sheet used as a backdrop and a prop—a fake mustache. Jackie Bulger posed like his tough older brother and Weeks selected the best four photos to use as he compiled the fake documents needed to deliver his boss a new driver's license, birth certificate, and Social Security card.

Whitey and Catherine couldn't leave Grand Isle without saying good-bye to the Gautreauxs. "Bruiser" was in bed when he heard a knock on the front door late at night.

"We gotta go, there's been a family emergency," Bulger told them. "You probably won't see me again, at least not in person. You may hear about me or read about me."

Oh shit, something must be really wrong, Glenn Jr. thought to himself.

Whitey and Catherine hugged each member of the Gautreaux family and left their home in tears.

CHARLIE GIANTURCO WAS STILL HOLED up in the Bayou in the midst of one of the longest stakeouts of his FBI career. While waiting for Whitey to reappear, he and a small team of agents interviewed everyone who'd come in contact with "Tom and Helen" on the sleepy barrier island and in nearby Galliano. Another team member, FBI agent Mike Carazza, hunted down the Gautreauxs, but they weren't saying much.

"Ain't no way that's him," Glenn Jr. said when he was shown an FBI wanted poster of Bulger. "You got the wrong guy."

Bruiser Gautreaux had no idea where the couple had fled, but even if he did know, he sure wasn't going to tell the FBI.

His mother, Penny, refused to talk also.

"She had to be compelled by a federal judge in Boston to testify before the Grand Jury," Carazza recalls. "It surprised us because here was a guy [Bulger] who was wanted for murder and she was pleading the Fifth until a judge ordered her to cooperate."

There was no doubt now that Whitey had been living in Grand Isle. The only question now was, would he return?

During a trip back to Boston, Gianturco visited Teresa Stanley, who confessed that she'd tipped off Whitey through Kevin Weeks. Gianturco knew there was no way that the fugitive crime boss would return to the Bayou now, knowing that the FBI had infiltrated Grand Isle.

Teresa figured she was now in big trouble, but Gianturco understood the incredible strain she was under.

"I told Teresa not to worry about it," Gianturco recalls. "This woman had been used all her life. I wanted her to know that we weren't the same as the bad guys."

While in Boston, Gianturco interviewed Whitey's former FBI handler, John Connolly, in Connolly's executive office at Boston Edison inside the Prudential Center. At this point in 1996, the extent of Connolly's crimes remained hidden—in fact not only was Connolly's corruption still unknown, he'd landed the cushy job with Billy Bulger's help upon his retirement from the Bureau.

For his part, Gianturco knew Connolly well. He and Connolly had played handball together, but more importantly, Gianturco's brother Nick had been Connolly's longtime partner in the FBI. Still, Gianturco refused to allow old friendships to get in the way of his investigation. He knew Connolly well enough not to trust him.

"He was in it for himself, always. He [Connolly] never did any real work. You gotta question a guy like that."

When he was first assigned the case, he asked Dick Swensen, then special agent in charge of the Boston Bureau, if they'd ever interviewed Connolly about Bulger's possible whereabouts. Shockingly, Swensen said no.

"We're now two years into the hunt for Whitey and no one's ever talked to John Connolly?" Gianturco says. "You do that on Day One!"

During their interview, Connolly nonchalantly told Gianturco and another agent that Bulger and Stevie Flemmi had been offered protection against prosecution by the FBI because they'd been "such good informants." While Gianturco and his partner knew that Bulger and Flemmi had been informants, they were floored by the news that they'd been offered protection against prosecution.

"I've known Jimmy Bulger since I was a kid," Connolly told them. "He used to buy me ice cream at a soda fountain in Southie. It's a great story and I'm thinking about using it in a book I'm working on about our relationship." Connolly had dreams that a

Hollywood superstar like Tom Cruise might even play him in an eventual movie.

Connolly then recounted a dinner with Bulger and Flemmi at the home of FBI supervisor John Morris in the historic town of Lexington, Massachusetts.

"He was in his cups," Connolly said of Morris, meaning he was drunk. "He told Bulger and Flemmi that they were so good as informants that he could get them off for anything short of murder."

Morris would later confess to taking $6,000 in bribes from Whitey Bulger, including $1,000 to bring his girlfriend to a 1982 Drug Enforcement Administration conference in Georgia as well as cases of French Bordeaux.

Connolly stressed that Morris promised Bulger and Flemmi they could continue to commit crimes like loan-sharking and illegal gambling as long as they fed the FBI information about Italian Mafia operations in Boston's North End. Connolly credits Bulger with providing him with knowledge used to obtain a wiretap of local Mafia boss Gennaro "Jerry" Angiulo's headquarters on Prince Street in the North End back in 1981. Connolly and a team of agents then arrested Angiulo as he sat down for a plate of pork chops at his favorite restaurant.

"I'll be back before my pork chops get cold," Angiulo said defiantly as Connolly placed him in handcuffs. Jerry Angiulo would spend the next twenty-four years in prison before dying a free man at ninety years old.

In Gianturco's opinion, Bulger and Flemmi should have been closed as informants after the Angiulo case. Instead, once the Mafia was crippled by prosecutions, Whitey's gang quickly filled the underworld void.

"Everyone knew this but no one wanted to go up against Connolly," Gianturco says.

Connolly also told Gianturco and his partner that Bulger and

Flemmi were indicted for things that they'd been told they wouldn't be indicted for.

"Bulger probably feels like he's been framed by the government," Connolly said incredulously. "I hope you guys never catch him."

For a long time, Connolly got his wish.

10

KEVIN WEEKS HAD MONEY INVESTED in a local orthopedic rehabilitation office and he often used the space for clandestine conversations with Whitey. Weeks would go to the office on Sunday nights and wait for further instructions from his boss. Sometimes, Bulger would order Kevin to drive from South Boston all the way to New Hampshire just to take a quick phone call at a secluded spot. During one of these calls, Bulger told him to meet up in Chicago. He and Catherine had ditched their car by then and were traveling by train from New York to the Midwest under the names Mark and Carol Shapeton.

Weeks met up with Whitey and Catherine at Water Tower Place, a huge shopping mall in downtown Chicago. Kevin had driven fifteen hours in a rented car from Boston, stopping overnight in South Bend, Indiana. He had the photos of Jackie Bulger with him.

They dined for lunch alfresco and walked around the city. Weeks had brought along a girlfriend to keep Catherine company. Greig looked good, radiant even, with smooth tanned skin and a toned body. Bulger looked better than he had in years, fit and happy and free of the anxiety he'd felt earlier while hiding with Teresa Stanley. Kevin was a giant ball of stress, however. So far, he'd escaped the noose of federal prosecutors, but he was looking over his shoulder every minute of every day waiting for an indictment against him to drop.

"If anything ever comes down, put it on me," Bulger told him during their walk.

But when Weeks showed Whitey the photos he took of Jackie, the boss shook his head in disgust. The mustache was all wrong. The fake one was much bushier than the pencil-thin facial hair Whitey was now sporting. They bought another Polaroid camera and a set of blue bedsheets to use as a backdrop and then went to Bulger's hotel room to take more photographs. The fugitive crime boss came up with four new aliases complete with Social Security numbers.

Evening had fallen and Whitey was hungry. He suggested they all go to a Japanese restaurant close by. The couples left the hotel and Catherine walked ahead with Weeks's girlfriend. Three young men catcalled the women as they walked by. Whitey exploded with rage.

"What're you looking at, you motherfuckers?" he shouted as he pulled a switchblade knife from a sheaf on his calf. Weeks whipped out his own knife, both blades now shining in the moonlight. They were ready for war, but the three young guys took off running down the street before any blood could be spilled.

When they entered the Japanese restaurant, Whitey pulled his protégé aside.

"Every day out there is another day I beat them, every good meal is a meal they can't take away from me."

They took a table in the back of the restaurant and devoured several dishes of chicken, beef, and vegetables while washing them down with some cold beer.

The next morning, Whitey and Catherine hopped on an Amtrak train and returned to Penn Station in New York while Kevin drove back to Southie to finish making Whitey's new IDs. Weeks was more paranoid than ever now. He swore that he heard the rotor blades of helicopters hovering over his house and he felt that he was being tailed everywhere he went. Instead of traveling himself, he asked a friend to deliver the phony identification cards to Whitey in New York. Bulger later convinced Weeks to meet him for one last rendezvous back at "the Lions," outside the main branch of the New York City Public Library. Whitey was feeling good, brazen even. While walking with Weeks and Greig in Manhattan, he stopped to ask a police officer for directions.

"The best place to get lost is a big city," Bulger said, trying to comfort Kevin after the brief encounter with the cop. "People are just walking around thinking about their own problems. You don't stand out there."

When Bulger put Weeks on a train back to Boston, the protégé had no idea that it would be the last time they'd see each other during Whitey's time on the run.

"I'll be in touch," Bulger told him. Weeks never heard from him again.

CHARLIE GIANTURCO HAD WATCHED BULGER slip through the FBI's net back in Grand Isle and he felt down, but not defeated. He knew that Bulger would not be careless enough to return to the Bayou, but his instincts told him that Whitey was still crisscrossing the South.

"We only have to be lucky once," he told himself over and over again. The feds were still monitoring the phone lines of Whitey Bulger's family and friends, and they got two hits for calls coming into the Southie address of a Bulger family neighbor from a calling card. One call was made in Slidell, Louisiana, and the other in Mobile, Alabama. The calls were both placed at gas stations along busy Interstate 10. Gianturco and his partner drove the route from Texas to Jacksonville, Florida, stopping at every resident FBI agency along the way. The trip took two weeks. Gianturco showed up at each FBI branch office with a stack of Bulger wanted posters.

"This guy's very familiar with the territory," he told his fellow agents. "And you may see him."

In the fall of 1997, Gianturco picked up a ping on a phone call to Southie while tracking Whitey in Mississippi. He says the call was made to one of Whitey's relatives from a pay phone near Biloxi.

Gianturco believes he was close to nailing Whitey in Mississippi when suddenly he got a call from a superior at the Bureau.

"We'd like you to return to Boston ASAP to discuss an important matter," the superior said.

"Now? I'm about to collar Whitey *fucking* Bulger!" Gianturco responded incredulously.

"Yes, right now. It can't be helped. Another agent will take the lead on Bulger."

Gianturco was frustrated, but he followed his orders and returned to Boston. The lead died there. Looking back now, it's hard for him not to have suspicions about the timing of that call back to Boston.

"I was about to arrest Whitey Bulger," he says today. "And someone inside the Bureau did not want that to happen."

In reality, Whitey Bulger was a ghost. Just as Gianturco and other agents were getting close to him in the Deep South, Bulger and Greig both vanished again, returning to Chicago, where Whitey met up with an old buddy from Alcatraz named Barney "Dirty Shirt" Grogan. A convicted bank robber, Grogan had earned his nickname by smuggling steaks under his shirt out of the prison kitchen. His real name wasn't Grogan at all, but John Joseph O'Brien. Whitey always found a way to connect with his prison pals, especially those who'd served with him at Alcatraz—his alma mater. Before he'd gone on the run, Whitey visited with another old inmate friend in Youngstown, Ohio. The former prisoner was down on his luck until Bulger appeared and lifted the trunk of his car. Inside were stacks upon stacks of dollar bills. Whitey took a few stacks out and placed them in the man's hands before going on his way.

After his brief reunion with "Dirty Shirt" Grogan, Whitey and

Catherine boarded a train headed west. They rode the Southwest Chief through the Great Plains and the Rocky Mountains until tall pine trees gave way to desert palms before arriving at Union Station in Los Angeles.

They booked a modest, quiet motel nearby and camped out there while Whitey plotted his next move. He considered heading north to Washington State, but the weather there was too damp for his aging bones; the same with San Francisco, which would have allowed him a sweeping view of his former home on Alcatraz. Bulger bought a map and unfolded it on the bed, studying it for several hours until Catherine urged him to get some sleep. Sleep would not come easy for him, though. It never did. Whitey had suffered from insomnia followed by frightening nightmares since his prison days in the 1960s, when he'd volunteered to take part in a covert CIA program called MK-Ultra in exchange for time shaved off his sentence. Bulger and the other prisoners were lied to and told that they were participating in a study to find a cure for schizophrenia. In reality, the CIA was working on a mind control weapon. Whitey was injected with LSD for weeks at a time, and he suffered terrifying hallucinations as he envisioned blood pouring from his cell walls while his prison bars transformed into slithering black snakes. He felt his head change shape and heard haunting voices. Years later he read that LSD also caused chromosome damage, and he blamed the drug for the death of his only son.

On one of their first days in Los Angeles, Bulger awoke in the early morning to the sound of a helicopter hovering over their motel. It was no hallucination. It was real.

This is it, he thought to himself. *It all ends here.*

He rushed to the window for a peek outside and saw a caravan of television news trucks passing by without stopping. Bulger then flicked on the television set to see what the commotion was all about. Turns out, the media including the news chopper hovering overhead were all scrambling to cover the O. J. Simpson civil trial, which was now unfolding nearby at the Santa Monica Courthouse. Instead of breathing a sigh of relief, Bulger ordered Catherine to pack her stuff immediately. They were leaving the motel as soon as possible to find something quieter and far away from the O.J. media circus. Their next stop was Venice Beach.

11

BEFORE HE'D EVEN ACCEPTED THE job to join the Bulger task force in 2008, Tommy Mac knew the story of Kevin Weeks. Every FBI agent did. Weeks's decision to flip had been one of the most important moments in the hunt for Bulger, not only because it provided them with fresh intelligence on Whitey, but because it had finally laid bare the FBI's role in Whitey's criminal enterprises.

Reading through the FBI's paperwork on Weeks, it was hard not to be shocked all over again by what had transpired. The capture and confession of Weeks would have huge ramifications on the search for Bulger, ramifications that even in 2008, as Tommy Mac was joining the task force, continued to reverberate. Weeks's eventual testimony implicated high-level officials at the Boston FBI office, but it also overshadowed all of the aggressive work that agents had been doing to catch him. All those near misses, all that good detective work, had been lost in the taint of scandal.

Suddenly, the whole hunt for Bulger became suspect. And somehow, in 2008 it still was.

BY THE MID-1990S, THE CAPTURE of Weeks had been building for some time. After he and Bulger met for the last time in the spring of 1996, Kevin Weeks gravitated toward John Connolly. Having no contact with Bulger, Weeks and Connolly met more than three dozen times. If Weeks wanted a sit-down with the former federal agent turned private-sector security chief, he'd call Connolly's office and give the receptionist a fake name.

"Tell Mr. Connolly that Chico called."

Connolly would then call a relative of Weeks to set up the meeting.

Bulger's onetime man on the inside at the Bureau told Weeks about a turf war being waged between the FBI on one side and the Massachusetts State Police aligned with the DEA on the other. Connolly was right. Nobody trusted anybody when it came to the Bulger investigation.

"I called State Police Colonel Tom Foley early on in my investigation and asked that we share information and resources," Charlie Gianturco recalls. "But he wanted no part of us."

Foley and others had long suspected that John Connolly, John Morris, and other federal agents were protecting Whitey Bulger and Stevie Flemmi and that this bad blood extended to every other agent in the Boston FBI office—corrupt or not. Foley had launched his own investigation and search for Bulger and Greig. He had a strong hunch that the pair was now living in Cuba, but the lack of diplomatic relations between the Clinton White House and Fidel Castro destroyed any chance of going there to find out.

"He had all the money in the world," Foley said in an interview later. "It was one of the areas we thought could be a real good spot for him."

What Foley didn't know at the time was that Bulger and Flemmi had also corrupted a member of the state police. A former lieutenant named Richard Schneiderhan had been feeding Flemmi information for years. It was Schneiderhan who had tipped off the gang to a state police bugging operation of their headquarters, a garage on Lancaster Street in Boston, back in 1980. He'd later tell Weeks that the FBI was tracking phone calls made from the homes of Billy and Jackie Bulger.

Schneiderhan had a warm spot for Billy Bulger. The dirty state cop was a member of a Catholic church that was spared from the wrecking ball when Billy helped it gain designation as a national historic site.

Kevin Weeks was now managing the relationship with Schneiderhan, who enjoyed playing wise guy as it boosted his ego. The gang had penetrated the ranks of the FBI and the state police, and they were relationships that kept on giving. But Weeks never asked himself what the feds wanted in return.

He found out one night in the spring of 1997, when he learned through a TV news report that Flemmi had testified during an evidentiary hearing that he and Bulger were longtime FBI informants—*rats*.

Weeks was stunned. At first he didn't think he'd heard it right. He continued to flip through the channels, and every local station had topped its newscast with the blockbuster revelation.

"It made no sense. We *killed* guys because they were informants," Weeks would later write in his memoir. "And now I was learning that Jimmy [Whitey] and Stevie were informants themselves."

For more than two decades, Kevin Weeks, Whitey's loyal soldier and surrogate son, had believed that it was Bulger who was corrupting the FBI, paying them for information that allowed him to stay two steps ahead of the law. But instead it was the FBI that had struck a Faustian bargain with the Irish mob boss to supply them with a steady stream of intelligence that would put his friends and criminal associates behind bars.

Whitey Bulger's life of crime had been fueled by one big lie. While rumors had swirled in the criminal underworld and among law enforcement for years that Bulger and Flemmi might be protected informants, the first time the duo was publicly accused surfaced in a 1988 report by the *Boston Globe*'s Spotlight Team. Although the documentation was a bit veiled in the story, the newspaper reported that the Southie crime lord had a "special relation-

ship" with the FBI. James F. Ahearn, who was then special agent
in charge of the FBI in Boston, denied any improper relationship
between the Bureau and Bulger, telling the Spotlight Team, "That
is absolutely untrue . . . We specifically deny that there has been
special treatment of this individual."

KEVIN WEEKS HAD MADE HIS reputation as a tough guy who
preyed on criminals and the innocent alike. But now he was the
target. Weeks figured that rivals on the street would believe that he
too was an informant for the FBI. He carried two pistols with him
at all times under a long coat with the pockets cut out so he could
keep his hands gripped tightly on two .45s that were sticking out of
his large waistband.

He met with Flemmi behind bars and accused him of putting
a bull's-eye on his back. Flemmi tried to downplay the situation,
but Weeks stormed out of the jailhouse visit. Later, John Connolly
offered his own take on the double dealing. To him, it was a simple
case of survival of the fittest.

"The Mafia was going against Jimmy [Whitey] and Stevie,"
Connolly explained to Weeks. "So Jimmy and Stevie went against
them."

As Weeks was trying to put the pieces together in his own head,
the Massachusetts State Police and DEA swooped in and plucked
him off the streets. He was arrested in November 1999 with a con-
cealed weapon—a knife in his pocket.

Weeks was charged with twenty-nine counts including extortion, money laundering, and racketeering and held without bail.
He was forty-three years old, the father of two teenage boys, and
he was facing hard time. He was sent to a federal holding facility in
Rhode Island. Normally, he would have been placed in Plymouth,
but that's where Flemmi was and authorities didn't want them communicating now that both were in jail.

Weeks's lawyer pulled the 661-page ruling from Mark Wolf, the federal judge assigned to the Bulger and Flemmi case, and gave it to his client to read. Weeks studied each page outlining their relationship with the FBI. Flemmi had been ratting on his friends since the mid-1960s, while Whitey was brought into the Bureau's fold a decade later.

Bulger's surrogate son had a decision to make: either keep protecting his boss and his boss's lies, or protect himself and cut his own deal. It was a no-brainer. Kevin Weeks offered to cooperate with prosecutors. He knew where the bodies were buried—literally.

On the frigid morning of January 13, 2000, Weeks took investigators on a tour of the gang's greatest hits. He brought them to Hallet Street in Dorchester, across from Florian Hall, which is the Boston firefighters' union hall, as well as a banquet facility where Boston politicians hold rallies and many Irish wakes are celebrated.

Weeks pointed to the patch of snow where underneath lay the bodies of three Bulger victims—a safecracker named Bucky Barrett, a boat mechanic turned smuggler named John McIntyre, and a twenty-six-year-old woman named Deborah Hussey, the stepdaughter of Stevie Flemmi.

Weeks had reburied the bodies there more than a decade earlier. On Halloween 1985, Weeks served as an armed lookout while Flemmi and Bulger dug the ditches under the cover of darkness. While Whitey and Stevie were working their shovels, the area was illuminated by headlights as a car pulled in and stopped a few yards away. Flemmi and Weeks hid as the driver got out, stumbled a bit, and unzipped his fly to take a piss. He got back in his car a few moments later and drove away. Weeks kept his eye and his trigger trained on the drunken motorist but didn't act.

"I told you that if anybody spots us, to shoot 'em," Flemmi told Weeks.

"Ah, c'mon Stevie, the guy's drunk. He just stopped to take a leak. He didn't see us and won't remember anything in the morning," Weeks replied.

"If anybody else comes here, you put 'em in the ground," Flemmi ordered. "Or one of these ditches will be for you."

As snow began to fall on the night of January 13, 2000, the sound of a large backhoe could be heard near Florian Hall, where state police and the DEA performed the grisly task of recovering the bodies, or what was left of them.

A short time later, investigators found bones. Deborah Hussey's tibia was still connected to her ankle and her foot was covered by a rotting shoe. Weeks told authorities that Hussey was choked to death by Whitey Bulger in early 1985. Kevin had witnessed the whole thing. It happened inside a home on East Third Street in Southie, which was owned by the brother of Bulger associate Pat Nee. They called the place "The Haunty," because of the grim undertakings that took place in its basement. Whitey was on the floor strangling Hussey with his bare hands, his legs wrapped around her. The attack was violent and took several horrific minutes. Her body was carried to the basement. Flemmi feared that she wasn't quite dead, so he strangled her some more and then pulled her teeth out to prevent identification before he buried her in the dirt basement.

Hussey's murder was a violent end to a long and abusive relationship she had with Flemmi—her stepfather, the one she called Daddy and who had driven her to school as a child. The young woman had threatened to expose the incestuous relationship to her mother, Marion, Flemmi's common-law wife. Before luring the younger Hussey to her death, Flemmi brought her on a shopping spree, buying her clothes that he knew she'd never wear.

Deborah Hussey's bones were found buried near the remains of John McIntyre. He too met his fate in The Haunty, on November 30, 1984. Whitey was worried that McIntyre was snitching about Bulger's involvement in a 1984 shipment of seven tons of guns including 163 assault rifles from Gloucester, Massachusetts, to

Ireland to support the Irish Republican Army's war of terror against Great Britain. McIntyre was a crew member aboard the fishing boat *Valhalla*, which carried the weapons, all hidden in caskets, and transferred them to a boat off the coast of Ireland. The guns never made it to shore, as the second vessel was quickly seized by Irish authorities. After McIntyre returned home, he wanted to go clean and start living a normal life. He reached out to the DEA to make a deal and word got back to John Connolly, Whitey's man on the inside. Bulger brought McIntyre to The Haunty and interrogated him at gunpoint while Flemmi tied him up with handcuffs and leg shackles. McIntyre confessed to everything, including tipping the DEA off to a large boat shipment of marijuana that was supposed to earn Bulger and his gang $3 million.

"I'm sorry, I was weak," McIntyre cried.

After six hours of questioning, McIntyre was led to the basement in chains. Whitey pulled out a rope and wrapped it around the smuggler's neck. Bulger tightened it with his strong forearms, but the rope was too thick to do the job. McIntyre just gagged and vomited. Whitey then reached for his pistol and waved it at his victim.

"Would you like one in the head?" the executioner offered.

"Yes, please," McIntyre pleaded.

Bulger shot him once in the back of the head and then several more times in the face, turning McIntyre's flesh into hamburger. Flemmi later pulled the man's tongue out with a pair of pliers. When McIntyre first disappeared, his family believed that he'd been taken out by a hit squad sent by British Intelligence because of his support for the IRA. When McIntyre's father began demanding answers, he was approached by a mysterious man who offered a warning: "Remember, you have another son."

But the first man murdered inside The Haunty was Arthur "Bucky" Barrett, a safecracker who was involved in a daring burglary at the Depositors Trust Bank in Medford, just north of Boston, in 1980. The robbers had entered the bank by breaking through a four-inch concrete wall from an adjoining eye doctor's office. Then they had to drill through another eighteen inches of steel and concrete to gain access to the vault, where they stole $1.5 million worth of cash, gold, silver, and jewels. The gang included several cops. Barrett's role was to bypass the bank's security system. Whitey was due $100,000 from the heist as a tribute, but Bucky refused to pay. Bulger was patient, though. He waited three years before making his move. On July 26, 1983, Whitey had a friend invite Barrett to The Haunty to inspect a cache of stolen diamonds. When he got there, Bulger met him with a nine-millimeter machine gun with a silencer.

"Bucky Barrett, freeze!" Whitey ordered, pointing the gun at the safecracker's heart.

Barrett was chained to a chair and grilled for information about a rival's drug business and then was ordered to pay Whitey the money he was owed.

Bulger and Flemmi stuffed Barrett in a car and drove to his home in Quincy, where Bucky retrieved $47,000 in cash and collected another $10,000 from a bar that he owned at Faneuil Hall Marketplace. They returned to The Haunty and Whitey announced that Barrett was going downstairs to "lay down."

Flemmi and Kevin Weeks knew what this meant.

As Barrett was led down the basement steps, Whitey stuck his gun to the back of his head and pulled the trigger, but the gun safety was on. Bulger fixed the problem and fired again, and this time the back of Barrett's head exploded and his body tumbled down the stairs.

Whitey went back upstairs and ordered Weeks to help Flemmi clean up the mess.

"I'm gonna lie down," Bulger said as he walked toward a bedroom and closed the door.

Barrett was buried in the dirt basement, where he was later

joined by McIntyre and Hussey. The macabre decision to unearth the bodies from The Haunty and move them to the Hallet Street site was made by Bulger because Nee's brother sold the house.

Now they were getting dug up again—this time by authorities.

Another Bulger death pit would be unearthed later that year. By this time, his brother Billy had retired from politics and was serving as president of the University of Massachusetts, earning more than $200,000 per year. Billy's crowning achievement as president was securing the first debate of the 2000 presidential election between Texas governor George W. Bush and Vice President Al Gore for the UMass Boston campus. Just so happens, while the candidates were taking the stage, excavation crews were digging for more Bulger victims nearby.

"The victims include strangers who happened to be in the wrong place, longtime criminal associates, friends and others," said US Attorney Donald Stern at the time.

12

WHITEY'S WELL-CRAFTED PERSONA AS A gentleman gangster and the Robin Hood of South Boston was virtually shattered once the city's newspapers and television stations described his death pits in gruesome detail. As the facts came to light, investigators continued forensic work day and night on Hallet Street, utilizing sifting screens, spoons, and small tools under yellow-and-white-striped tents to keep the burial ground out of sight.

The unearthed bodies ended any doubt about Bulger's murderous ways and ran counter to the image of Whitey that many people, especially those in Southie, had fixed in their minds. Before he went on the run, Bulger was spotted handing out turkeys to needy families in the projects on Thanksgiving. He sent money to the canteen accounts of jailed Southie prisoners. He donated to youth sports programs. He literally helped old ladies cross the street.

"You had a husband giving a wife a hard time, that's the stuff you went to him for," said then–City Councilor Peggy Davis-Mullen, a South Boston native who represented the district. "Even growing up, there was this dichotomy. You knew that he was a guy that was involved in organized crime, but you also had—I've got to be honest with you—regard for the man. I don't know what he did when he was doing his business, whatever his business was, but I know that he was a guy on the street and that he was good to people that were poor."

This myth was even perpetuated by the local media, especially longtime *Boston Globe* columnist Mike Barnicle, now a high-paid talking head on MSNBC's popular *Morning Joe* program. After Whitey had scammed his way to the lottery jackpot in 1991, Barnicle insisted that he had won it fair and square and told his readers so.

"So, lay off Jimmy Bulger. For the first time in his life, he got lucky, legitimately, and won the lottery," Barnicle wrote at the time. "Knowing him, he probably already handed out money to St. Augustine's, figuring that when he goes—and the odds on that are better than winning Mass Millions—there will be some people left behind who will say, 'Not a bad guy.'"

While he still had friendly columnists in his back pocket, the burial ground's discovery finally provided incontrovertible evidence of what an evil, murderous man Whitey Bulger truly was.

One person who knew the real Whitey Bulger was John Connolly, and now the former FBI agent found himself in handcuffs. He was arrested just before Christmas 1999 at his home in Wakefield, Massachusetts. Connolly was recovering from the flu when agents yanked him out of his stately colonial home and escorted him across his well-manicured lawn and into an FBI vehicle. Connolly, who wore expensive suits and $100 haircuts, was sick and disheveled on this day. His hair was a mess and he was dressed in a jogging suit. He looked like any other mobbed-up thug.

Charlie Gianturco and others had been chasing Connolly for some time and they finally got the break they needed when Frank Salemme, the cagey head of the Boston Mafia, testified that it was Connolly who had tipped him and Whitey off to the impending indictments years earlier, allowing them to escape.

Connolly was soon out on bail and was called a scapegoat by his attorney. He also received a phone call from Billy Bulger, who later told a federal grand jury that he was "just expressing interest in his situation and giving him a call to tell him that I still have confidence in him."

Gianturco was elated by Connolly's arrest, but he soon got pulled down and nearly drowned in the corrupt agent's wake.

Kevin Weeks, still wheeling and dealing, told a federal judge that Whitey had six FBI agents on his payroll including Connolly, John Morris, and an FBI supervisor named James Ring who received cash and gifts from the gang. He then pointed an accusing finger at Gianturco and his brother Nicky.

Nick Gianturco was Connolly's longtime FBI partner, and he'd been cozy with Bulger since Whitey allegedly warned him that he'd been marked for death by other gangsters. Nick dined with Whitey and even presented him with the Alcatraz belt he still wore proudly around his waist. In return Bulger gave him some expensive crystal stemware, an attaché case, and an Oriental figurine.

"At the time it did not dawn on me that it was something that I probably should not have done," Gianturco said later.

Nick Gianturco had long since retired and like Connolly, found a job in corporate security. But his younger brother Charlie was still an active agent and presumed guilty by association.

"The Bureau didn't back me," Charlie Gianturco recalls. "They said go down to Washington, you need to get polygraphed."

Charlie passed the lie detector test, but he knew that he was dead in the water when it came to the Whitey Bulger investigation. He asked Barry Mawn, then special agent in charge of the Boston office, whom he had worked with on the FBI's bank robbery squad in New York City, to take his name off the case as case agent but to keep his team intact. Gianturco was ready to jump ship but offered to assist on the Bulger case behind the scenes.

"This was personal to me. My reputation was on the line. I understood Whitey Bulger better than anyone," Gianturco says. "I got deep into his head. He didn't follow the criminal code and would sacrifice anyone and anything to survive. He was a vicious killer of women and yet he depended on a woman to survive. But there were other forces working against me, including some of my so-called *friends* in the Bureau."

Charlie Gianturco went on to work several other cases, including helping nab infamous terrorist Richard Reid, the "Shoe Bomber," and breaking up a human trafficking ring that included the kidnapping and exploitation of a thirteen-year-old girl.

"I took a beating from feds in Washington who whispered that I was dirty, when in fact they were the dirty ones," Gianturco says with disgust. "Collaring Richard Reid at Logan Airport in Boston was like redemption for me. I had arrested this notorious terrorist and gained information from him that put him behind bars for life."

More satisfying for Charlie Gianturco was saving the thirteen-year-old girl from the gang of sex-traffickers. "I celebrated each birthday with her and was there when she finally graduated high school. She had lost her innocence but we fought hard to get her life back."

While he remained on the outside looking in when it came to the Bulger case, Gianturco routinely called his FBI colleague Roberta Hastings in the Boston office with new information and fresh ideas.

"We all wanted that son of a bitch caught, but none more so than Charlie Gianturco," says Hastings.

13

WHILE HIS DARK SECRETS WERE getting dug up from the frozen ground in Boston, Whitey and Catherine were enjoying all the sunshine and warm weather that Southern California had to offer. He was now facing nineteen murder charges back home in addition to the extortion and bribery counts. Stevie Flemmi, his partner in crime, was charged with participating in ten of those slayings.

But Bulger was deep underground now, and the west coast provided him with the perfect place to hide. He'd vacationed there years before with Teresa Stanley, although he didn't mention that to Catherine. Whitey was playing the role of devoted husband now and Greig soaked up all the attention.

After leaving the motel near the O. J. Simpson media circus, they stayed in Venice Beach, an eclectic artsy community that was plagued by an exploding homeless population with desperate forgotten people huddled in encampments living in tents under murals of rock icons like Jim Morrison and Jerry Garcia. The down-on-their-luck crowd were easy marks for the aging gangster on the run.

Bulger was always looking for new identification cards. Fake IDs were as good as gold to him. While in Venice Beach, he spotted a homeless woman lugging an old suitcase down the street. Whitey and Catherine approached her and offered to buy her a new suitcase at a store nearby. The woman had moved to California decades before in hopes of finding stardom, but now she was living on the

streets and in and out of hostels. Bulger pulled out $40 cash to pay
for the luggage and then offered the woman another $200. He told
her that he and Catherine had moved to California from Canada
and they needed some documentation to stay in the country. The
homeless woman offered him her Social Security card and another
ID in exchange for the money.

Catherine had grown tired of life on the road, bouncing from
one motel room to the next. She yearned for somewhere to call
home. They found a place to settle down in nearby Santa Monica.
The seaside community cultivated an interesting mix of people,
from the Hollywood elite to college students, pensioners, and vacationers, who flocked to its famous pier with its towering Ferris
wheel and other amusement rides that glimmered off the Pacific
Ocean each night after sunset. The city's name also had a special
meaning for Whitey. Living in Southie as a child, he'd attended
St. Monica–St. Augustine Church. Now he was living once again
under the protection of the patron saint of difficult children.

With the Tom and Helen Baxter names compromised, the couple was now going by Charlie and Carol Gasko. Bulger took the
name from a mentally disabled homeless man he'd encountered
during one of his walks through town. The homeless guy's name
was actually Charles Gaska. Whitey paid him cash for his Social
Security card and altered the name slightly to Gasko. Then, he and
Catherine placed a $300 cash deposit on a two-bedroom apartment
with a balcony overlooking the street at the Princess Eugenia. The
rent there was $837 a month.

The twenty-seven-unit building was just a few blocks from the
beach. It wasn't a slum, but it was plain-looking and worn. Princess
Eugenia's best days were behind her. The complex had originally
housed art students from the J. Paul Getty Museum. There were
still some students there now, along with retirees. The place was
rent controlled when they first moved in, which was attractive to
Whitey and Catherine. Plus, they didn't have to sign their names

on a lease, provide any references, or undergo a credit check. The building's management had made it all too easy for the mob boss turned fugitive. After moving in, the couple kept mostly to themselves, which was the way Whitey wanted it.

When he got to Santa Monica, he tried to track down one of his former Alcatraz associates, a bank robber named Frank Hatfield, who'd served six years on the Rock. Hatfield was known for his ability to use printing presses to craft fake checks and identification cards. Bulger searched for Hatfield hoping he could create fake IDs for him and Catherine. He never connected with Hatfield, perhaps not knowing that the man had actually gone straight and become a US park ranger who gave guided tours of Alcatraz.

Whitey got lucky one day while walking through Palisades Park when he struck up a conversation about the weather with a man who appeared to be down on his luck.

"Do you have a driver's license?" Bulger asked.

The man said he had a license from the state of Nevada.

"Do you have any drunk driving charges or points against it?" Bulger pressed.

The man shook his head no.

"I'll give you $200 for it."

"I've got a Social Security card and a Sam's Club card," the man told him.

"I'll give you another $50." Bulger smiled.

He paid the man, stuck the IDs in his pocket, and walked away.

Their first few months living at Princess Eugenia were like a honeymoon. Whitey loved the old-time penny-crushing machines he found in the boardwalk arcade at the Santa Monica Pier. He enjoyed crushing the pennies and giving them to Catherine as little tokens of his affection, once handing her one engraved with the words "I love you."

Together, they would stroll to the Rose Garden at Palisades Park and shop at Barnes & Noble, where Bulger would browse the true crime section looking for books written about him or other mob figures. Once they returned to Third Street, Whitey would remind Catherine that the neighborhood had once been home to one of his favorite comedians, Hollywood legend Stan Laurel. Bulger explained that one of the few luxuries he had enjoyed while behind bars at Alcatraz was watching Laurel & Hardy movies on a screen in the mess hall.

When Catherine would get her hair done at a local salon, a place appropriately called The Haircutters on Wilshire Boulevard, she'd chat with her hairdresser Wendy Farnetti about her husband "Charlie." For her, it was much-needed "girl time."

Greig appeared every two to three weeks wearing a visor to protect her face from the sun while pulling a cart filled with groceries from a nearby Whole Foods. She was no longer coloring her hair, which had turned white like Bulger's. Catherine kept it short in the front, long on the sides, and shaggy in the back. It was a bit punkish, and she resembled some aging 1980s rocker.

Catherine told Farnetti that her husband suffered from prostate problems and other ailments.

The hairdresser noticed that Catherine, or "Carol," spoke with a Boston accent and surprisingly, Greig told her that she was originally from Massachusetts. She also seemed to be always stressed out. Farnetti never saw her client's beau and began to jokingly refer to him as Carol's fictional husband.

Despite occasional forays out in the bright sunshine, Bulger became a virtual shut-in while his girlfriend hungered for contact with the outside world.

"Why don't you bring him in so I can cut his hair?" Farnetti asked.

"No, he doesn't go out for a haircut," she replied. "He's bald and just does a buzz on his hair."

Farnetti offered Carol her own tale of woe and confided to her that she was a "bum magnet" when it came to men.

The two had much in common.

"I like the bad boys," Catherine confided to the hair stylist. "I knew he was a bad boy when I married him, that's what attracted me to him. But he's older and has mellowed out now."

There was once a gap between visits to the beauty parlor that lasted over a month, and Farnetti was concerned until suddenly Catherine reappeared one day. Her hair was a mess and she acted distraught and nervous. Farnetti believed that her client had been pulling her own hair out because of some kind of stress.

"What's wrong?" the hairdresser asked.

"You don't know, you just don't even know," Greig replied.

Farnetti thought it was best to not pry further and just left it alone.

Catherine also struck up a friendship with their elderly neighbor Catalina Schlank after bumping into her one day. Catalina had been living in the United States since emigrating from Argentina in 1963.

"When she saw that I was trying to get my newspaper from the front entranceway, she said, 'Don't do that, I will pick it up for you,'" Schlank remembers.

Whitey and Catherine didn't own a car, so she'd wake up every day at 6 a.m. and push a shopping cart eight blocks to the nearest market for food and other supplies. Greig would also walk to Pavilion's Place at the corner of Montana and Ninth Street or over to the farmer's market on Arizona and Third Street. Whitey never came downstairs to help her haul the groceries. Schlank thought it was unusual for the couple not to have a car, especially in California.

"I thought they just had a big accident and maybe had their driver's licenses taken away," she says.

When Greig picked up Catalina's newspaper each morning, she'd place a piece of fruit or another food item on top. The elderly neighbor wanted to return the favor, but Catherine would always smile and wave her off. Still, Schlank would place sweets and chocolates, perfumed soaps, and mango slices outside their front door.

"She felt that it was important to give something to me, and not to receive it," Schlank says. Catherine sent their elderly neighbor cards for each major holiday and showered her with thank-you notes.

Good morning Catalina, thank you for the "yummy" surprise. We are saving it for dessert. I know you appreciate these "neighborly gestures," please no need for gifts. My gift—I love seeing your plants again on the balcony!!!

Whitey did show some kindness to Catalina when the woman received a visit from a relative from Argentina.

"My niece arrived and I went to pick her up at the airport. I drove her to my building and we were unloading in the carport," she recalls. "He [Bulger] came up and offered to take the suitcases to my apartment and he did."

Schlank says that Bulger had a nice, sweet face and that she never knew he was bald because he always wore a hat with the brim down.

Greig continued to shower Catalina with kind notes and greeting cards celebrating Passover and other religious holidays. Nearly every card ended with the words, *If we (Charlie and me) can ever lend a hand or do an errand—just give this neighbor a call. Thank you again, Carol and Charlie Gasko (303).*

Greig always included their home phone number.

If Whitey wanted to call his family back home, he certainly wouldn't use his landline. Instead, he and Catherine would buy a car with cash. They'd choose something dependable but not flashy and take off for a few weeks at a time, making their way from Santa Monica to Detroit, Michigan, some 2,297 miles away. Bulger and Catherine wouldn't drive straight there. Instead, he'd take a winding path through several states, staying at motels and buying food and gas with cash. Once he made it to Detroit, he'd leave his girlfriend and purchase a throwaway phone to call his brother Billy back in Boston.

Whitey later said that he strategically chose Michigan in an attempt to confuse any listening ears—especially the FBI if they were tracing the call. The crafty gangster said that he wanted the feds to believe that he and Catherine were living in Canada, not California, and coming down to Detroit to make phone calls to his family.

Catherine Greig wasn't as careful. Once back in Santa Monica, she'd sneak out to call her sister Margaret McCusker to check on life back home and the well-being of Nikki and Gigi, the French poodles she missed so much.

"She called me from California," McCusker says. "We probably talked once a month or every two months. We'd also talk about everyday things like the weather and such. I knew they were in Santa Monica. We didn't talk about her coming home. That was her business but I wasn't concerned about her being on the run with him. He'd always been very kind."

Despite the regular conversations, McCusker never told anyone where her sister and her boyfriend—the nation's most wanted fugitive—were living.

14

LIKE MOST EVERY OTHER AMERICAN, Whitey Bulger was glued to the television set watching in horror as the World Trade Center towers collapsed into themselves on September 11, 2001. Despite being a gangster and a cold-blooded killer, Bulger also considered himself a patriot and a proud veteran. Making the tragedy feel even more personal to him, one of the doomed flights, American Airlines Flight 11, had taken off from Boston's Logan Airport before crashing into the World Trade Center's North Tower.

The attacks on 9/11 also impacted his life as a fugitive in two important ways.

With the murders of nearly three thousand Americans in Lower Manhattan, the Pentagon, and a field in Shanksville, Pennsylvania, at the hands of Islamic terrorists, the FBI would need to shift much of its focus to fighting the War on Terror. This meant that resources being used to track him and Catherine down would need to be shifted elsewhere.

Michael Sullivan, a Republican former district attorney in southeastern Massachusetts, was awaiting confirmation from the US Senate to become the next US attorney in Boston on the day the planes struck the towers. Sullivan grew up on the South Shore of Massachusetts and knew the toll that the Winter Hill Gang's crimes took on countless lives in Boston and neighboring communities. After being appointed by President George W. Bush, he read books on Whitey to get up to speed as he prepared to lead the global manhunt. After September 11, 2001, he was quickly confirmed and his mission, like that of all federal prosecutors, drastically changed, especially since two of the hijacked planes came out of Boston.

"Leading up to my appointment, not once did national security or terrorism come up as a priority interest for the US Attorney's office in Boston," Sullivan recalled. "After 9/11, that was the only priority of the Department of Justice. All your resources should be put against national security, anti-terrorism.

"Still, in the back of your mind, you're saying there are other things that are important as well and one of them was the Bulger investigation," he added.

While the infamous terror attacks took much of the heat off Bulger, the ensuing security crackdown impacted him too. Now, he was stuck in the United States. Any dreams of taking off to Europe or South America were gone. Airport security was tightened to the highest levels in American history and there was no way that his phony IDs would pass inspection.

Following 9/11, terror mastermind Osama bin Laden, a man whose name had been unfamiliar to most people, had now catapulted to the top of the FBI's list of Most Wanted Fugitives, right above Whitey.

The FBI was offering a $250,000 reward for Bulger's capture. His case had been profiled several times on *America's Most Wanted*, the popular Fox television show hosted by John Walsh. After one broadcast, the FBI received a tip from Fountain Valley, California, a city in greater Los Angeles whose motto is simply "A Nice Place to Live." Actress Michelle Pfeiffer graduated from high school there before going on to play the girlfriend of fictional Miami mob kingpin Tony Montana in the Al Pacino flick *Scarface*.

Catherine Greig, the girlfriend of a real mob kingpin, had almost blown their cover while getting her hair colored at a Vietnamese-owned salon called Fountain Hair & Nails, where the prices were cheap. Catherine showed up with her own blond hair dye and apologized to the owner that she was pressed for time, as her husband was waiting outside with their car idling. The owner later described Greig as pretty and petite, with lovely blue eyes.

Catherine paid $16 cash for a coloring plus a healthy tip. She thanked the owner with a smile and walked out the door toward Whitey's car. Catherine climbed in and they disappeared.

After seeing Bulger's story on television, a salon customer called the tip line saying that she recognized him as the man who was watching Catherine closely from his car parked right outside the store.

Years later, there was suspicion that Bulger could have been involved in a string of bank robberies in Orange County and as far south as San Diego. The robber, known as the "Geezer Bandit," sported a baseball cap and dark sunglasses, which had become a Bulger trademark. The thief hit fourteen banks in all and routinely handed a note to the tellers that read *Give me $50,000 or I will murder you.*

The "Geezer Bandit" was never caught, but it wasn't Whitey Bulger. He was shorter than the man identified as the bank robber. Catherine had done a marvelous job keeping her man out of trouble while on the run, despite his natural instincts and urges to create mayhem.

When occasionally traveling by car, Whitey and Catherine hit the casinos in Las Vegas and Reno, Nevada, once again to wash their money. Bulger would use some of the cash to stockpile weapons from local gun shows. He browsed tables at the Big Reno Gun Show and at the Crossroads of the West Gun Show in Las Vegas under signs reading *Got Ammo?* and *Buy—Sell—Trade*, always looking to add to his growing arsenal. As one of America's most wanted fugitives, Bulger shopped with little fear of getting caught, thanks to a gaping loophole in federal law that allowed him to buy weapons and ammunition from private sellers without showing any identification or submitting to a background check. Unlike sellers at a gun store, private vendors at gun shows didn't even need to record the sale. Bulger paid cash, carried the weapons and ammo to his car, and drove away without peeking over his shoulder.

WITH FBI AGENT CHARLIE GIANTURCO off the case and John Gamel in retirement, coupled with the focus on terrorism, many people, including members of the media, thought that the FBI was spinning its wheels and had no real intention of catching Whitey Bulger. They criticized the Bureau for, among other things, taking fifteen months to question Teresa Stanley after his escape and even longer to interview John Connolly.

"They were sniffing for footprints that were 15 months old with Teresa Stanley. That's a tangible example of a fugitive hunt that really wasn't real," argues Jonathan Wells, a former *60 Minutes* producer who also had headed the *Boston Herald*'s investigative team for years and led the paper's aggressive Bulger coverage. "John Connolly and by extension Whitey Bulger still had people in the Bureau, in the Boston office, who believed this was ridiculous, that they were hanging this longtime informant out to dry and indicting him. And now they're going to chase after him? Because they believed Whitey did his service and he was one of them. He was an Irish guy and the whole office back then was all Irish."

Conspiracy theorists were convinced the FBI was hiding Bulger, perhaps on a military base somewhere, to prevent him from revealing more of their dirty secrets. Others even suggested Whitey had been murdered—taken out by a team of government assassins.

The reality was far less nefarious: there just weren't the same resources being devoted to the hunt the longer it dragged on. For all that the FBI had gotten close over the years, the pursuit of Bulger had never relented. Even after the Boston office became the epicenter of one of the largest corruption investigations in FBI history, there were still agents working hard to try to catch Whitey. But as bad as the stain on the Boston office was, perhaps nothing changed the search for Bulger more than 9/11.

By the mid-2000s, both the FBI and Massachusetts State Police had little to show for their efforts and had spent millions of dollars chasing down leads across the globe in places like Piccadilly Circus in London and later in Manchester, England. It was a cushy gig for agents working on the Bulger Task Force.

While the Bureau was focused on enforcing President George W. Bush's Patriot Act to combat terrorism after 9/11, the Bulger Task Force operated under the radar, jetting around the world to picture-postcard locales in Britain, Ireland, France, and Italy with little oversight. The notion that agents assigned to hunt down Whitey were out seeing the world on the Bureau's dime gnawed at many law enforcement officers who believed that more attention should have been paid to Bulger sightings around the United States.

15

I F THE FEDS COULDN'T FIND Whitey and Catherine, they could still make life hard on their loved ones.

Margaret McCusker and her friend Kathleen McDonough were indicted for lying to a grand jury investigating the case about receiving calls from Catherine. Both pleaded guilty and were sentenced to six months' house arrest and fined $2,000.

According to court testimony, McCusker and McDonough would go to the home of McDonough's aunt to make or receive calls from Catherine. When the aunt asked why they needed to call from her home, the women replied, "You never know who's listening."

One topic that Margaret tried to stay away from during the calls was how Catherine's prized poodles were doing. McCusker, who was grieving the death of her only son from suicide, had made a strange decision to euthanize her sister's beloved dogs Nikki and Gigi.

She never told Catherine. Greig heard the news from someone else and was devastated.

"Their relationship was always dysfunctional at best," says FBI agent Mike Carazza. "There was a love-hate thing going on between Catherine and Margaret and this is an example of that."

Jackie Bulger was also indicted for lying to the grand jury about his communications with his brother and about paying the rent for Whitey's safe deposit box in Clearwater, Florida. His lawyer said that Jackie had made a mistake, but that he only lied out of "brotherly concern."

The family loyalty excuse was dismissed and a federal judge sentenced Jackie to six months in federal prison, as his family members, including Billy Bulger, looked on.

BILLY BULGER AVOIDED CHARGES LIKE those faced by his relatives, but he was put on the hot seat before Congress when he was ordered to testify in a sweeping congressional probe of the FBI's use of informants, namely his brother.

On June 19, 2003, wearing a dark suit and powder-blue tie, he testified before the House Committee on Government Reform on live TV. This was Billy's second appearance before the committee. The first time around, he pleaded the Fifth and refused to answer any questions.

Lawmakers were investigating the FBI's decades-long misuse of informants starting with another Boston-area gangster, Joe "The Animal" Barboza, who had served as a guinea pig for the Bureau's Top Echelon Informant program. The program began in the 1960s and was essentially created by infamous FBI director J. Edgar Hoover and his longtime nemesis, US Attorney General Bobby Kennedy, in a campaign to bring down the Italian Mafia.

Barboza was recruited to rat for the FBI by Boston agents Paul Rico, who had collared Whitey Bulger for a bank job back in the 1950s, and his partner Dennis Condon. The agents convinced Barboza, a notorious hit man who had collected as many as twenty-six mob pelts, to lie on the stand in three criminal trials against the most powerful gangsters in New England, including La Cosa Nostra boss Raymond Patriarca of Providence and Gennaro "Jerry" Anguilo of Boston's North End. Barboza was hidden by the FBI and the US Marshals Service on Thacher Island off the coast of picturesque Rockport, Massachusetts. There, "The Animal" practiced his testimony while the Mafia did everything in its power to kill him, including sending a hit squad to the island by boat in hopes of blowing Barboza's head off with sniper rifles. Ultimately, Barboza's testimony put Patriarca and others behind bars, including four men framed for the murder of a gangster named Edward "Teddy" Deegan, which had actually been carried out by Barboza and Stevie Flemmi's brother Vincent "Jimmy the Bear" Flemmi, a true psychopath. J. Edgar Hoover had strong evidence that Barboza was lying at the time but still allowed him to send the men, many of whom were noted gangsters, to jail for life. Some of the men died in prison while two others, Joe Salvati and Peter Limone, were eventually freed after spending thirty years behind bars. The case would lead to the biggest settlement in the history of the United States Justice Department as a federal judge ordered the government to pay $101 million to the families of the wrongly accused.

The House committee heard from the innocent men and their families and also from Paul Rico, now retired from the FBI. Rico represented all that was wrong with the Boston office of the FBI, so perhaps it wasn't surprising that he and his partner Condon recruited Stevie Flemmi as an informant. It was Rico and Condon who groomed a young FBI agent from Southie named John Connolly to cozy up to Whitey Bulger. Rico would later face murder and conspiracy charges for his role in one of Whitey's most brazen hits, the assassination of millionaire businessman Roger Wheeler in Tulsa, Oklahoma. Rico died in the hospital before he could be brought to trial.

After Rico's testimony it was Billy Bulger's turn. As Bulger, president of the University of Massachusetts, took his seat behind a microphone, committee chairman Tom Davis of Virginia called the hearing to order.

"We are here today to receive testimony from William Bulger," he announced. "James 'Whitey' Bulger was an informant for the FBI in Boston. Whitey Bulger was repeatedly able to avoid arrest due to information illegally leaked to him by his FBI handler John Connolly . . . This hearing will focus on whether the relationship between John Connolly and Whitey Bulger benefited Whitey Bulger's brother William Bulger while he was a high-ranking elected official in Massachusetts."

Being granted immunity by the committee, Billy Bulger was sworn in and then read from a prepared statement.

"Please allow me to speak plainly, I do not know where my brother is," Billy claimed. "I do not know where he has been over the past eight years. I have not aided James Bulger in any way while he was a fugitive. Do I possess information that could lead to my brother's arrest? The honest answer is no!"

The hearing was carried live on C-SPAN and barrooms across Southie were packed as patrons sipped from pints of Guinness, glued to the television screens hung over the beer taps as if it were the fourth quarter of a close New England Patriots game.

Meanwhile, in apartment 303 at the Princess Eugenia, Whitey and Catherine watched intently as Billy, once the most powerful politician in Boston, squirmed on the national stage.

Under oath, Billy claimed to have had just one telephone conversation with Whitey back in 1995 and said that after that, he was "unable to penetrate the secretive life" of his older brother. He also criticized the FBI's leaking of information about Whitey's status as an informant to the *Boston Globe*.

"I believed that the FBI wanted James Bulger killed," Billy told the panel. ". . . I know my brother stands accused of many things, serious crimes, brutal crimes. I do still live in the hope that the worst charges against him will prove groundless."

When questioned by lawmakers, including Congressman Steve Lynch of South Boston and Massachusetts representative Marty Meehan, who would go on to become president of UMass, Billy admitted that he had maintained a close friendship with Connolly but denied any real relationship with Kevin Weeks and others, including corrupt former state trooper Richard Schneiderhan.

Another Massachusetts congressman then asked Billy if he'd been interviewed by the FBI before being compelled by a grand jury investigating the case.

"If you have a memory, were you interviewed by the FBI prior to 2001 as to the whereabouts of your fugitive brother?" asked Representative William Delahunt.

"I don't believe I was," Billy replied.

"Were you not?" Delahunt stressed again.

"I don't think I was," Billy repeated.

He later claimed that the first direct effort by the FBI to question him about Whitey came eight years after his brother went on the lam.

Congressman Chris Shays of Connecticut later jumped in on the same topic.

"I'm asking you whether you gave a signal to the FBI that you did not want to answer their questions, and that they should not ask you and that they should leave," Shays pressed.

"I don't recall meeting the FBI. I really don't recall it."

"Did the FBI ever come to your offices?"

"No, I don't think so."

Right there, federal investigators suspected Billy Bulger was lying before Congress. Shortly after Billy's hours-long testimony, someone from the Bureau reached out to John Gamel, now retired, as he was about to go on a fishing trip.

"Did you ever contact Billy Bulger?" the investigator asked.

"Of course, I went to his office myself," Gamel replied. "He later called me and said he refused to help us find Whitey. He slammed the phone down on me. I wrote up a 302 about it right after. It's gotta be still there in the files."

An FD-302 form is used by FBI agents to summarize interviews they conduct while working a case. The Bureau went digging for the 302 regarding Gamel's conversation with Billy Bulger from early 1995 and found it. The FBI wanted to use this piece of evidence to bring formal perjury charges against the university president, but for some mysterious reason, those actions were not taken by the US Attorney's Office.

Billy's lawyer argued that his client didn't perjure himself before Congress. "He [Bulger] offered his memory. He reserved the notion that his memory might not be perfect," Attorney Tom Kiley insisted. "The truth is, memories do change and memories do fail over eight years."

Still, Billy Bulger wasn't out of the woods yet. He'd been appointed president of UMass in 1996, nearly a year after Whitey had gone on the run, with support from then-Governor William Weld. Billy's annual salary was a whopping $357,000.

Mitt Romney now sat in the corner office of the Massachusetts Statehouse and Billy's testimony was nothing short of an embarrassment for Romney, who was eyeing a run for president of the United States. Romney, the future Republican presidential nominee, launched an immediate campaign to oust Billy from UMass.

"The shadow over the university is real and . . . the interests of the university are being harmed," Romney told the press.

Romney exerted pressure on the UMass Board of Trustees, who then applied their own pressure on Billy.

Less than two months later, Whitey's brother resigned from his prestigious post. On his way out the door, Billy blasted Mitt Romney for targeting him with "a calculated political assault."

The congressional hearing had resulted in a death blow to Billy's reputation and his career in public life. After his resignation, he disappeared from view, only to be comforted by a pension that would pay him more than $200,000 each year for the rest of his life.

Meanwhile, the hunt for his fugitive brother continued.

16

S AN DIEGO SHERIFF'S DEPUTY RICH Eaton knew the Whitey
Bulger story well. A native of Hyannis, Massachusetts, Eaton
grew up on Cape Cod surrounded by news stories and neighborhood tales that mythologized the Irish mobster, who had vacationed in Provincetown at the tip of the Cape in years past.

Hollywood was first attracted to the dark world of Whitey
Bulger in the early 2000s when acclaimed director Martin Scorsese
decided to fictionalize the crime boss's exploits in the Oscar-
winning film *The Departed,* starring Jack Nicholson, Leonardo Di-
Caprio, and Boston native Matt Damon, who'd put Southie on the
Tinsel Town map with his own Oscar-winning effort *Good Will
Hunting.* Like that movie, *The Departed* was filmed on location in
Boston, on the same neighborhood streets that Bulger had once
controlled in his death grip.

Rich Eaton was living in San Diego at the time and working as
a detective in the North County Regional Gang Task Force. His
job brought him in close contact with killers from the Mexican
cartels. In early October 2006, Eaton found himself testifying in a
drug trial at the federal courthouse. The judge had called for an extended break, which gave the detective and his partner three hours
of free time.

"Hey, *The Departed* just opened," Eaton's partner James Mancuso
told him. "First showing is at eleven. We should go check it out."

"It'd be good to see if Scorsese gets the Boston mob story right,"

Eaton responded as the two walked across the street to a multiplex cinema adjacent to a galleria mall called Horton Plaza.

They purchased their movie tickets and entered the theater, which was surprisingly crowded for a weekday.

Eaton dug into a bucket of popcorn and briefly scanned the crowd before the lights dimmed. His eyes immediately focused on a man sitting alone four rows away. The man looked to be in his seventies. He was wearing a black floppy bucket hat and a neatly trimmed white beard covered his jawline.

Is that Whitey fucking Bulger? Nah, that's absurd, he thought to himself. *Who would imagine that Whitey would be sitting in this theater with me watching Jack Nicholson act out his life story?*

Yet as the film ran, Eaton paid little attention to the screen and instead studied the man just a few rows away.

"I could see him reacting viscerally to Nicholson's portrayal," Eaton says, sharing his full story exclusively with the authors. "He was laughing at certain moments, shaking his head in disagreement at other times. My weird hunch suddenly became very real to me."

As the screening ended, Eaton slipped out of the theater ahead of his partner and waited for the mysterious older man to walk out. Several matinee-goers filed past him until the older man finally came into view. He was wearing cargo shorts, New Balance sneakers, and an oversized polo shirt that could not hide a peculiar bulge.

He's carrying, Eaton thought to himself.

As the older man walked by, Eaton caught his stare. The man looked at him menacingly with his pale blue eyes before quickly looking away, and the detective was convinced.

"I had just found Whitey Bulger," he recalls.

Eaton felt for his pistol, which was normally strapped to his ankle, and remembered it was not there. He'd had to turn over his service weapon and his handcuffs earlier that morning as he entered the federal courthouse for trial. He forgot to retrieve them at the break.

Fuck. He's armed and very dangerous, the detective reminded himself. There was no way he could approach the fugitive without a gun to protect himself.

Eaton watched Bulger walk out the door and kept a safe distance as he monitored the mobster's next move. The detective saw Whitey walk toward an oncoming Blue Line trolley that was headed for San Ysidro, California, on the border with Mexico.

"That made sense to me," Eaton recalls. "We'd all heard that Bulger might be living in or close to Mexico, where he could get cheap heart medication. I watched him get on the train and then hightailed it back to the courthouse to grab my gun and cuffs."

Once armed, Eaton and his partner jumped into a police car and raced to San Ysidro in hopes of beating the train. With one hand on the steering wheel, Eaton fished for his cell phone and dialed the number for the San Diego office of the FBI.

"We have the fugitive James 'Whitey' Bulger on a southbound trolley headed for the Mexican border," Eaton told the FBI officer assigned to the fugitive squad. "We will meet the train and are in need of assistance for his apprehension."

The detective arrived at the station several minutes later and ahead of the train. Eaton was shocked to see that he and his partner were the only law enforcement agents on scene. The FBI was nowhere in sight.

"We saw the train pull in and braced ourselves for what was to come," Eaton recalls. "We didn't believe that Bulger would be taken without a fight and we feared that a shootout could lead to innocent people getting killed."

The detectives watched as all the passengers stepped off the train at what was the last stop on the line, but James "Whitey" Bulger never appeared.

"Fuck, he got off early and gave us the slip," Detective Mancuso told Eaton.

"Yup. He's a crafty bastard," Eaton replied. "But he couldn't have gone too far."

Eaton called the FBI once more and was connected with the agent in charge of all Whitey Bulger sightings in Southern California.

"That's when I realized the fix was in," Eaton says. "This agent didn't have a clue. She didn't know what Bulger looked like, didn't have any real understanding about the case, and this was one of the agents that the FBI had placed in charge of finding Whitey Bulger on the west coast. She couldn't solve a murder if it happened in front of her."

Detective Eaton recognized the problem immediately. He believes that the old guard of the FBI did not want Bulger captured, fearing that the fugitive mob boss had more secrets to reveal and more careers to ruin regarding his long-standing relationship with the Bureau, while the younger agents had no idea who Whitey was, even though he was now the Bureau's number-two-ranked fugitive behind Osama bin Laden.

"Corruption and sheer incompetence allowed this killer to remain on the run," Eaton contends.

Eaton continued to hunt for Bulger in San Diego, establishing patrols on the beaches of Coronado Island and anywhere else an elderly couple could blend in, but just like the elusive character Keyser Söze from the movie *The Usual Suspects—poof* . . . he was gone.

Eaton then pulled the surveillance video from Horton Plaza, which showed an elderly man fitting Bulger's description riding an escalator. He immediately called his friend Danny Simmons, a Boston native now working as a DEA agent in San Diego. Simmons forwarded the clip to fellow DEA agent Dan Doherty back in Boston. Doherty promised to run the tape by Kevin Weeks.

"Weeks tends to think not," Doherty told Simmons in a phone call. "He said that Whitey was a germophobe and he's touching the handrails of the escalator in the video. Plus the guy has cargo shorts on and Whitey only wore long pants."

"Remember, Whitey's on the run," Simmons countered. "You're gonna mix it up a little bit when you're on the run. You'll wear a hat when you wouldn't have, wear shorts when you wouldn't have."

Simmons believes that Eaton had found his man. "Right time and right place for Richie, yeah. Unfortunately he couldn't get his hands on him. That was more than likely him [Bulger] despite what Kevin Weeks has to say."

An FBI agent who worked closely with Eaton in San Diego is also confident that he'd spotted the fugitive crime boss. The agent is still active with the Bureau and asked us not to use his name for this book.

"Over the years, there were allegations that Bulger was seen in San Diego years before and they were investigated very hard, but deemed not to be credible," the agent says. The FBI had interviewed Bulger look-alikes walking the beach or at their homes and met with dead end after dead end.

"But it was different here," the agent points out. "I had worked previously with Rich Eaton and he had identified a homicide fugitive that I had that I would not have been able to identify myself. We even knew where the guy was, but he looked completely different and Rich identified him within a fraction of a second correctly. Rich is so sharp and such a good detective that if he's said he'd just seen Jesus, I would have believed it."

Eaton called the agent immediately and informed him of the sighting. The agent then contacted the FBI's organized crime squad and he said, "This is the real thing."

The agent provided the contact information for Eaton, but those assigned to the case never bothered to reach out to the detective directly about this highly promising lead.

"I can't justify that. The first thing that I would have done is call the detective," the agent says. "In any case, you need to interview the source and that wasn't done here. You don't interview a detective like Rich with his creds. Are you kidding me?"

The agent doesn't believe that the FBI purposely avoided following up on Eaton's tip in an attempt to keep Whitey out in the cold. Instead, the agent says that colleagues in the Bureau just weren't competent enough at that point to track him and Catherine down successfully.

"The other agents out here didn't understand the background of the case or the bigger picture here."

17

THE GAME FINALLY CHANGED WHEN Noreen Gleason took over the case in February 2008. There would be no more missed opportunities or lack of effort in following up credible leads. Indeed, this was a unit designed with one purpose in mind: catching Whitey Bulger. Gleason provided much-needed leadership to the task force and she had the full support of her boss Warren Bamford, who allowed her to bring in valuable resources from outside the Boston FBI office.

Gleason now had Agent Tommy MacDonald on the case, while she worked hard to deconstruct the Bulger mythology and paint for the public an accurate portrait of an insidious criminal.

When the FBI announced that it was increasing the reward for Whitey's capture from $1 million to $2 million on the gangster's seventy-ninth birthday in 2008, Gleason used that opportunity to speak directly to those who still thought Whitey was a man of honor.

During a press conference, Gleason went off script and announced publicly for the first time that the FBI had uncovered evidence that Bulger was not just a killer, but a pedophile.

"He preyed on innocent girls, as young as twelve years old," Gleason told reporters. "These are sad, troubling, and disturbing stories that most people have not been privy to . . . [Bulger] is a truly deadly crime figure, not a folk-hero. The gravity of Mr. Bulger's crimes is egregious and has not been diminished over time."

The child molester rumors had been around for years, but had first gone public in 2001 when a low-level former Bulger associate named Eddie MacKenzie claimed that members of the Winter Hill Gang regularly preyed on underage girls—including some from a Southie parochial school. Girls were lured to MacKenzie's gym— nicknamed "The Dog Room"—where they were secretly watched and videotaped having sex through a two-way mirror. Whitey was a regular participant in the sex romps and was also known to have trysts with underage girls at Triple O's.

Gleason knew that she was potentially digging a hole for herself, as her comments were not part of the official statement that had been approved by the US Attorney's Office.

"I got so emotional about this stuff because Southie thought he was a hero," she recalls. "This guy [Bulger] was the biggest piece of crap on so many levels."

US Attorney Michael J. Sullivan went wild. He'd been caught completely off guard by Gleason's comments and immediately called her boss Warren Bamford, screaming.

"We could press charges against her for saying that," Sullivan yelled. "He's not charged with being a pedophile."

Gleason's frustration with the US Attorney's Office had reached its peak. She'd long held the belief that federal prosecutors were working against the FBI and blamed them for the malaise that had nearly derailed the manhunt for Bulger.

"When case agents brought strong prosecutorial cases to the US Attorney's office, they were turned down," Gleason claims. "The office wasn't eager to work with the Bureau. That was really frustrating for a lot of people in the Boston office. I'd never experienced that before. You could see it was very deflating to the agents. And now they were threatening to come after me."

Gleason also blamed federal prosecutors for dropping the ball on pursuing charges against Billy Bulger for obstruction of justice. Under her leadership, the task force learned years later that Whitey had been communicating with Billy by telephone. According to Tommy Mac, he'd get word to a neighbor and order them to bump into Billy on the street in Southie and tell him to be at their house at a specific time, usually in the afternoon, because that was when Whitey would call that house.

"We had a strong case against Billy," Gleason says. "We knew he'd been in contact with his brother. It made me wild. The US Attorney was as complicit as anyone in not finding Whitey. How do you not hold Billy accountable and why are you making the Boston FBI office pay for our father's sins regarding John Connolly? It made me question where their loyalties lie."

Billy has always denied helping his brother while he was on the run, but he eventually confirmed that he did in fact take at least one call from him while he was a fugitive. It strains credulity, given how close the brothers were, their relationship with Connolly, and how their lives intertwined, that Billy Bulger did not stay in contact with Whitey during his years on the run. Gleason was surprised to see that her team was losing support from some within the FBI family, most notably retired agent John Gamel. She'd seen him interviewed on television saying that he didn't think Bulger would ever be caught.

"I was livid, I got to the office and said, 'Gimme that guy's number. I gotta call him,'" Gleason remembers. "I called Gamel and laid him out. I said, 'Now you've become part of the problem we're facing. How dare you?'"

Gamel met with Gleason in her office and the two finally cleared the air.

"You gotta stay positive," she stressed. "You can't be focused on old history. This is a new day."

Gleason wasn't paying lip service to this problem. The new day meant a new stable of agents, including Tommy Mac and another manhunter Gleason had appointed to the team, Special Agent Phil Torsney.

Torsney was working out of the FBI office in Cleveland at the time. He'd been running the Fugitive Task Force there for nearly two decades.

"I've always been an adrenaline guy," he says. "I'm not an accountant; I'm not a foreign language guy. I'm just an FBI cop; I chased people for a living. Finding guys and bringing them in, I loved the work."

Before working the Bulger case, Torsney's most high-profile fugitive pursuit involved an Ohio doctor who'd killed his wife by feeding her calcium capsules that he'd emptied and refilled with hand-crushed cyanide. The doctor's name was Yazeed Essa. He'd vanished in 2005 shortly after being questioned by police. He had a license to practice medicine, but Essa was a stupid criminal. When mourners gathered at his home immediately after his wife's death, the doctor tossed back shots of liquor and joked with his buddies that at least he wouldn't have to sneak other women into their house anymore. Using fake travel documents, Essa made his way to Lebanon, leaving the couple's young children behind. Working with INTERPOL, Phil Torsney created a flier with Essa's photo, his fingerprints, and details of the murder. That document was then translated into several languages and sent to law enforcement agencies across the globe. But since Lebanon had no extradition treaty with the United States, the accused killer was untouchable while living in Beirut. Torsney and his partners at INTERPOL kept track of the doctor's movements and waited for their break. Fortunately for the manhunters, Essa had wanderlust and decided to book a trip to the island of Cyprus. That's when Torsney and the team sprung into action, arresting the doctor the moment he stepped off the plane. Yazeed Essa would eventually be brought back to Ohio to face charges. He was tried for the murder of his wife and sentenced to life in prison.

When Torsney got the offer to join the Bulger Task Force, he felt that he'd already had a bit of a head start on the case.

"When Whitey was first indicted, I was following him right away," he recalls. "He'd been featured on *America's Most Wanted* and we were getting inundated with look-alike sightings. Any older guy with a baseball cap and sunglasses was fair game and we questioned a lot of them. Noreen Gleason brought me up to Boston because I knew how to work fugitives. I knew there was some bad shit happening there previously with Connolly. At one point, it felt like everybody in the Boston office was corrupt. But when I got there, I found out that wasn't the case at all."

Torsney reported to Boston on October 6, 2009. He checked into a hotel in Charlestown and went for a run. The crisp fall air felt refreshing, opening his lungs and clearing his head for the major task at hand. When he returned to the hotel sweaty but reenergized, he met his new partner, Tommy Mac, in the lobby. They'd spoken on the phone for a few months to familiarize themselves with one another, but they never mentioned where they'd be staying. Both were excited to know they'd be living under one roof, because this was the type of case that would be all consuming. The agents would have to work day and night.

"The Bulger case was like a bird flying around in my head," Tommy Mac recalls. "I'd wake up in the middle of the night and wonder, why am I thinking about this case? We're coming into this case fourteen years after he's been on the run. They'd already made a movie about him with Jack Nicholson, so what the hell are we gonna do?"

Phil Torsney felt the same way. But Noreen Gleason had placed her faith in the agents and together they devised a sound plan.

"We put an emphasis on facial recognition, as the technology had improved vastly and we felt that Whitey wouldn't be able to keep up with it," Torsney explains. "So we're looking to find any and all IDs for either of them. Another big thing was knocking on doors, even if witnesses had already been interviewed four or five times. We also wanted to recommit ourselves to tracking phone calls."

Phil and Tommy Mac were told that they'd be assigned to the Bulger case for three years of temporary duty unless they caught him first.

The clock was running.

They'd barely had time to unpack when the new partners requested a meeting with the US Attorney's Office. Despite a mutual mistrust, the FBI agents understood they'd need cooperation from federal prosecutors, especially in the effort to place taps and trace orders, or pen registers, on the phones of the four people closest to Whitey and Catherine: Billy Bulger, Jackie Bulger, Jean Holland, and Margaret McCusker.

"If I wanted to find out about your life, I'd look at who you talked to on the phone," MacDonald explains. "Those conversations tell us all the little things that may lead to big things. We wanted to have that information on the key Bulger family members who may still be in touch with the fugitives."

Next, Torsney and Tommy Mac went exploring through Whitey's old neighborhood in Southie. The previous investigative team had long given up on knocking on the doors of Whitey's friends and family, but the partners wanted everyone to know that this was a new day and the heat was back on.

They first approached the home of Billy Bulger and asked to speak with the former lawmaker and college president. His wife, Mary, answered the door.

"We're from the FBI and would like to ask your husband a few questions," Phil asked kindly.

Mary Bulger nodded, smiled, and informed the agents that her husband wasn't home. Phil found it odd, as Billy's car was parked in the driveway. "By all accounts, I'd heard that Mary Bulger was a saintly woman," Phil says. "When she said that to us, I'm thinking to myself, 'She's probably gonna have to go to confession because she just lied to me.'"

The visit to Billy's house prompted a call from his lawyer, Tom

Kiley. The attorney left a voice mail for Tommy Mac saying that he represented Billy Bulger and all of his siblings along with their spouses and children. Kiley stressed once again that the Bulger family—the entire Bulger family—would not assist or support the hunt for Whitey.

Tommy Mac shook his head in frustration. "Who the fuck does this guy think he is?" he asked aloud. "Does he represent half of Boston? We're not gonna back down."

The Bulger family's posture was firm and clear. Collectively, they were saying, "Fuck you, FBI."

18

JOEY HIPP MOVED TO SANTA Monica with his wife in 2007 when she was offered a position in a local law firm. Hipp's brother lived on Third Street and Joey wanted to be nearby, so the couple grabbed the first apartment they saw—which happened to be across the street from the Princess Eugenia.

They moved in with their tiny white dog, a West Highland terrier named Joplin, and as they walked Joplin one afternoon, they were approached by a nice older couple.

"Can we talk to your dog?" the woman asked.

She was with a man who dressed all in white and was impeccably groomed.

"The whole town is filled with rich film industry people, so I thought he was a retired studio executive," Hipp recalls.

In fact, the young man had just come face-to-face with one of the most wanted men in America.

The older couple patted the dog and Joplin took a quick liking to them. The couple introduced themselves as Charlie and Carol Gasko.

"He shook my hand," Hipp says. "He's one of those guys who looks you right in the eye and tries to break your hand and sees if you break eye contact. I let it go."

"Where are you from?" the old man asked.

"Philly."

"You Irish?"

"Yeah," Hipp replied. That seemed to lighten Charlie's mood. Still, he kept up with the line of questioning. Bulger was making sure their story added up.

"Once he realized that we were just a couple across the street with a white dog, we were okay," Hipp says.

Catherine told him they were both dog lovers but couldn't have a dog of their own. Joe and his wife would see them from time to time on afternoon strolls, and Joplin would strain at his leash and wag his little tail when he knew they were close by.

"Carol and Charlie" always had chewy dog toys to present to Joplin. One day while the couple was playing with the dog, Hipp reached for his phone and wanted to take a photo for social media.

"Yeah, take a picture of the dog with the toy," Charlie said. He and "Carol" then slipped behind Hipp to make sure they were out of the shot.

Hipp was fascinated by stories about organized crime. His hometown had no shortage of classic real-life mob tales, including the bloody reign of Mafia boss Nicky Scarfo, who ordered more than a dozen gangland hits in the late 1970s and early '80s. He'd devoured mob books like T. J. English's *The Westies*, and he'd even read a book about Whitey Bulger.

"I was aware of who he was," Hipp says. "But I had no idea that it was the guy living across the street from us. Carol was very nice to my wife. She took care of the stray cat up on the corner. There's a hotel across from their building, the cat belonged to the owner, someone that died or left. It was a stray that never left the property. She would feed it and go make sure it was alright."

Joey and his wife walked Joplin each afternoon and they'd normally run into Carol, but eventually there was no sign of her husband.

"I haven't seen Charlie in a while," Hipp asked her one day. "Is he alright?"

"He's got a bit of Alzheimer's and gets scared and doesn't like to come out," she told him.

The last time Hipp saw his sweet, elderly neighbor, he asked her once again about "Charlie."

"He's not well," she said. "But he wants to know how Joplin is doing. Do you have any pictures that I could show him?"

"That's a shame," Hipp replied. "Tell him that I wish him well. I'll print out a couple of pictures and bring them over."

Carol showed concern on her face. She didn't want Hipp anywhere near their apartment. "Just print a couple out and put them in an envelope and write 303 on them."

Whitey was no doubt watching the exchange with a pair of binoculars from his third-floor balcony. That was the perch where he could study every face that came and went by the building. He was always on alert for a stranger who didn't belong there.

Just as Osama bin Laden had lived in seclusion inside his compound in Pakistan before he was killed by US Special Forces, Bulger too was technically a free man, but his movements were now severely limited. He was a prisoner of sorts inside the apartment building, where he'd sleep in the rear bedroom with tinfoil-covered windows to block out the light. Yet, his room was also filled with flickering candles.

"I need them to sleep," he later told investigators. "They help with all the nightmares." Nightmares caused by years of prison LSD experiments.

He'd spend his waking moments watching television, exercising, and keeping a lookout for the FBI or someone he'd double-crossed on the streets back home.

Whitey had a punching torso used by mixed martial artists standing inside the living room next to the sliding glass doors leading out to the balcony. He'd positioned it there with a fedora on its head to confuse any would-be assassin who might try to take a shot at him from the street or a nearby apartment.

"If you walked past at night, you'd see something in the window. He had a workout dummy torso that he would dress and put in the window, so it would look like someone looking out the window," Hipp remembers.

Bulger was also working on a manuscript about his life, one he hoped his family would get published for him. He didn't like what had been written about him by Kevin Weeks and others and wanted to set the record straight—at least his version of events.

When Hipp finally saw "Charlie" on the street again, his view of the man changed dramatically. The old man had already done the tough-guy routine by squeezing Joey's hand when they had first met, but this exchange was different. This was ugly.

"We were standing there and this young pregnant black woman walked down the other side of the street," Hipp recalls. "He let out a horrible racist rant just loud enough so she could hear it. According to him, every problem in Santa Monica was caused by minorities. He used the N word repeatedly."

"This is what's wrong with everything," the old man screamed. "Blacks and Mexicans!"

Hipp was appalled by the outburst. "I felt like just clocking the guy. But I thought, 'Ah he's an old man. He's not going to change his views.'"

After the racist rant, Joey took his dog Joplin and continued on his way. He promised to stay clear of "Charlie Gasko" from then on.

19

WHITEY AND CATHERINE STAYED HUNKERED down in Santa Monica but occasionally traveled to Las Vegas to gamble. He had a VIP playing card at the Four Queens Casino, located two miles off the famous Strip, where you could book a room for as low as $42. Bulger was obsessed with washing his money and keeping his cash flow clean. He also went there to buy guns and knives.

Catherine kept up with the monthly bills paying with cash or money orders, getting to know the manager of the Princess Eugenia, Birgitta Farinelli, shortly after they moved in. A native of Göteborg, Sweden, Farinelli took the job after years working at LAX for New Zealand Air and Swiss Air. She was fluent in several languages, which made it easy to communicate with foreign guests at the Princess Eugenia and its sister building, the Embassy Hotel apartments located across the street. Farinelli got to know "Carol Gasko" when she came into the office to drop off the rent. She always paid cash, and the two would often sit down and chat. Being from Sweden, the hotel manager couldn't place Carol's accent, so she inquired about it.

"I know that you don't have a New York accent," Farinelli told her. "But you have some kind of accent from the East Coast."

"Well, we're from Chicago," Catherine replied.

Despite Farinelli's inquisitive nature, Greig looked forward to their talks. If Farinelli was busy working in her office, Catherine would sit in the lobby and wait until she was free. Then she'd hand the property manager a white envelope stuffed with $1,165 in rent money. The bills, $100s, $50s, $20s, and $5s, always looked crisp and were neatly stacked.

"Well, did you rob a bank again, Carol?" Farinelli joked.

"Oh no," she replied nervously. "I just went to the bank and had to do some errands."

Greig asked Farinelli where she got her hair and nails done and would give her small gifts, like a silk scarf and a water bottle. One day, Farinelli knocked on the couple's apartment to notify them that the fire department had to cut the phone lines between the Princess Eugenia and Embassy Hotel apartments because of dangerous faulty wiring. When the manager entered the home, she could barely see. All the windows were covered by blackout shades.

"Oh, it's so dark in here," Farinelli observed to Carol.

Bulger was sitting in a fold-up chair, watching television.

"Charlie has a hard time sleeping," Greig said. "So he sleeps during the day." For once, Catherine wasn't lying, at least, not quite.

"We don't really need a phone," she told the manager. "Nobody ever calls us and we don't call anybody."

Farinelli was concerned about Charlie's health and would ask Carol about it.

"Well, he's always sick," Catherine explained. "He was smoking so much when he was younger that he has emphysema."

In truth, Bulger had never smoked and despised those who did.

Still, no one suspected a thing. Their cover stories worked well, and the fact that their case wasn't generating any media coverage in Southern California allowed Whitey and Catherine to conceal their true identities with ease.

Despite his being featured on the *America's Most Wanted* television show sixteen times, including a final appearance in October 2010, few people on the west coast knew who Whitey Bulger was and that's exactly how the elderly fugitive wanted it.

Whitey was spending less and less time outside their apartment at the Princess Eugenia. When he'd see Catherine chatting with neighbors in the hallway, he'd grumble for her to get back inside.

They'd occasionally visit a local dentist, signing in under the names "John R." and "Mary R."

After one agonizing trip, Bulger complained about his tooth pain to Farinelli.

"It's really hurting," he told her.

"You should get some Vicodin," she advised. "That makes you fly up to the sky. I have some. I can give it to you."

"No thanks," Whitey said, waving her off. "I'll tough it out."

Coupled with his tooth pain, Bulger was also suffering from severe arthritis. During a visit to an urgent care clinic in Los Angeles, the aging gangster was offered a cortisone shot for relief but said no. The shot cost $160, but it wasn't the money that Bulger was concerned about.

"I'm scared of needles," he told the doctor.

It was a childlike response that belied a mean temper. According to clinic physician Dr. Reza Ray Ehsan, Bulger shouted at the nurses and demeaned Catherine by introducing her as "his girl."

Greig smiled through the humiliation and did her best to stay healthy. She cut out new diet recipes and kept a thick binder in the apartment on the warning signs and treatment for osteoporosis, as their bones were starting to degenerate with age. She'd done everything she could to turn their tiny apartment into a home and made sure that Bulger realized how thankful she was, despite the circumstances. On Valentine's Day, Catherine expressed her love with a card that featured a drawing of a puppy on the cover with the whimsical wish for a day "that's tail waggin' fun." Under it she wrote: *"Happy Valentine's Day, 'Valentine'. Love always, Cxxxxoooo"*

There were photos of dogs and cats placed into frames on the walls, and pictures of her beloved poodles Nikki and Gigi were posted on a large piece of cardboard in the small kitchen. She bought everything in bulk, from Q-tips to Kleenex to bars of Dial soap, all stacked in orderly fashion in closets.

Catherine slept with a Claude Monet print above her bed, which stood opposite a pretty dresser with a makeup mirror and various blushes and perfumes spread out neatly across a table covered by an embroidered cloth.

While her bedroom was decorated with a woman's delicate touch with accented lace and linen, his looked like a military barracks. A large map of the world was tacked up on the wall, no doubt fueling Whitey's imagination as to where they could flee to if they were ever spotted in Santa Monica. The map shared wall space with a poster of the US flag with the banner *God Bless America*.

Bulger collected dozens of books, which covered his desk and lined his small bookcase. His favorite subject was World War II, but he also read books on pirates and of course, tales about the mob. He even kept a copy of *Brutal*, the memoir penned by his protégé Kevin Weeks, on his shelf. He also owned a prized copy of *Escape from Alcatraz*. Whitey wasn't just reading for pleasure, though; he was also honing his skills as a fugitive.

He read *Soldier of Fortune* magazine religiously, along with a handbook on how to find missing persons and another that offered tips about how to survive worst-case scenarios including high-rise hotel fires and UFO abductions. One book that he studied cover to cover was *Secrets of a Back Alley ID Man: Fake ID Construction Techniques of the Underground*. The book promised to reveal the most effective "new school" and "old school" techniques for fake IDs, including hologram reproduction, do-it-yourself templates for driver's licenses and official seals, and other evasive tricks for those on a tight budget, which most certainly appealed to Whitey.

He put this knowledge to work on another desperate man he'd met while strolling through Palisades Park named James William Lawlor.

Whitey did a double take when he first spotted Lawlor sitting on a bench. The man was bald, bearded, and Irish—just like Bulger. But Lawlor was also shorter than Whitey and paunchier, details that could possibly be overlooked on an ID card. Whitey sat with Lawlor and soon learned that he'd moved to California from New York after his wife died and that he had lost contact with his family. Lawlor also confided to Whitey that he had a drinking problem and was low on cash.

Bulger spotted a tattoo on Lawlor's right arm that read *US Army Irish*. Whitey offered him a few dollars but asked for nothing in return—at least not yet.

The two men would continue to talk in the park several more times and discovered they shared a mutual passion for history and reading. Finally, "Charlie" gave Lawlor his cover story—that he'd moved down from Canada illegally and he needed a valid California driver's license to get work.

Whitey forked over $1,000 for Lawlor's license, Social Security card, and birth certificate and morphed into Lawlor. He opened a bank account in the man's name and smartly convinced Lawlor to order a new senior citizen's identification card by mail. This time, Lawlor changed his description to say that he was five foot nine, 170 pounds, and had blue eyes. For this, Bulger gave him an additional $2,500 and even paid Lawlor's rent at a local hotel. Whitey also bought a car with cash and had Lawlor register it in his name so that he could drive around.

Bulger would continue to pay Lawlor's rent while urging him to seek help for his alcohol problem. In 2007, a couple of days after paying his rent with the money Whitey had given him, Lawlor died in his room. Bulger would never get over it. He couldn't claim the body as it would blow his cover, but Whitey was happy to learn later that Lawlor, an army veteran, was buried at a military cemetery some sixty miles away. Whitey drove the car back to Lawlor's neighborhood and parked it close by. He splashed some vodka around the front seat and left the keys in it. Bulger never drove again.

The years he'd spent prowling South Boston and preying on his neighbors were a distant memory for him now, but Whitey's criminal brain never stopped working. Bulger had amassed great power in the underworld over several decades by using people on both sides of the law to serve his diabolical needs. Now, in the lion-in-winter phase of his life, Whitey exploited vulnerable men like James Lawlor to keep law enforcement at arm's length. His day-to-day life might have been more about toothaches and drawn shades, but his schemes were in constant view.

Whitey later befriended a young man named Josh Bond, who was hired to work with Birgitta Farinelli as a property manager for the Princess Eugenia in 2007. Bond was a musician and a recent graduate of Boston University, so he recognized Whitey's accent right away, although Bulger told him that he and his wife were from Chicago. He also lied and claimed he'd fought in the Korean War.

Bond lived in the apartment next to Whitey and Catherine and he played loud music at all hours. Surprisingly, Bulger didn't mind the noise. In fact, he liked the music.

"The first time I met Charlie, he brought me an old black Stetson hat and carrying case," Bond later recalled. "I thought that was strange."

The black cowboy hat was the same one he'd worn when he had first taken Catherine on the run years earlier. Now they were known in the neighborhood as the couple that always wore white. She wore white blouses and slacks, and "Charlie Gasko" was never seen without his floppy hat and sunglasses.

The couple hung a sign on their front door asking people not to knock at certain times of the day. Like Farinelli, Josh Bond was one of the few people to ever get a look inside apartment 303. His eyes were immediately drawn to the torso dummy, which he thought was strange, but nothing else stood out to him.

It was clear that Charlie kept himself physically fit, and he gave Bond workout equipment including a curling bar and stomach crunch machine as gifts.

"If I didn't think the Gaskos were such a nice old couple, I would have thought that Charlie was trying to get me in shape because he was attracted to me," Bond says. "But since they didn't have any children of their own, they sort of treated me like a son."

Other presents included an Elvis Presley coffee-table book, a beard trimmer, and a bottle of Grand Marnier liqueur. As the apartment manager got closer to the couple, he learned that Whitey carried a knife at all times for protection after someone had creeped up on him from a flophouse down the street. Bond made the same mistake once and approached Bulger from behind. Whitey yelled at him for it.

He didn't like to be startled and tried to be observant about his surroundings at all times. Bulger would leave copies of the local newspaper outside Bond's apartment door highlighting neighborhood crimes and other articles.

"He'd stay up all night," Bond remembers. "I could see him through a window sitting in his apartment with a pair of binoculars."

Josh Bond thought that Charlie Gasko was some kind of neighborhood watchman, an aging vigilante whose aim it was to protect his fellow residents. No one could have known that the man in apartment 303 was keeping a lookout for the FBI and was one of the most wanted killers alive.

20

SPECIAL AGENT PHIL TORSNEY HAD an idea. There was still much debate within the FBI about whether or not Whitey remained in communication with Billy Bulger or any of their siblings.

"What if we tell them that we think Whitey might be dead?" he told Tommy Mac. "What might their reaction be, shock? Or will they know we're lying because they're talking to him regularly? Let's get them out of their comfort zone."

The partners returned to Billy's house, knocked on the door, and were once again met by his wife.

"Mrs. Bulger, we have a DOA that may be James Bulger," Phil told her. "We'd like to make a determination on this, but we need your husband's cooperation by supplying his DNA for testing."

There was no reaction on Mary Bulger's face. She merely smiled and said that she'd pass along the request to her husband.

Torsney and MacDonald visited the other siblings, with only Whitey's younger sister Sheila consenting to an interview. Sheila McKeon was estranged from the family and lived with her husband in Hull, Massachusetts, twenty-five miles away from Southie. Out of all the Bulgers, Sheila looked to be the best bet.

"We need a sample of your DNA to compare it with this John Doe," the agents told her. "Because if it is Jim Bulger, we can put this thing to bed and stop bothering you folks and we can close the case."

Estranged or not, Sheila McKeon wouldn't assist them by giving up her DNA. Neither would any of the other Bulger family members.

When they returned to their office, the voice mail button on MacDonald's phone was flashing. He sat down at his cubicle and pressed play. Once again, the booming voice of Bulger family lawyer Tom Kiley could be heard loud and clear.

"You come to us with a body, and then maybe the family will talk," Tommy Mac recalled Kiley stating in the voice mail. "But we're not going to do anything to help you find James Bulger."

Tommy Mac was not dissuaded.

"Previous agents would have backed off, but Phil and I don't work that way," MacDonald says. "Whitey was wanted for killing nineteen people; this wasn't a tax case. We had a right to be there. I wondered how the Bulgers could sleep at night."

After interviewing Sheila McKeon, they waited and watched the pen registers on the phones of Billy and other family members. Would they immediately call each other? Would they call someone else?

FBI analyst Roberta "Bobby" Hastings was tasked with figuring it out. The only team member who'd been tracking Whitey since he went on the run back in the mid-1990s, Hastings had more skin in this game than anyone. For her, the hunt for Whitey was personal. Unlike the new members of the team, Hastings had enjoyed a friendship with disgraced agent John Connolly and felt burned by his betrayal.

A native of Clinton, Massachusetts, and a graduate of Western Kentucky University, Hastings joined the Bureau in 1980. As an FBI investigative analyst in the Boston office, Hastings had worked hand in hand with Charlie Gianturco before he was taken off the case. She analyzed and kept records on all tips, telephone calls, and meetings with those in Whitey Bulger's inner and outer circles. She cross-referenced every bit of information that was brought in and helped to put all the puzzle pieces together, and then told the agents which pieces were still missing.

"We had a lot of good days, but a lot of bad days too. I'd wake up in the middle of the night with phone numbers running through my head. We'd get excited about a tip one minute and then learn it wasn't him. It was all-consuming," Hastings remembers. "Everybody, especially those in the media, also thought that we were all corrupt because of Connolly. We were all put into a category of liars and cheats. We were kicked down so low, but we had to pick ourselves up each morning and do the job. I knew John [Connolly] and I actually liked him. He was a flashy guy, but he treated me well. I had always thought of him as a nice guy, but then I reminded myself that nice guys don't murder people. We didn't know what he was doing behind closed doors. Connolly never brought me into that circle of his life."

By the time Gleason took over in 2008, Hastings was the unit's mother hen—the one who had been through it all and hadn't given up the fight. She was also a wizard when it came to researching data. And when it came to Billy Bulger's phone records, she analyzed all the phone numbers to narrow down common calls. One series of calls that stood out came from Billy's house to a location in Oxnard, California. The agents figured that Billy was too smart to phone his brother directly, but it was still an unusual lead worth chasing.

Had Billy finally let his guard down? Tommy Mac traced the call to a woman living in Oxnard and flew out to interview her.

"She told us that she was an old classmate of Billy's," MacDonald says. "The woman said that the phone calls with Bulger concerned an upcoming class reunion and had nothing to do with Whitey."

MacDonald wasn't convinced.

After the interview, Tommy Mac drove south along the Pacific Coast Highway toward the FBI's Los Angeles office. After about an hour on the road, he stopped off in Santa Monica. The weather was gorgeous and MacDonald was hungry. He and a fellow agent on loan from the LA office parked their car and took a walk on the Santa Monica Pier, staring out at the Pacific Ocean and breathing in the salt air. While they grabbed lunch at the Bubba Gump Shrimp Company and discussed the case, MacDonald explained the unit's frustration, the mythology surrounding Whitey, and his determination to capture the mob killer, who unbeknownst to them was sitting in his apartment less than a mile away. After lunch, Tommy Mac and his fellow agent got back in their car and continued on to Los Angeles, not knowing just how close they had come to solving this case once and for all.

Upon his return to Boston, MacDonald and Torsney took a new approach. If they couldn't unnerve the Bulger family, they'd do their best to embarrass them.

Tommy Mac printed up hundreds of fliers with photos of Whitey and Catherine on them. Under the pictures, the FBI wrote *Fugitives Wanted by the FBI* in the color blue for law enforcement, *19 Murder Victims* in the color red for blood, and *Reward $2 Million* in the color green for cash. MacDonald scribbled his cell phone number on the pieces of paper and then blanketed Billy Bulger's neighborhood, sticking the fliers in mailboxes and under windshield wipers. To the agents, this was psychological warfare and another attempt to get the family out of its comfort zone.

One of the fliers would later find its way to Whitey himself.

"We handed out business cards with New York printed on them for me and Cleveland for Phil," MacDonald says. "We also wanted to show them that the Bureau was investing its resources from outside the Boston office and we weren't going anywhere. We were getting the fire going. It had been years since a lot of the key people were approached. The answer we were getting from folks in Southie was that we weren't really looking for Whitey. Or he's dead and we're wasting our time. We wanted people to know that we were committed to finding this guy. We didn't come to Boston to drink pints of Guinness at Faneuil Hall. This was no vacation."

Another investigator who was brought in to help supervise the Bulger probe was Rich Teahan, an agent who had spent a decade working in the FBI office in New Haven, Connecticut. Like Torsney, Teahan was a veteran manhunter, but he was also one with deep local roots. Teahan was Boston Irish. He grew up in Quincy, where his father worked as a trooper in the state police. When he landed in Connecticut, Teahan was handed one of the biggest fugitive cases in the country, the hunt for Alex Kelly, the "preppy rapist." Kelly was a former high school wrestling champion from Darien, Connecticut, who was accused of raping two teenage girls. Before his trial was set to begin, Kelly fled to Europe, where he stayed for seven years, bouncing around as a ski bum and living off money sent to him by his wealthy parents. The FBI long believed that Kelly's mother and father were supporting their son from afar. Finally, Rich Teahan and a team of agents swarmed the family home, executing a state police search warrant. Teahan discovered letters from the accused rapist and recent photos of the parents enjoying time with their son overseas. The parents were charged with obstruction and Kelly finally surrendered in Switzerland. He was extradited back to the US to stand trial, where he was ultimately found guilty and sentenced to sixteen years in prison.

While on assignment in New Haven, Teahan also spent time chasing down Bulger leads and sightings, including one at a posh yacht club in Groton, Connecticut. The agent even had his own brush with a Bulger look-alike while touring World War II battlefields in Tunisia.

"I was sitting by the hotel pool having a beer when I look over and there's a guy who looks just like Whitey, and he's wearing a Boston Red Sox hat," Teahan recalls. "I listened to him speak and recognized a thick Boston accent."

Teahan observed the man for several more minutes. He'd heard Bulger's voice on surveillance tapes and remembered that his Southie dialect was more subtle. It turned out that the look-alike was a tourist from Somerville, Massachusetts.

"I thought you were someone else," the agent told the tourist. "I thought you were a top-ten FBI fugitive. I was gonna get a real nice reward for it."

Of course, federal agents were ineligible to cash in on the $2 million prize, but catching Whitey Bulger in North Africa would have been the ultimate reward for any lawman.

In 2002, Teahan moved to Washington to work on the executive protection detail for then–FBI director Robert Mueller before jumping over to the national joint terrorism task force. Like Noreen Gleason, Teahan was known for his leadership and organizational skills. In 2006, he applied for Office of Preference, which was a wish list of where agents wanted to go. Rich Teahan wanted to go home for the first time in fifteen years. He had a wife and three kids and yearned to be close to his father, who was recently widowed. Teahan had a special bond with his father, who had retired as a lieutenant colonel in the state police and had inspired his son to join law enforcement. The father had been assigned to South Boston in the 1970s during a violent period of neighborhood unrest over a federal judge's decision to desegregate Boston schools. State troopers mobilized to protect African-American children as their school buses entered and left Southie while residents hurled bottles and racist insults in their direction. Whitey Bulger was among those who didn't want black students bused into his neighborhood. He tried to burn down an elementary school in the judge's hometown of Wellesley and then tossed a Molotov cocktail through the back door of President John F. Kennedy's birthplace in nearby Brookline. The home, a historical landmark, was targeted by Whitey because Senator Edward Kennedy, JFK's younger brother, had been a vocal supporter of forced busing. Before fleeing the scene in a green

Chevy Impala, Bulger spray-painted *Bus Teddy* on the sidewalk in front of the home.

When Rich Teahan agreed to supervise the Bulger Task Force, he too discovered the impenetrable wall that was put up around Whitey's siblings, especially Billy Bulger.

"What made me mad about that family was they wouldn't even talk to us without an attorney," Teahan recalls. "I had hunted enough people to know that the family was always the central thing. It's the central theme, and that's where you start and work your way out. It's like a dartboard and you focus on the family. That's what we did in the Alex Kelly case and just look at what that did for us. But the Bulgers were so insulated and so powerful. We were dealing with another level of power inside Massachusetts, like no other. Billy Bulger was titanium and we were not gonna break through."

Whitey Bulger meets with fellow Winter Hill mobster George Kaufman at the crew's headquarters at the Lancaster Street garage in Boston in 1980. *(United States Attorney evidence photo)*

Bulger *(center)* eventually learned that law enforcement was bugging and videotaping clandestine meetings at the Lancaster Street garage. *(United States Attorney evidence photo)*

Stephen "The Rifleman" Flemmi *(left)*, Whitey *(middle)*, and Kevin Weeks *(right)* stroll Castle Island on the South Boston waterfront. *(United States Attorney evidence photo)*

Whitey (*left*) and Weeks on Castle Island in Southie just before Whitey went on the run in 1995. This is one of the last known photos of Bulger in Boston. (*United States Attorney evidence photo*)

Whitey's de facto headquarters, Triple O's Lounge, was a blood-soaked barroom on West Broadway in South Boston. Today, it is home to an upscale gastropub and a luxury condo building. (*United States Attorney evidence photo*)

Whitey holds mob executioner John Martorano's son, John Jr., at the boy's christening in Boston in this undated photo. Martorano admitted killing twenty people as the Winter Hill Gang's top triggerman and implicated Whitey in more than a dozen killings. *(United States Attorney evidence photo)*

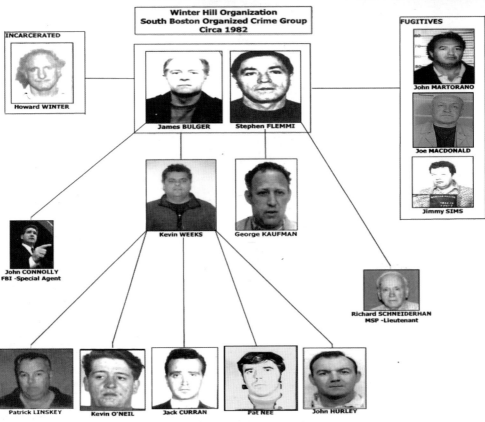

US Attorney's office organization chart for the Winter Hill Gang, including corrupt FBI agent John Connolly and corrupt Massachusetts state trooper Richard Schneiderhan as associates of the gang. *(United States Attorney evidence photo)*

Boston-born businessman Roger Wheeler, the fifty-five-year-old president of World Jai Alai, was executed in his car by John Martorano as he left a Tulsa, Oklahoma, country club in 1981. Wheeler was targeted for death after discovering Bulger and his crew were skimming from the Jai Alai operation. *(United States Attorney evidence photo)*

The bullet-riddled blue Datsun driven by Michael Donahue after an ambush by Whitey outside a bar on the South Boston waterfront in 1982. Whitey, wearing a wig, fake mustache, and floppy hat and brandishing a machine gun, executed Donahue, an innocent bystander, and Brian Halloran, who Bulger feared was cooperating with the FBI. *(United States Attorney evidence photo)*

FBI mugshots of Whitey and Flemmi taken in 1983 when they were suspects in the 1982 murder of former World Jai Alai president John B. Callahan in Miami. Callahan, forty-five, was from the Boston suburb of Medford and was killed because of what he knew about the Wheeler murder. *(United States Attorney evidence photo)*

Stephen Flemmi's mistress Debra Davis was strangled to death in the basement of The Haunty because Whitey feared she would talk to the FBI. While Flemmi testified Bulger killed the twenty-six-year-old beauty, the jury made no finding on Bulger's guilt in her slaying. The no-finding verdict on the Davis murder was labeled a victory for Whitey by his lawyers. *(United States Attorney evidence photo)*

Cops dig up bones at Tenean Beach in Dorchester. Three badly decomposed bodies were found at the site, including the remains of Paulie McGonagle, Debra Davis, and boxer Tommy King, who had the distinct honor of once having beaten up Whitey at Triple O's. *(United States Attorney evidence photo)*

Remains of one of three bodies unearthed from the burial site on Tenean Beach in 2000. *(United States Attorney evidence photo)*

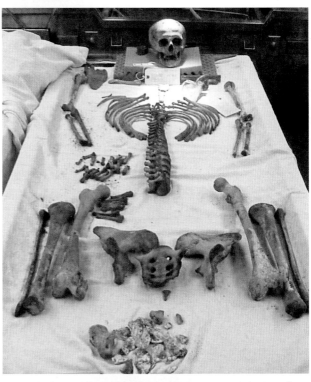

Below: Masks used by the Winter Hill Gang in armed robberies and shootings were unearthed, along with dozens of guns, in 1980 from the East Third Street home of Flemmi's mother, Mary, who lived across a courtyard from Whitey's powerful politician brother, Billy Bulger. *(United States Attorney evidence photo)*

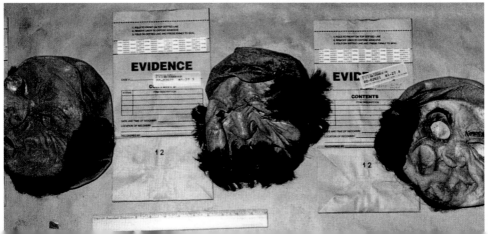

Whitey's brother, former Massachusetts State Senate president Billy Bulger, spoke to the authors for hours at this South Boston home on the left in the summer of 2019. The house on the right across the courtyard, 832 East Fourth St., was home to Flemmi's mother, Mary, for decades. It is now vacant. *(Photo by authors)*

Bulger and his crew killed at least three people and buried them in the basement of "The Haunty" murder house at 799 East Third St. in Southie. Built in 1890, the house was purchased for just $120,000 in the 1980s and sold for $3.5 million in 2019. At publication, it was slated for demolition for a new condo building in the heavily gentrified neighborhood. *(Photo by authors)*

Whitey's girlfriend Catherine Greig (*left*) and her twin sister, Margaret McCusker, in an undated photo. (*Photo courtesy of Margaret McCusker*)

A never-before-published fake ID used by Bulger in New York, immediately after he went on the run, under the name "Charles Gaska." He would later amend the name to Charles Gasko. (*United States Attorney evidence photo*)

LEGAL / 1ST AMENDMENT, NON-GOVERNMENT, PHOTO ID CARD FOR RESIDENTS OF

New York

1996   1998

#1321

SOCIAL SECURITY NUMBER   DOCUMENT No.

December 16, 1936   **1998**

D.O.B.*   DMV NO.   EXPIRATION DATE

Male   **Brown**   **Blue**   **5'9"**   **165**

SEX   HAIR   WEIGHT

NATION

Charles W. Gaska
188 W. 44 Street
New York NY 10036

Issued by authority from Washington, D.C. Signature

Charles W. Gaska

Authorized Dealer of The National Card Center © Copyright 1996

Whitey got this California driver's license by paying a US Army veteran named James Lawlor for his personal information. (*United States Attorney evidence photo*)

CALIFORNIA

DRIVER LICENSE

EXPIRES 11-09-07   S0620560   CLASS:C

JAMES WILLIAM LAWLOR
1538 SAWTELLE BLVD APT 29
W LOS ANGELES CA 90025

SEX:M   HAIR:WHT   EYES:BLU
HT:5-08   WT:170   DOB:11-09-36

RSTR:CORR LENS

09/23/2002 235 RB   FD/07

Whitey stood watch on the third floor of the Princess Eugenia Apartments (*top right unit*) in Santa Monica, California, where he hid in plain sight for years as an unassuming retiree while the nation's number one fugitive. Bulger was arrested in 2011 by FBI agents in the underground garage in the bottom left of the photo. *(Photo by Authors)*

Whitey and Catherine lived in this unit, #303, at Princess Eugenia Apartments in Santa Monica for years until cops lured him out of the apartment and arrested him in the building's underground parking garage in 2011. *(Photo by Authors)*

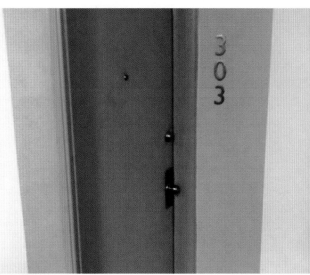

Charlie and Carol Gasko—the aliases of Whitey Bulger and Catherine Greig—befriended their elderly neighbor Catalina Shlank. The Argentinian woman thought they were retirees and said Whitey regularly helped her with her groceries. *(Photo by Authors)*

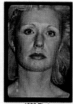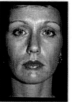

The FBI scored a major breakthrough in the case when agents found photographs of Catherine Greig that were taken when she underwent plastic surgery. *(Photo courtesy of the FBI)*

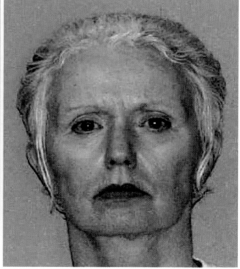

Booking photos for Whitey and Catherine following their arrests in 2011.
(Photo courtesy of US Marshals Service)

FBI Special Agent Scott Garriola handcuffs James J. "Whitey" Bulger in the underground parking garage at the Princess Eugenia Apartments in Santa Monica, on June 22, 2011. *(Photo courtesy of Scott Garriola and LAPD/ Miguel Mejia)*

FBI Special Agent Scott Garriola escorts Whitey in cuffs while FBI agent James Ross escorts Catherine Greig to a federal prison detention center in Los Angeles in 2011. *(Photo courtesy of Scott Garriola and LAPD/Miguel Mejia)*

Authorities retrieved more than $800,000 and dozens of guns and weapons stashed in wall hides such as this one inside unit #303 at the Princess Eugenia Apartments in Santa Monica. *(United States Attorney evidence photo)*

A cache of guns belonging to Bulger that were seized following his capture in Santa Monica. *(United States Attorney evidence photo)*

Whitey's living room in Santa Monica where he used a punching dummy wearing a fedora as a decoy for anyone who might want to shoot him through the window. *(United States Attorney evidence photo)*

Sgt. Richard Eaton of the San Diego County Sheriff's Department claims to have identified Whitey at a screening of the Oscar-winning film *The Departed* in 2006. *(Photo courtesy of Sgt. Richard Eaton, San Diego County Sheriff's Department)*

FBI Assistant Special Agent-in-Charge Noreen Gleason led the Bulger Task Force and put together the team that ultimately captured the fugitive crime boss. Gleason is credited with making the call to focus the investigation on tracking Catherine Greig, a pivotal move that ultimately led to the key break in the case. *(Photo courtesy of Noreen Gleason)*

US Marshal Neil Sullivan is the agent who got the tip that led authorities to Bulger's hideout in Santa Monica. *(Photo courtesy US Marshals Service)*

Assistant US Attorney Brian Kelly was part of the prosecution team that put Whitey away for good in 2013. Kelly received death threats that required security for him and his family because of his work on the Bulger case. *(US Attorney's office photo)*

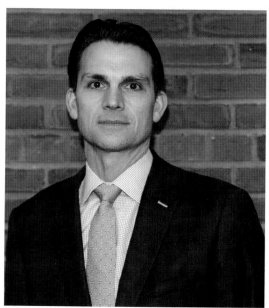

Zach Hafer, a seasoned organized crime prosecutor, had a front seat to the courtroom theatrics as part of the team in the Boston US Attorney's office that brought Whitey to justice. *(US Attorney's office photo)*

Unit 303 in the Princess Eugenia Apartments where Whitey and Catherine hid out for years was renovated in 2019 and rented to a new tenant. *(Photo by authors)*

FBI manhunters Tommy MacDonald and Phil Torsney were brought in to spearhead the task force that captured Whitey. *(Photo courtesy of Federal Bureau of Investigation)*

A rare photo of Whitey Bulger in prison, seen here with his art teacher Clement "Chip" Janus at USP Tucson in 2014. *(Photo courtesy of Clement "Chip" Janus)*

Another rare photo of Whitey Bulger in USP Tucson in 2014 with his art teacher "Chip" Janus and others. *(Photo courtesy Clement "Chip" Janus)*

July 2014

On Right Chip - "The Artist"
A man who found himself in this place where so many waste away accomplishing very little.
Oscar Wilde said it over a hundred years ago
"Vile Deeds, Like Poison Weeds
Bloom Well in Prison air
It is only what is Good in Man
That Wastes and Withers there."
So True. But Chip is the exception - fortunately for us who appreciate the fruits of his Talent.
James Whitey Bulger 1428 AZ

A letter written by Whitey to his friend Clement "Chip" Janus in 2014.
(Courtesy of Clement "Chip" Janus)

Springfield mobster Fotios "Freddy" Geas, one of Bulger's accused killers, was a lieutenant in the powerful western Massachusetts Mafia faction run by Alfredo "Big Al" Bruno. The crew answered to John Gotti and the New York La Cosa Nostra and used this Springfield, Massachusetts, strip club as its headquarters. *(Photo by authors)*

Suspected Bulger killer Fotios "Freddy" Geas, who is serving life for murder and racketeering in the United States Penitentiary in Hazelton, West Virginia, where Whitey was killed, is shown with his daughter Taylor in this undated photo from the 1990s. *(Photo courtesy of Taylor Geas)*

Whitey is buried here with his parents, Mary and John, in a cemetery in the West Roxbury section of Boston. Whitey's name is not on the grave. *(Photo by authors)*

21

TOMMY MAC KEPT THE HEAT on Whitey's family while Phil Torsney traveled across the country, chasing down Bulger's old pals from Alcatraz to see if there was any piece of information that had been missed over the past decade. Phil also flew up to Canada to check on Whitey sightings across the border. It made some sense that he and Catherine would be hiding there since Bulger had contacts in Canada through Teresa Stanley's son-in-law, former NHL player Chris Nilan, who had dragged money up there for Whitey in the past.

Back at the Boston FBI office, Rich Teahan also went on the offensive, giving media interviews to discuss the lack of cooperation offered by the Bulger family. It was Noreen Gleason's idea to lift the curtain and show the public what was being done to solve this case.

"You either feed the beast, or the beast feeds on you," Gleason says. "The FBI had been quiet for too long and that led to all the outrageous conspiracy theories about us hiding Whitey. It was so ridiculous to even think about."

Teahan was more than willing to engage with local reporters who had lost respect for the Boston office. It was his chance to turn them around. Still, most journalists working the Bulger beat remained skeptical about the Bureau's efforts.

"That was the single most frustrating thing about working this case," Teahan recalls. "We got the shit beat out of us every day. We were all very principled and ethical, but having the press beat you down every day and lump you in with John Connolly, Morris, and all the other dirty law enforcement that got into bed with this guy, it got to us. It gets down into your soul a little bit."

On a Sunday night in November 2009, Tommy Mac and Torsney decided to leave their hotel and drive to Quincy to pay a surprise visit to Kevin Weeks. It had been some time since anyone had spoken with Whitey's right-hand man, and the agents wanted to check his pulse and see if there was any nugget of information he had that previous agents could have overlooked.

"We didn't call the FBI first and ask permission to speak with Weeks," MacDonald says. "We knew we wouldn't have gotten the okay. The guy was part of the John Connolly conviction, so the US attorney had always told us to back off."

They found Weeks's apartment and knocked on the door. The former mob thug let the agents in and pointed them to a couch in the living room. Torsney looked around the well-kept apartment. The finely decorated digs were a far cry from the prison cell where Weeks had been locked up for five years before his parole in early 2005.

Weeks had a throw blanket wrapped around his large body and he was watching the fourth quarter of a tight New England Patriots game as his girlfriend hovered close by. Despite the interruption, Kevin patiently answered their questions for two straight hours.

"Do you think they're still together?" MacDonald asked him about Whitey and Catherine. "Could he have killed her by now?"

"I don't know about that," Weeks said. "They had a good relationship, they had a loving relationship, but there was one time where I witnessed violence between them that I had to pull Jimmy off Catherine because he was choking her to death."

Weeks was referring to the incident at Greig's house after she had confessed about their relationship to Teresa Stanley.

The agents scribbled in their notepads, thanked Weeks for his time, and then left.

The next morning, MacDonald and Torsney had breakfast together in the hotel restaurant. Tommy Mac had a plate stacked high with eggs, while his partner ate cereal with no milk. MacDonald had a hard time knowing that Phil was a vegetarian, as Tommy considered himself a proud carnivore and never met a steak he didn't like. Despite the differences in their diets, both got along well.

"Is Bulger a guy who's slick enough to kill or is he your typical old Irish guy who needs a good woman by his side to get through the day?" MacDonald asked.

"If he had killed her, she'd be a Jane Doe," Torsney replied. "Remember, she's never been arrested before so her fingerprints aren't on file. How can we search, dental records?"

"What about plastic surgery? What about breast implants?" MacDonald countered. "She was meticulous in her appearance and always tried to look young. If she's had a boob job, wouldn't the implants have serial numbers? If a medical examiner was performing an autopsy on a Jane Doe and she had breast implants, you'd think they would take them out and record the serial numbers for identification."

Earlier in their investigation, police had found the torso of a female in the waters close to Grand Isle, Louisiana. It wasn't Catherine, but it got the agents thinking.

The agents posed the question to Bobby Hastings, who reminded them about a source close to Greig that was cultivated by agent Mike Carazza. That source had mentioned that Margaret McCusker had once dropped her twin sister off at a local hospital for a plastic surgery procedure.

On December 3, 2009, MacDonald and Torsney drove out to Newton-Wellesley Hospital with a subpoena. They quickly learned that Catherine had not only undergone breast enhancement surgery, but also had liposuction and other procedures performed at Plastic Surgical Associates in Newton, Massachusetts. Catherine was a woman who'd spent a lot of her time under the knife.

The medical practice now was run by Dr. Matthias Donelan and the FBI called his office requesting a meeting.

"Let's set up a time to talk by phone," the doctor told his secretary.

"No, the FBI wants to meet with you in person," she replied.

The Bureau didn't tell Donelan's assistant what the agents wanted to speak to him about, but the doctor knew all about Whitey Bulger and remembered that his longtime partner Dr. Eugene Curtiss had treated Catherine Greig as a patient before his retirement.

"She came into the office to have her eyelids done," Dr. Donelan recalls. "It was standard practice to take photographs for both face-lift patients and eyelid patients."

A few years later, Catherine had breast augmentation surgery performed by the same surgeon in the same office. When Donelan first met Tommy Mac, he told him that it was likely they had preserved her records. MacDonald was surprised at how willing the surgeon was to cooperate with the investigation.

"My father was an FBI agent," Donelan told him. The doctor's father, Charles Donelan, was a lawyer who worked for the Bureau for thirty-seven years and retired as assistant director and trainer at the FBI Academy at Quantico. He'd also served in the Bureau's New York office, just like Tommy Mac. For once, things were going right for MacDonald in the Bulger case.

"I'll check our files in storage; they're located in the bowels of our building," Dr. Donelan told him. "I'd be happy to help you catch Whitey Bulger."

A short time later, the plastic surgeon called MacDonald back. It was late in the day and the agent was pressed for time. Tommy Mac was just about to leave the office and head back to Connecticut to catch one of his son's baseball games.

"I've located the files you've been searching for," Dr. Donelan said. "I had to pull them out of storage."

"That's great," Tommy replied. "I'll swing by and pick them up in the morning."

"Do you want the photographs too?"

"You have photos?" MacDonald asked excitedly. "In that case, I'll be over in fifteen minutes."

Tommy Mac was dumbfounded. He didn't think that any photos of Greig existed outside the grainy surveillance pictures of her taken at a distance during a walk with Whitey several years before in Southie. In those images, Catherine wore a thick pair of sunglasses that took up half her face. To the investigators, they were useless.

When MacDonald arrived at the doctor's office, he was presented with a collection of high-resolution photographs of Catherine Greig. Unlike the surveillance pictures, these images were tight close-ups and side profiles of Bulger's longtime girlfriend. They were face, neck, and breast shots both before surgery and after.

"You could see every pore in her face," MacDonald remembers.

"We always had crappy pictures of her," adds Torsney. "Those pictures of Catherine became the backbone of the case."

But how could the FBI use them effectively? The agents huddled with Teahan and Noreen Gleason and came up with the strategy to target the medical and dental fields.

They took out advertisements showcasing the photos in industry news outlets like *Plastic Surgery News* and the American Dental Association's newsletter under the banner *Have You Treated This Woman?*

The advertisement listed all the plastic surgery procedures that she'd undergone and even listed the serial number of her breast implants, alerting doctors that Greig had the procedure done in 1982 and might be looking to replace them, along with information that she also suffered from a ragweed allergy and was sensitive to Valium.

Soon they were flooded with more tips, including a highly promising one from a dental office in Vancouver, British Columbia.

"She used to work here," the office manager told the FBI.

Was Whitey hiding in Canada after all?

MacDonald and Torsney flew out to Vancouver and rifled through the employment records. But like all the sightings of Whitey, this tip about his girlfriend proved to be another dead end.

Still, knowing they had the photos, the agents believed that it would be only a matter of time before someone came forward with the right information.

"We find her, and we'll find him," Noreen Gleason told her team.

But the Bulger Task Force unit needed support. Since both Tommy Mac and Phil Torsney were on temporary duty assignment in Boston, they would occasionally get pulled back to their home offices in New York and Cleveland.

"The powers that be thought, why are my agents in Boston chasing some old white guy when we have real fugitive cases in our own office?" MacDonald says.

Tommy was ordered back to Manhattan to investigate a rash of shootings in Yonkers, New York, while Phil was ordered home to Cleveland to handle a serial murder case. Anthony Sowell, the "Cleveland Strangler," had murdered eleven women inside his home. Sowell buried the bodies of his victims in the basement and in crawl spaces in the house.

"I was assigned the case, and when I got back there, I found that all the work had been done," Torsney recalls. "We'd recovered all the bodies and the killer had confessed to the murders. There was no need for me to be back in Cleveland as I had an active fugitive that I was chasing out of Boston."

22

PHIL TORSNEY PLEADED HIS CASE to the Bureau and was finally granted a permanent duty assignment in Boston with the sole purpose of catching Whitey Bulger. Torsney was fifty-five years old now and close to retirement. He hoped that he'd never have to look back on Whitey as the one that got away.

But with Tommy Mac still back in New York, Noreen Gleason needed additional assistance, so she looked outside the FBI to the US Marshals Service. It was a humbling experience, as there was still great animosity between law enforcement agencies and the FBI regarding Bulger, but Gleason wanted to be transparent about her efforts and the need for help.

"Look, there's not been a lot of collaboration and cooperation," she told David Taylor, the chief deputy marshal of Boston. "I'm very sincere about this; let's try to get along. I know you don't trust us and I understand why. But it's a new day. Let's try to bury this hatchet and catch this guy. This affects all of us. This is a really bad dude who continues to have this terrible influence over this region."

In September 2010, the marshals assigned one of their own, a Massachusetts native named Neil Sullivan, to the case. When he reported to the Bulger Task Force, it consisted of two FBI agents (Teahan and Torsney) and an analyst (Hastings), along with a few state police detectives and correctional officers. The unit had once operated out of the Coast Guard building on Atlantic Avenue in the North End, but now, the Bulger team was back under the FBI's roof at its Boston headquarters at One Center Plaza, the so-called Land of Misfit Toys.

Sullivan grew up on Cape Cod and graduated from Barnstable High School, the same school that had produced another Bulger manhunter, San Diego sheriff's deputy Rich Eaton, although the two did not know each other.

Neil's father, William, worked a civilian job for the US Air Force on Cape Cod while his mother, Carrie, tended to their home. Neil joined the Air Force after graduating from high school and was assigned as a security police officer, patrolling bases in the US and South Korea while undergoing heavy weapons training with Mark 19, 50-caliber, and M16 rifles and mortar teams.

"I wound up loving it and I knew that's exactly what I wanted to do in the civilian world," Sullivan says. "I enjoyed security police and saw some of the older guys get out of the service and into law enforcement jobs, so I followed their lead."

He enrolled at Salve Regina University in Newport, Rhode Island, where he studied criminal justice but left early to join the US Marshals. "When the Marshals offered me a job, I knew I had to take it as I didn't believe there would be any other good jobs out there when I graduated," he recalls.

Sullivan entered the US Marshals Academy in October 1995, eleven months after Whitey Bulger had gone on the run. As a young marshal, he worked court duty in Manhattan escorting gangsters like Gambino crime family honcho Vincent "Vinny the Chin" Gigante back and forth to trial.

"Gigante never gave me any trouble," Sullivan says. "He was the one feigning insanity. He was in character pretending that he was crazy at all times."

Two years later, he joined the warrant squad, earning the same salary, but this job was completely different. Now Sullivan was on the streets breaking down doors and arresting accused killers, robbers, and rapists. It was a dangerous but rewarding job. Sullivan experienced a few close calls with fugitives, including one where a suspect rammed Neil's vehicle with a heavy-duty Ford Expedition. Sullivan jumped out of his car and opened fire on the Ford as it barreled toward him before crashing into a stop sign just a few feet away.

"If he'd been a foot or two to the right, I'd be dead," he says.

Sullivan admits that he was shaken by the incident and decided to take voluntary court duty for the next couple of months to heal himself psychologically.

"There had been a slew of marshals killed in the line of duty in recent years because we go after the most serious and desperate criminals," he explains. "When you're going after people like that, violent things are gonna happen."

After working a decade in New York, Sullivan joined the Boston office in 2010. At his going-away party in Albany, a colleague urged him to reach for the brass ring in Boston.

"When you get up there on day one, demand to work the Bulger case," the colleague said. "Say it immediately."

Sullivan packed his car and drove from upstate New York to Boston with his wife, Eileen, a social worker who had counseled families of lost loved ones after 9/11.

After getting approached by Noreen Gleason, the marshals were searching for someone to join the FBI's team, and Neil Sullivan was the ideal candidate.

"My superiors recognized my work in New York and that I was good in the fugitive unit and a good investigator," he remembers. "The Marshal in Chief asked me if I'd be willing to go to the FBI and help them with the Bulger case. I said yes immediately."

There was no sophisticated layout at the Bulger Task Force headquarters. The unit didn't have its own office and instead had to share space across from the FBI gang squad (GS14), where agents worked violent street gang cases and other organized crime cases.

There were photos of Bulger and Greig tacked on bulletin

boards, along with a world map covered in pins identifying all the places that the fugitives had been sighted since 1994, both real and imagined. Sullivan, Torsney, and Roberta Hastings were dropped into a pen surrounded by investigators who rolled their eyes and snickered, comparing the team to Mulder and Scully, the fictional agents in the hit show *The X-Files*, who chased after aliens and paranormal phenomena.

Were they hunting Whitey Bulger or the Abominable Snowman?

Roberta Hastings handed Sullivan a stack of case files and told him to start reading. The marshal could hardly believe the trail of blood left by Bulger and members of his gang through the streets of Southie, Dorchester, and other Boston neighborhoods.

"I had first heard about Whitey Bulger in the late 1990s. I had no idea who he was when he went on the run," Sullivan admits. "Growing up on Cape Cod, I was isolated from all the Boston crime news. My family only went to the city once a year for a Red Sox game and that was it."

It didn't take Sullivan long to hit a stone wall. He'd been handed the baton from Tommy Mac and he'd inherited the same resistance from those closest to Bulger. The marshal even flew down to Clearwater, Florida, and checked out Whitey's other old haunts to see if the fugitive had returned.

"I shared with my wife Eileen the frustrations I had about interviewing people who'd already been spoken to seven times," Sullivan recalls. "No one was giving us anything. There was a code of silence. In fact, they were offended that we were chasing after an old man."

The task force was beginning to lose ground on leads from the first campaign that utilized new photos of Catherine Greig to target plastic surgeons and dental offices. The investigators needed to rethink their strategy once again. Sitting around the conference room at One Center Plaza, the agents spit-balled fresh ideas.

"What can we do to take control of our own message?" Rich Teahan asked the group. "We shouldn't be controlled by a media outlet like Fox's *America's Most Wanted* because Whitey's been aired on that show more than a dozen times and we have nothing to show for it."

Someone floated the idea of creating a commercial. The team brought in the FBI office's resident public relations professional to discuss whether it was feasible.

"We'll need a production company to build a public service announcement, and we'll need to target markets," the PR flack informed them. "We need to have a budget for those markets because one market may be more expensive than another market."

Teahan brought the idea to Noreen Gleason, who went to FBI headquarters to secure funding for the project. The FBI had never done something like this before and the approval process was painstakingly slow, but the team was confident that the strategy would net results.

Gleason managed to get only $50,000 allocated for the PSA's production and commercial costs.

"It wasn't a lot of money, but you can't look a gift horse in the mouth," Teahan says.

The FBI worked with a production company out of Maine on the content for the spot and then chose fourteen markets to run it in.

"The common theme for us now was that Whitey had never left the country," Neil Sullivan remembers. "We created a chart of where we knew he was during the first two years and it was always in the US. If he was gonna go to Europe to hide, he would have done it in those first two years."

The team was also convinced that Bulger would be hiding someplace warm and near the ocean. That eliminated places like Oklahoma and Minnesota.

"We believed that he'd want to surround himself with fellow retirees someplace where he could walk and get around," Sullivan adds.

The investigators drew a map across the bottom of the United States from the Carolinas south to the Florida panhandle and over to the Gulf of Mexico and the west coast. Those were the regions they would spend money in.

But in California, the spot would only run in San Francisco because of Whitey's ties to Alcatraz, and not in the Los Angeles area, where the media market was too expensive to advertise.

While the FBI was plotting airtime, in Santa Monica, Catherine had been busy feeding and fretting over a stray cat they'd named Tiger. Tiger had helped her make new friends, including a woman from Iceland named Anna Bjornsdottir, who struck up a conversation with her while Greig was feeding the cat outside. Anna was a former model who'd been crowned Miss Iceland in 1974. She'd moved to Southern California to kick-start her acting career and managed to get a few gigs, including a guest spot on the hit television show *Remington Steele*. She also appeared in Hollywood films including *More American Graffiti* and *The Sword and the Sorcerer*. Like Catherine, Anna was a cat lover, and they spent time together, especially at night, when Greig was feeding Tiger and Anna was returning home from one of her walks. Catherine, or "Carol," told Anna that she had a niece who'd once lived in Santa Monica and that's why they'd decided to move there.

It was as casual and innocent as every other stray conversation Catherine had since moving there—and it would be Whitey's undoing.

23

O N Sunday night, May 1, 2011, Americans across the country and people around the world watched the breaking news coverage about the death of Osama bin Laden at the hands of US Special Forces in Abbottabad, Pakistan. President Barack Obama made the announcement from the East Room of the White House, interrupting a nationally televised baseball game between the New York Mets and the Philadelphia Phillies.

"Tonight I can report to the American people and to the world, the United States has conducted an operation that killed Osama bin Laden, the leader of al-Qaeda, and a terrorist who's responsible for the murder of thousands of innocent men, women and children," President Obama declared.

In Santa Monica, at Barney's Beanery on the Third Street Promenade, bar patrons broke into cheer; "USA, USA," they shouted. At an Italian restaurant nearby, diners waved American flags. At the popular Santa Monica pub Britannia, one grizzled barfly hoisted his mug in the air. "The bastard's dead. I'll drink to that!"

Inside apartment 303 at the Princess Eugenia, Whitey Bulger sat in his living room with Catherine, watching the announcement with a mixed feeling of pride and dread. The patriotic side of Bulger was elated to learn that members of SEAL Team 6 raided bin Laden's secret compound and sent the terror mastermind back to his maker with a bullet above his left eye. But with bin Laden's death also came an unnerving reality for the eighty-one-year-old former crime boss. James "Whitey" Bulger was now elevated to number one on the FBI's list of most wanted criminals, and that meant the pressure to find him would be intensified.

Would a Black Hawk helicopter soon land on the roof of their apartment building? Would armed men kick down his door and instigate a bloodbath?

He'd been planning for such a showdown for years as he built up his personal arsenal while purchasing weapons at Nevada gun shows. Whitey now owned more than thirty firearms, including a Ruger pistol and several Smith & Wesson and Colt revolvers that he kept hidden inside cut-out walls and hollowed-out books, along with killing knives and $822,000 in cash. He also had two shotguns and two rifles stored under his bed and a pistol at his bedside.

All the weapons were loaded, and there was enough ammunition on hand to defend against a small army. Bulger was armed to the teeth and had vowed that he'd never be taken alive.

BACK AT ONE CENTER PLAZA, Noreen Gleason and Rich Teahan were busy building a command post and call center to support the leads they had hoped to generate from the Catherine Greig PSA.

"We didn't really care how he was going to be found," Teahan says. "We didn't care if it was a local cop in Iowa or the DEA in Bogotá. All that mattered was catching the motherfucker."

The FBI bought 350 time slots during daytime TV shows that appealed to women, including *Live with Regis and Kelly*, *The View*, and *Ellen DeGeneres*. On June 21, 2011, the Bulger Task Force let the thirty-second commercial spot fly.

"This is an announcement by the FBI," a female narrator declared. "Have you seen this woman?" The high-resolution photos of Catherine Greig discovered by Tommy Mac slid into the video frame next to the FBI shield, along with a reward in bold type of $100,000.

"Greig has had plastic surgeries," the narrator continued. "She's wanted for harboring James 'Whitey' Bulger, a fugitive on the FBI's Ten Most Wanted List."

Both Teahan and Gleason made sure that the commercial also evoked a sense of fear for Catherine's safety. They added a line about Bulger's violent temper, along with the fact that he was wanted for nineteen murders, in hopes of mobilizing a sisterhood of female viewers that might help rescue the girlfriend and pull her from harm's way.

What the investigators didn't realize was that the spot would generate major news because of the FBI's unique and innovative strategy to roll out a commercial on its own behalf. Rich Teahan's phone was inundated with interview requests from local, national, and international press, including CNN and the BBC. It didn't matter that the spot ran in only fourteen media markets, as Catherine Greig's photos were now plastered on TV screens and websites around the world.

Whitey Bulger was sitting in his apartment watching CNN when the news story flashed on the screen. He realized its significance right away. He then turned to Catherine.

"That's it," he said somberly.

Neil Sullivan was manning the command post at One Center Plaza that day. The team got a series of tips including several from Biloxi, Mississippi. The young marshal was excited because the tips had come from such a small geographical area.

"I was the one sending all the information from the day shift to the cities, especially to Biloxi, and then just eliminating them one by one," Sullivan says.

Sullivan and Phil Torsney made a pact that if they got enthusiastic about a lead, they wouldn't just jump on the next plane, because that would have left all the other tips not being vetted by the right people.

"We knew more about the case now than anyone else and we

didn't want any information to be dissected by other agents who didn't know what to look for," Sullivan adds.

By the end of the first day, they had run down all the Biloxi leads. Again, the sightings all wound up being look-alikes. Sullivan ended his day shift and handed over the duties to Torsney in the hope that he'd have better luck at night.

When the marshal returned to work the next day, he was faced with a big pile of tips that had come in before dawn. Some of the leads had been written down by call center operators who'd answered them overnight, while others were e-mailed to Sullivan's computer. He and analyst Roberta Hastings began to sift through them all and recognized three different inquiries that had come from the same tipster—a woman named Anna Bjornsdottir from Reykjavik, Iceland. One tip was in the pile, another was buried in Sullivan's e-mail in-box, and a third was a voice-mail message. Anna Bjornsdottir had called frantically three times and it was clear that she wasn't getting the answer she wanted.

"The person that I think is him is living at Princess Eugenia Apartments in Santa Monica, California. Call me back immediately," Anna said in accented English. "They call themselves Charlie and Carol Gasko."

It was Anna Bjornsdottir who had once befriended Greig over their mutual love for the stray cat named Tiger. She had even provided an actual location and a name, which differentiated this tip from all the rest.

Sullivan and Hastings checked all the federal law enforcement databases available and found a Carol and Charles Gasko living at the Santa Monica address. The strange thing was that the couple had no birth dates listed, no Social Security numbers, no California driver's licenses or state identification cards. They were ghosts.

"Right away, red flags started going off in my head, so I called the tipster," Sullivan says.

She spoke with a trace of a Scandinavian accent and she was

frustrated. Anna Bjornsdottir was adamant that she knew the couple Sullivan was looking for.

"Between the databases and what she was saying, I was quite convinced we had them."

Sullivan held his excitement in check. Although he was the newest member of the team, he'd heard enough stories from Torsney about dead ends and red herrings that he almost couldn't believe his own ears now. After sixteen long years and the near collapse of the Boston FBI office, had the team finally found its man?

Neil motioned Rich Teahan over and explained what was happening. Teahan then got in touch with Randy Jarvis from the FBI's Violent Crimes Task Force.

Scott Garriola is the best guy in L.A., Teahan wrote Jarvis in an e-mail. *We need him to chase down a promising lead on Whitey Bulger.*

Special Agent Scott Garriola had been working out of the Los Angeles office since 1991 and already had a colorful and celebrated career in the FBI, having hunted and captured dozens of dangerous fugitives, including many violent killers from the LA gang world and the murderous Mexican drug cartels. He'd also taken down a fugitive from the FBI's Top Ten List.

"Agent Garriola is a legend in the Bureau," Teahan says. "He's the only one I could fully trust for a job like this where we couldn't be boots on the ground ourselves. There's a small cadre of fugitive hunters in the FBI and he's on the top of the list with Phil Torsney."

But Garriola was on vacation and enjoying some well-deserved time off. He was with his kids at a local sporting goods store when Jarvis forwarded Teahan's e-mail. Garriola had worked Bulger leads in the Los Angeles area before. He also was very familiar with the east coast organized crime world, having grown up in the Bronx before attending college and law school in Southern California.

This is a 281, an organized crime case, Garriola typed back in a group e-mail to Teahan and Jarvis. *I'm off this week. Why don't you call in one of the O.C. guys?*

He stared at the message before sending and decided to delete it. This was Whitey Bulger after all.

Why don't you give me a call and show me what you got? Garriola responded instead.

Teahan phoned Garriola and brought him up to speed.

"I was still so pessimistic, having already covered so many Bulger leads over the years," Garriola says. "But something told me that I should go cover this one, so I went and got a babysitter. My mother-in-law was home at the time, thank God, so I dropped my kids off and got to work."

Garriola summoned four members of his fugitive team from the LAPD to join him on the hunt in Santa Monica. He was very familiar with the area, having lived one block away from the Princess Eugenia while attending law school at Loyola Marymount.

We got a lead on Whitey Bulger and I'll see you there in about an hour, Garriola wrote in a group text.

A response came immediately: *Who's Whitey Bulger?*

You ever see the movie The Departed*? It's kinda based on him,* Garriola texted back.

Although Bulger's face and a list of his crimes, including nineteen murders, were plastered all over the FBI website and now on television, a generation of younger agents and law enforcement professionals had little or no institutional knowledge about America's most wanted fugitive.

Garriola had to get his team up to speed quickly while also devising a plan to capture Bulger properly and safely. Most importantly, he wanted to make damned sure they were looking for the right guy. He called Teahan back during the drive to Santa Monica.

"Who talked to the tipster?" Garriola asked.

"A US marshal," Teahan told him.

"Well, as you know, Rich, the FBI and the marshals don't really get along, so I need to speak to the tipster myself."

Once again, his pessimism set in. He recalled that an influx of

Russian Jews had immigrated to Santa Monica during his time living there and figured that's what this was. The couple in question probably didn't have a big footprint in terms of identification cards because they didn't speak the language, didn't know the culture, and were unfamiliar with US document requirements.

Garriola's mind changed when he was put in touch with Anna Bjornsdottir.

"We called the Los Angeles office about this and didn't get a great response, so we called your headquarters in Washington and then Boston," Bjornsdottir told the agent on the phone. "He [Bulger] claimed he was from Chicago, but I have traveled around the country and I knew it wasn't a Chicago accent. It was a Boston accent. I got into several arguments with him. He's a racist and very anti-Obama. But the woman he is with was very pleasant."

"How sure are you that the couple you met are the fugitives we are looking for?" the agent asked her.

"I'm not 100 percent sure," the tipster replied. "I'm 200 percent sure it's them!"

That was good enough for Garriola. He started peppering Rich Teahan with requests. He needed a subpoena and was hyperfocused on the utilities of the apartment.

"Who controls the utilities?" Garriola asked him. "What were the names on the bill? Do they match the names that were called in on this tip?"

Teahan and Sullivan confirmed the information and then warned Garriola that they believed the aging crime boss was armed and would not give himself up without a fight.

"We had to get him away from the ability to shoot through walls and barricade himself inside with her [Catherine]. We feared that he'd use her as a hostage," Teahan recalls. "He wouldn't have come out of that apartment, not with the amount of firepower he had and everything he had to lose."

Scott Garriola went silent at that point. He was now operational.

Apartment manager Josh Bond was napping on the couch in his apartment when he was awakened by a coworker who told him that the FBI was in the office inquiring about a tenant. Bond then called Garriola's cell phone.

"Can we do this tomorrow?" Bond asked. "I'm off today."

"Well, I was off today too, pal. We need to take care of this now. It'll only take a few minutes of your time," Garriola said sternly.

Bond went down to his office across the street at the Embassy Hotel, where he was met by the FBI agent, who showed him photos of Whitey and Catherine.

"I'll make this real quick, I'm looking for a couple of fugitives," Garriola told him. "Are these the people living in apartment 303 at Princess Eugenia?"

Bond stared at the photos of his friends Charlie and Carol and put his head in his hands.

"That's my neighbor and his girlfriend," Bond said. "Yes, 100 percent it's them."

Garriola told the manager their real names and that they were wanted for serious crimes including murder. Bond was shocked.

"I know who Whitey Bulger is," Bond told him. "I went to school in Boston." The manager said that he'd lived in Boston for five years and had been working at the Princess Eugenia for five years too.

"You had ten years, and you never put two and two together that this was Whitey Bulger?" Garriola asked.

"I never saw a picture of him before."

"Well, it's him and I need some information from you."

Bond was unsure whether to cooperate.

"Umm, can we talk downstairs?"

Garriola didn't like that answer. He thought that maybe Bulger had set up a trip wire through the apartment manager to lure him somewhere long enough for Whitey to make his escape. The FBI agent called in his LAPD team members for backup.

"Okay, you should meet your team in the back of their building," Bond advised. "He's always on the balcony with a pair of binoculars looking up and down the street."

Garriola couldn't believe how clueless the manager was.

"And you didn't think that was odd as well?" he asked incredulously.

Bond was getting frustrated, as he didn't want to be late for a concert he was planning to attend that evening. He then inquired about a subpoena. Garriola quickly mentioned the big FBI reward for Whitey's capture and that certainly triggered the manager's interest.

"Somebody's already in line for the $2 million reward for leading us to Bulger's doorstep," the agent said. "But there's another $100 thousand reward for Catherine."

Garriola didn't know if the money was available or not. He was just throwing it out there to get the manager's cooperation.

"What can I do to help?" Bond asked.

Garriola asked for an apartment in the Embassy Hotel so that his team could run surveillance on Bulger's third-floor balcony. Bond complied.

"Where do you live?" he asked the manager.

"I live right next door to Charlie and Carol."

"Okay, I'd like to set up a ruse. We can shut the power off or tell him there's a plumbing leak going down from Bulger's apartment to the floor below. Or what if I get a UPS uniform and deliver a fake package?"

Josh Bond told Garriola that he didn't think any of the plans would work.

"No one's ever allowed in their apartment."

The agent told Bond to meet him in the back alley of the Princess Eugenia. The two men then went upstairs to the third floor and Garriola pressed his ear against the front door of apartment 303.

There was silence. He had to find another way inside.

Back in Boston, the Bulger Task Force waited patiently while Garriola and his team set the trap. Phil Torsney was now in, leading the command post as night shift commander. Both Sullivan and Teahan had reluctantly gone home for the evening but were monitoring all developments through texts with Garriola.

The Boston team felt it didn't need to micromanage Garriola from three thousand miles away. They had ultimate faith that the renowned manhunter would get the job done.

But the question remained—would anyone be harmed or even killed in the process?

After about thirty minutes of radio silence, Torsney texted Garriola for an update.

Busy, Garriola texted back.

More waiting . . .

Scott Garriola sneaked down to the garage underneath the apartment building and walked toward a set of storage lockers that were assigned to each unit. He found the locker for apartment 303 with the name *Gaskos* written in crayon.

The fugitive hunter had an idea. He'd retrieve a set of bolt cutters and cut the lock off. He'd then take some stuff out of the locker and toss it on the ground to make it look like a burglary in hopes of luring Bulger downstairs.

The agent then called in for more backup. He needed three more officers to guard the exits of the Princess Eugenia while Garriola's team took position in the garage. It took another hour for the officers to arrive, as they'd been stuck in traffic. Garriola told them to fan out across one block and keep an eye out for an older couple with white hair.

Garriola then phoned Bond.

"Call the Gaskos and tell them to meet you at their storage locker," Garriola ordered.

Bond placed the call, but there was no answer.

"What do I do now?" the manager asked the agent.

"I want you to go knock on the door."

Bond smartly wasn't willing to put his life on the line for his job.

"I don't want to do that. What if he pulls a gun on me? I just Googled his name. He's killed nineteen people!"

A moment later, a call came in to Bond's phone. It was Catherine Greig, or "Carol Gasko," on the line.

"Hi, Josh, did you just call?"

"Yes, Carol. I have some bad news. Your storage unit was broken into. Do you want me to call police or meet me down in the garage?"

Greig turned to Bulger and relayed the information.

"Charlie wants to meet you in the garage," she replied.

"Okay, I'll be over in a minute," Bond told her. "I'm helping a guest right now."

Moments later, Catherine appeared on the balcony. She looked down at the street and saw nothing unusual, so she went back inside.

"What do you want me to do now?" Bond asked Garriola.

"Stay where you are. We'll handle it from here."

Garriola fired off another quick text to Boston:

Looking good, standby

After receiving the call from Bond, Whitey Bulger grabbed his white hat, stepped out of the apartment, and took the elevator down to the garage. Bulger described the scene in vivid detail in a letter to author Michael Esslinger, which was shared with the authors of this book:

> *When I entered the elevator, I kind of hesitated. I stood there for a minute after the doors closed and stared at the button . . . looking intently at the worn buttons on the panel. I gathered my thoughts, but was thinking I didn't want the cops called or have this turn into anything big. When I got off the elevator and started to walk around a parked car, I could see my locker. I noticed that the door was hang-*

ing off. I knew something wasn't right. What first caught my eye was that I saw a few pieces of colored tape on the cement as if to mark positions like on a stage. There was a stillness that just seemed off . . . Hard to describe in words, but my instinct told me something was off.

As I started walking toward my locker, a light was shined on me and quite a few men in full combat gear and armed with M4 Carbines—fully automatic machine guns and a couple point Glock hand guns—took aim at me. I remember almost every word that was said in the garage that day. Some were omitted by the FBI on purpose. The agent in charge yelled: "Who are you?" He quoted me as responding back: "Who the fuck are you?" What I actually said was: "Who the fuck are you, Homeland Security?"

I felt I was the calmest person in the garage at that moment. Things were so tense I expected they may kill me.

The agents demanded that he get on his knees. But Bulger didn't want to kneel in the spot where they wanted him because there was a small pool of oil. Sixteen years on the run, millions in law enforcement spending, and years of unfathomable agony for his victims' loved ones, all had come to this moment: a deadly standoff over whether Whitey would get his pants dirty.

They were screaming, "We will shoot," and I responded, "Go ahead . . . I'm not kneeling down in the oil." I told them that there was a clean place to my right and for him to take two steps to the right to that area and then I'd comply.

He was screaming, "Don't try it or I'll shoot!" I thought, "I'm going to die," and I knew it might be my last step, but I told them, "Here is step number one," and I took it. I debated with myself: do I dare chance another step? The tension was rising, but I said, "Fuck it, I'm not backing down" and I said, "Here's step number two." They screamed, "Don't or we'll shoot!!!" I had that feeling I had as a kid waiting to feel the bullet in the back.

But the agents didn't shoot.

Shit, is this guy gonna try to run on us? Scott Garriola thought.

But cornered with no chance to escape, Bulger put his hands up. He'd feared this moment for the past sixteen years and now it was finally here.

"What's your name?" Garriola asked with his gun trained on Whitey's chest.

"You know who I am," Bulger said defiantly.

"Okay, Whitey. We have a warrant for your arrest!"

Garriola then took out a pair of handcuffs and tied them to Bulger's wrists.

"Is Catherine upstairs?"

Whitey nodded.

"Do you have any guns up there?"

"Yeah," Bulger replied. "And they're all loaded."

"What do you mean? Do I need to call a SWAT team to get her outta there?"

"No, no," Whitey assured him. "All the guns are mine. Most of them are in my bedroom. She's never held a gun and she's not allowed in my bedroom."

Bulger offered to call Catherine to get her down to the garage.

"No, give me your key," Garriola said. "I'll go up and I'll treat her like a gentleman and I'll bring her down here."

Garriola sent another group text to Teahan, Sullivan, and Torsney: *One in custody and one to go. Bulger captured. Standby for Catherine.*

The agent got a female detective to accompany him to apartment 303.

"Santa Monica PD," Garriola shouted. "Open the door."

Catherine walked to the door and turned the knob slowly. She opened the door and then let out an exasperated sigh.

"I knew it!" she said tersely. "I knew the FBI was here."

Garriola sent another group text to his fellow agents in Boston: *Catherine in custody without incident. Scene secure.*

EVERYONE STARED AT THEIR CELL phone screens in near disbelief.

"He's under arrest!" Torsney shouted to the young agents manning the phones at the FBI command center.

"They looked up at me as if to say, 'Holy shit!'" he recalls.

Agents started hugging one another.

"Tears came to my eyes. I've done a lot in my career and I'm not too proud to say that, but this was next level," Torsney says. "For the Boston office to finally put this to rest? I mean, are you shitting me?"

For Sullivan and Teahan, the moment was equally satisfying.

The marshal reached into the refrigerator of his rented condo on St. Botolph Street and grabbed a cold Stella Artois, popped the cap, and chugged. He then hugged his wife, Eileen.

"She couldn't believe it," Sullivan recalls, "that we'd actually completed the task that took sixteen long years to accomplish."

The celebrations were contagious.

"It was just unbelievable to me," Noreen Gleason says. "I almost cried when I heard. I sat down and thought, *oh my God, this is awesome!*"

The hunt for Bulger had been a team sport also involving the Massachusetts State Police, DEA, and US Marshals Service, but for the Bureau, it marked the beginning of a recovery. The stain of John Connolly and other corrupt agents had finally been lifted.

"I took my phone and threw it across the room and jumped in the air in celebration," Teahan remembers. "My wife had been dealing with my heartache and pressure. She was in the room when I got the text and she was just as thrilled. It was vindication. and the sweet thing was that it was the FBI that got him!"

Tommy Mac was attending a family celebration when he first learned of Bulger's capture. He threw his arms up like a boxer after a knockout win. He wasn't surprised that it had happened so quickly after the PSA was released. "If we never found those photos of Catherine Greig, Bulger would be sitting on the couch in Santa Monica right now scratching his balls and watching TV," MacDonald says. "Those images changed the case."

Roberta Hastings was also elated. She'd been working on the case longer than anyone. Her first phone call was to her former colleague, the now retired Charlie Gianturco.

"We got the son of a bitch!" she told him.

FBI director Robert Mueller called Rich Teahan, his former protector, at home.

"Rich, Director Mueller here. You did a great job. Your team did a great job."

The news had triggered a seismic reaction at FBI headquarters in Washington, DC.

"Oh my god, you gotta be kidding me. They just caught Bulger!" Andrew McCabe, the future director of the FBI, shouted when he heard.

McCabe had just been given an assignment to build the high-value detainee interrogation group and while the Bureau's focus remained on national security, the hunt for Whitey Bulger had always been a priority and a personal mission for every agent in every FBI office.

"The Bureau's Criminal Investigation Division [CID] had always bristled by the amount of attention that was generated by counterterrorism agents," McCabe explains. "That's why this was so special. It was a huge accomplishment for the FBI and one that echoes back to the core of who we are and what we do. FBI agents live their entire careers with the belief that we never forget, that we never stop looking. The search for Bulger was the perfect example of that. It was a highly significant event."

For Noreen Gleason, the magnitude of putting this operation into play and having it be successful was overwhelming. "Arresting Whitey was a team sport with the marshals, state police, and finally the US Attorney's Office involved, but for the FBI, it was much more personal. This marked the beginning of a recovery for the people of Boston and for every good FBI agent that ever worked in the office. I felt so proud of what we had accomplished together. Bulger was no hero. He was a dangerous sociopath who committed heinous crimes and eluded capture for so many years until we got him."

24

As Scott Garriola was placing Bulger into custody in the carport at the Princess Eugenia, a neighbor entered the garage to do her laundry.

"I think I can help you," Janus Goodwin told the agent. "This man has dementia. So if he's acting oddly that could be why."

Goodwin lived on the same floor as Whitey and Catherine and had been told like so many others that "Charlie Gasko" suffered from mental illness.

Garriola got nervous for a moment. Had he just arrested a delusional elderly man with Alzheimer's disease?

He turned to Bulger. "This woman over here says you have a touch of Alzheimer's."

"Fuck her. Don't listen to her. She's fucking nuts. I'm James J. Bulger."

A few minutes later, Garriola asked the captured crime boss to grant the FBI permission to search apartment 303. He signed the consent form *James J. Bulger.*

"That's the first time I've signed that name in a long time," he sighed.

Garriola asked Bulger whether he was relieved that he didn't have to look over his shoulder anymore as the sixteen-year manhunt had come to an end.

"Are you fucking nuts?" Whitey answered.

Catherine was wearing a revealing halter top and asked to

change into something more appropriate, so a female officer led her to the bathroom. Meanwhile, Whitey was busy walking Garriola through the apartment.

"He showed us where all his 'hides' were, where his stashes were," the agent recalls. "He had a Derringer in a hollowed-out book and of course all that money and weapons in the walls. Whitey was a tough son of a bitch. He looked pretty feisty when we got him. If we'd met up with Bulger a few years earlier, he would have given us a helluva fight."

Bulger and Greig were led out of the apartment building in handcuffs and placed into separate squad cars and driven off to Los Angeles, where they'd be jailed separately overnight as they awaited their first court appearance the following day. It was after 8 p.m., so Garriola had to get special permission from the Bureau of Prisons to bring the fugitives in at such a late hour.

With Bulger safely in custody, Phil Torsney left his Boston office in the early morning hours and drove home in the driving rain. He didn't have time to sleep, as he was to meet Neil Sullivan and Rich Teahan at Logan Airport to catch the first flight out to Los Angeles.

When Neil Sullivan saw Whitey Bulger for the first time in person at the Federal Courthouse in LA, the aging gangster was wearing an orange prison jumpsuit and was doing push-ups in his cell.

"He looked very fit and was doing a lot of push-ups for an old man," Sullivan remembers. "I'd heard some reporters whispering that Bulger may be senile, but that wasn't true. He was totally with it and physically strong for an eighty-one-year-old."

The marshal also saw Catherine Greig in her cell. She was subdued and didn't say a word.

Sullivan escorted Bulger into court, where it was standing room only. This was the biggest criminal case to hit Los Angeles since O. J. Simpson, and everyone strained to get a look at the Irish mob boss from South Boston and his aging moll. There were not enough seats available, so Neil had to stand with his gun on his hip. Both

Whitey and Catherine remained quiet during the proceedings, which was a relief to the marshal.

"I wasn't worried about security in court," Sullivan says. "The place was airtight. I wasn't worried either about someone sneaking in firearms or that he'd make an outburst. That didn't seem to be his style."

While Bulger and Greig were in court, an FBI team continued to canvass their apartment at the Princess Eugenia.

Agents couldn't believe the amount of weapons Bulger had collected and hidden or the nearly $1 million he had squirreled away. They were also surprised to see how the couple had stockpiled everyday items like cleaning products and soaps. When agents entered Whitey's bedroom, they spotted seven 64-ounce bottles with white tube socks stretched over the top. It looked like Bulger was busy trying to build Molotov cocktails, but that wasn't the case. He told investigators that he'd purchased the socks at a discount store and that they were too tight on his calves, so he was merely stretching them out.

"Some of the other stuff we found in the apartment showed a different side of Bulger," Phil Torsney says. "We found letters showing that he had assisted some people with their legal fees. If you were loyal to him, he was pretty damn loyal to you. He also reached out to people he didn't know in Alabama after seeing their story on TV. He sent some cash to someone who'd killed a family member for molesting a child."

Scott Garriola was exhausted and longing to return to his vacation. Instead, he was ordered to join a teleconference with FBI director Robert Mueller. That didn't sit well with the agent. He asked if his bosses could do it instead but was told no.

"The call with Mueller got a little testy," the agent recalls. "I was so tired at the time. I cracked a joke and the director didn't like it. I cracked another and he threatened to send me to Afghanistan and it went downhill from there."

Mueller had worked in Boston as the interim US attorney in 1986–87 and knew the Bulger case well. The FBI director was only interested in the facts and had no sympathy for the agent's fatigue. Mueller did recognize and express his appreciation to Garriola for his work on the case a few months later.

The FBI director then sent his own private Learjet for Sullivan, Teahan, and Torsney to escort America's most wanted man and his girlfriend back to Boston. Sullivan placed the belly chain and the leg restraints on Bulger and walked him carefully onto the plane. Whitey and Catherine were separated when they got on board. She was led to the front of the plane and was watched closely by a deputy, while he was placed in the back in a rectangular seating area with two chairs facing backward and two chairs facing front. Bulger was joined by Sullivan and the two FBI agents. They had only six hours to interview Whitey and they weren't going to let one second go to waste.

"It's not often that you get to chase someone and hunt someone and then get the chance to interview them—and they're actually consenting," Teahan says.

Phil Torsney led the questioning. He called the captured fugitive James and not Whitey or Mr. Bulger.

"It was really hard not to be a crook anymore," Bulger told him. "I really lost focus. Years and dates kinda ran together."

"Like any other retiree?" Torsney said.

"Yeah." Bulger smiled. "But I went back to Boston a few times to handle unfinished business. The last time was five or six years ago and I was armed to the teeth."

The agents didn't believe him. They felt that it was just Whitey's attempt to remain relevant in a criminal world that has passed him by. Bulger wanted the investigators to believe that he was still menacing and that he still had clout.

"I'm done," Bulger told them. "I'll plead guilty tomorrow if you let Catherine go. She's the only reason I don't commit crimes. She doesn't deserve to be in jail. She deserves a fucking medal. There won't be a trial. I need to face the consequences but she's innocent and doesn't deserve any of this."

Whitey also tried to protect his old handler John Connolly. "I feel responsible for John Connolly. I never really dealt with him though. I was dealing with John Morris, not Connolly."

Bulger even claimed that Morris, the former FBI supervisor, had offered him money to kill his wife. He was rewriting history to benefit himself.

Whitey then took the agents down memory lane, or his version of it anyway, reminiscing about the old days in South Boston during the busing crisis.

"If blacks came across my territory in Southie, I'd beat the shit out of those niggers."

Teahan was surprised by how racist Whitey was. "He threw the N-word around like he was drinking a cup of water. He complained about blacks in South Boston and black people in Santa Monica."

But the agents had to work around Bulger's nasty disposition. He was a killer and a liar after all. They didn't want him to shut down. They needed him to keep talking.

"Do you have any money left in safety deposit boxes?" Rich Teahan asked.

"Why the hell would I tell you?"

Bulger then confided that he had a plan if he ever got real sick. He said he was going to go to Nevada and fall into a mine shaft, killing himself so that no one would ever find his body.

"I wanted to keep the mystery going," Whitey told them. "Fuck the FBI. I never wanted you guys to find me. I wanted you to all look like failures. I don't know why I'm telling you all this. I'm giving you the fugitive's playbook."

Rich Teahan watched Whitey Bulger in amazement as the elderly gangster's personality shifted. One minute he'd be normal and the next minute he'd snap.

"His eyes would turn steel blue," Teahan recalls. "You could see it. It was like a lion watching its prey, totally disarming one minute and devouring you the next."

As the Learjet flew over the Grand Canyon, Torsney took his attention off Bulger and looked out the window, as he'd never flown over the majestic site before. Whitey wasn't amused.

"He looked at me as if to say, 'You've finally got an opportunity to interview me and you're looking at the fucking Grand Canyon?'" Torsney says. "'Don't you know who I am? I'm Whitey fucking Bulger.'"

"I couldn't believe his ego and his bragging," Sullivan remembers. "He'd describe crimes in vivid detail but he refused to admit his involvement."

Instead of placing himself at the scene of a mob murder, Whitey spoke as if he were a narrator reading a true crime book in the third person.

Bulger would play word games like "This guy did this thing or that thing and that's what got him killed." When one of the investigators asked Whitey if he'd ever spent time in San Diego, the mobster smiled. "They have nice theaters there," he said, corroborating the earlier sighting by Sheriff's Deputy Rich Eaton at a screening of *The Departed*.

Six hours later in late afternoon, the Learjet carved through the clouds above South Boston. Whitey Bulger was coming home.

On the approach to Logan Airport, Whitey looked out the window of the jet and down onto the rooftops of Southie.

"Where's that?" he asked. He didn't have a smile on his face. He wasn't joking. Whitey didn't recognize his old neighborhood. It had been that long since he'd fled.

PART II

THE TRIAL

25

IN LATE JUNE 2011, WHITEY Bulger made his first court appearance in Boston. Billy was seated in the second row of the John Joseph Moakley Courthouse, named after a former congressman and childhood friend of the Bulgers. Whitey's eyes lit up when he spotted his brother.

"Hi," he mouthed.

Billy smiled back.

It was the first time that the disgraced politician and former college president had seen his gangster brother in more than a decade. It was also the first time that many reporters had ever set their eyes on Whitey in person. To them, he was a specter known only through grainy surveillance images, court documents, and neighborhood rumors. One spectator compared the hearing to something from the days of Al Capone in Chicago.

"If you could go back in time to be in that courtroom [for Capone] wouldn't you?" she asked.

Another gawker stood outside the courthouse amazed at the amount of television cameras present to cover the proceeding. "It's quite a bit of celebrity for a criminal," he remarked. "But around these parts, he's pretty famous so it doesn't surprise me."

But among the curious onlookers were those who had felt the pain of Bulger's brutality and reign of terror up close and personal. Tommy Donahue, whose father had been gunned down by Whitey during the hit on Brian Halloran in 1982, seethed when he saw

Bulger for the first time in court. Donahue wanted the judge to inflict as much bodily harm on his father's killer as possible.

"He should get the electric chair," Donahue told reporters. "I'm an electrician, I know."

Security was beefed up around the courthouse for the hearings. The US Coast Guard sent two boats with mounted machine guns, along with a state police boat and a Boston police patrol boat, to guard against an attack on Bulger from the adjacent Boston Harbor.

Whitey looked fit and bronzed by the California sun, wearing a white hooded shirt and blue jeans as he was led into court. America's most wanted, now caught, fugitive sat quietly while the judge read the laundry list of indictments against him, including nineteen counts of murder.

"Can I have a public defender represent me?" Bulger asked.

The request was shot down immediately as prosecutors reminded the judge of the more than $800,000 seized from the Santa Monica apartment. "He clearly didn't make that on a paper route on Santa Monica Boulevard," quipped prosecutor Brian Kelly.

He then stared out at the courtroom, spotting brother Billy and other family members. "We feel he has access to cash," Kelly argued.

During the second of back-to-back hearings that day, the magistrate judge asked Whitey if he could afford an attorney.

"I could if you give me my money," Whitey groused, inciting laughter in the courtroom.

Bulger didn't enter a plea that day, leaving all to wonder if he had any more cards to play.

Catherine appeared in the same courthouse later in the day with her twin sister, Margaret, watching from the front row. Unlike Bulger, she appeared gaunt and exhausted. All the stress of the past sixteen years on the run was now evident in the lines across her once delicate face. As the judge recited the charges against her, including harboring a fugitive, Greig started shaking and her court-appointed lawyer had to place his hand on her frail shoulder to support her.

After the initial court hearing, Catherine was sent to the Wyatt Detention Center in Central Falls, Rhode Island, which had housed some notorious Mafia figures and also one of the prime suspects in the infamous art heist at Boston's Isabella Stewart Gardner Museum. Whitey was taken by motorcade to the Plymouth County Correctional Facility, the former home of Stevie Flemmi and the so-called Shoe Bomber, Richard Reid.

Whitey had not seen the inside of a prison cell since the early 1960s, when he spent time at Atlanta, Leavenworth, Lewisburg, and of course Alcatraz. The town of Plymouth had its own rock a short drive away where the Pilgrims had landed. No feast awaited Bulger when he arrived, though. It was back to bland prison food.

The elderly former mob boss was placed into the administrative segregation unit, where he had no contact with any other inmates and was never allowed to mix with anyone besides the guards and his visitors.

Both Billy and their brother Jackie made the hour drive south to Plymouth on a weekly basis. Since Jackie was now an ex-convict himself, he needed special clearance to meet with Whitey.

Bulger was housed in Unit G of the prison, where he was in lockdown twenty-three hours per day with one hour for recreation. There were fourteen cells in the unit. On the top tier, inmates were doubled up. Bulger had a single cell on the bottom floor called Southwest 108, tucked away in the corner. The guards kept cell 107 empty to provide Whitey with a buffer.

As he'd done at the federal courthouse in Los Angeles, Bulger made the most of his confined space, doing hundreds of push-ups every day. When he was allowed to walk the floor, he'd chat up other inmates through their cell doors. One jailhouse snitch always tried to get Whitey to discuss mob murders that he'd either ordered or carried out on his own, but Bulger would never take the bait.

Ken Brady worked in the investigations unit at Plymouth. The biggest concern for authorities there was that Bulger would attempt suicide. Brady spoke with Whitey every day.

"He was frustrated that he wasn't the feared gangster that he used to be," Brady recalls.

Instead, Whitey felt that he was being humiliated on a regular basis. There was an incident on the floor of Bulger's unit that prompted a search of all the inmates' cells. Ken Brady had to conduct a strip search of Whitey. The old man stood up from his bunk and clenched his fists, preparing to fight.

"I'm not fucking doing it," Whitey growled. "I'm sick of this shit. I'm not doing it!"

Brady didn't want to pin down the geriatric prisoner and tear off his clothes, but he would if he had to. Bulger wasn't giving an inch of cell space.

"Listen, Whitey, I'm not playing games with you anymore," Brady commanded. "Knock it off and let's go. Strip or I'm ripping off your clothes anyway!"

Brady had always called him Mr. Bulger. It was the first time he'd called him Whitey and that got him even angrier. He wasn't the intimidating figure he'd once been or feared like he was decades ago in Southie. Whitey could show Brady that he was still tough, but attacking the prison guard would not help his situation, so he finally backed down.

"I'm sorry," Bulger apologized the next day. "I was frustrated."

To keep his brain alert, Whitey traded books with people, mostly history books. He also wrote letters and responded to anyone who wrote him. He talked about his time in Grand Isle, Louisiana, and his friendship with the Gautreaux family.

"These people were so poor and desolate, I'd buy them new appliances for their house," Bulger bragged as he tried to resurrect the image he'd carefully crafted as a Robin Hood–style bandit. He wrote Glenn Gautreaux Jr. a letter, asking him about the family and describing his time on the run and also the circus in Boston:

> *When they brought me back here, it looked like a parade. We traveled a lot over the years and even visited Tombstone, Arizona. But Grand Isle is the best place we ever visited.*

Glenn Jr. wrote Whitey back, telling him how much the family loved and missed him and "Aunt Helen."

Bulger was also doing anything he could to gain leverage with the guards. He'd try to guess their lineage. "Are you Irish?" he'd ask. "Do you have a family? Where do you live?"

The prison guards wouldn't entertain the questions. To them, Bulger wasn't the crime lord he once was. He wasn't running the Winter Hill Gang anymore. In fact, the gang no longer existed. Whitey was just an old man who was about to be put away for the rest of his life, however long that lasted.

Ken Brady monitored all of Bulger's calls and visits from his family. Emotions got high during one jailhouse meeting with his brother Billy. Separated by a partition of thick glass and speaking over the phone, Whitey complained about his unfair treatment in prison and had questions about his emerging defense. He was in full martyr mode, blaming everyone else including the FBI for his predicament. Finally, his younger brother had heard enough.

"Do you have any idea what this has put the family through for the past sixteen years?" Billy asked him.

Those words turned Whitey red with anger.

"What I've put the family through? Look at me. I'm locked up!" he shouted. "My girlfriend is in jail! If you could give me a poison pill right now, I'd take it!"

Ken Brady was listening in on the conversation and ran into the room to put an abrupt end to the visit. He then placed Whitey

Bulger under suicide watch. If anything happened to Whitey while in Plymouth, the punishment for the guards would be severe. The US Attorney's Office was in charge now and they wanted Bulger treated with white gloves as he awaited trial.

WHILE WHITEY WAS ADJUSTING TO his life behind bars, Catherine was trying to avoid hers. A month after Catherine's initial court appearance in Boston, her new lawyer was fighting hard for her release. Attorney Kevin Reddington asked the judge to release Greig on bail pending her trial and painted her not as Whitey's girlfriend, but as another one of his victims.

"This woman is not a violent person," Reddington argued during her bail hearing. "Her only crime is a crime of passion—falling in love with this gentleman [Bulger]."

FBI agent Mike Carazza, who had followed Bulger's trail down to the Bayou with Charlie Gianturco, testified at the hearing and described how domineering Whitey was toward Catherine and how subservient she was toward him. Prosecutors asked Carazza whether the Gautreaux family had ever said that Greig was being held against her will while living with Whitey in Grand Isle, Louisiana.

"They never indicated that," the agent replied.

Carazza looked over at Catherine sitting at the defense table. She was no longer the fragile prisoner that had first appeared in court a month before. She had regained her strength and projected a new attitude at the hearing.

"She was stoic, defiant, and loyal in court," Carazza recalls.

Attorney Reddington also claimed that Catherine was unaware of all the weapons and money stashed in the Santa Monica apartment.

Prosecutors argued that she was no unwitting accomplice and pointed to her efforts to help Bulger secure fake IDs and how she called her sister regularly while on the run.

"The defendant learned the tricks of the fugitive trade," said Assistant US Attorney James Hebert. "She was a willing, active participant in their joint effort to avoid arrest."

Tommy Donahue, son of victim Michael Donahue, then took the witness stand and called Greig "a creep." He said that allowing Catherine to be free would be unbearable to his family and the loved ones of Bulger's eighteen other murder victims.

"The sixteen years with her lover on the run are the sixteen years that we cried," he told the judge.

Reddington did his best to attempt to separate Bulger's crimes from his client, who was accused only of helping Whitey elude capture.

"She has nothing to do with any of those murders or acts of violence," the defense attorney said.

One year later, in 2012, Catherine Greig was sentenced to eight years in prison after pleading guilty to charges of conspiracy to harbor a fugitive, identity fraud, and conspiracy to commit identity fraud. As part of the plea deal, Catherine could not be compelled to testify against Whitey.

Attorney Reddington had appealed to the judge for leniency and asked that she serve only twenty-seven months behind bars.

"Catherine Greig fell in love with Mr. Bulger, and that's why she was in the situation she was in," Reddington argued again. "Miss Greig did not believe that Mr. Bulger was capable of these homicides."

The lawyer's claim drew both heavy sighs and laughter in the courtroom.

Prosecutors pushed for a stiffer sentence, saying this was no "romantic saga."

Whitey and Catherine weren't Romeo and Juliet. Theirs was a modern-day version of Bonnie and Clyde.

"We are all responsible for what we do," US District Court judge Douglas Whitlock told Greig. "There is a price to be paid."

After Catherine was escorted out of the courtroom in shackles, her attorney was asked whether she felt any remorse for sticking by Whitey Bulger.

"He's the love of her life and she stands by him," Reddington noted. "Of course she has no regrets."

There was still a question about additional money, believed to be in the millions, that Whitey had stashed away in safe deposit boxes. The US Marshals had already taken control of everything that was found in the Santa Monica apartment. The asset forfeiture, including the $822,000, would go to the families of Bulger's victims, but investigators believed that was just the tip of the iceberg.

"We wanted to bring Catherine in to the grand jury to talk about the money, but she wouldn't do it," says Rich Teahan. "So she was held in contempt of court."

For her unwillingness to cooperate, Greig, then sixty-one years old, would have an additional twenty-one months tacked on to her prison sentence.

26

THE MOAKLEY COURTHOUSE STOOD AS an impenetrable fortress on the Boston waterfront. The city was still recovering from the deadly Boston Marathon bombings that tore through downtown in April, leaving three spectators dead, including an eight-year-old boy, and hundreds more critically wounded.

Terror suspect Dzhokhar Tsarnaev had been brought to the courthouse for his initial hearings, bringing with him throngs of media from around the world.

Now armies of reporters had returned as James "Whitey" Bulger, the city's proverbial white whale, was on deck. Network satellite trucks were fixtures on Seaport Boulevard, drawing gawking stares from tourists and locals alike. There were lines wrapped around the courthouse for spectators seeking to witness history.

"I'm sick to my stomach," said Tommy Donahue.

"He's a cold-hearted murderer," Donahue told reporters. "Got a kick out of it like most of these people would . . . His demeanor is still the same. He could care less about what's going on, what feelings were hurt, who was killed."

Inside the courtroom, prosecutors were preparing for what they knew would be difficult weeks of proceedings. Of all those on the prosecution team, Zachary Hafer was the one true outsider. Raised in Philadelphia, Hafer graduated cum laude from Dartmouth College and got his law degree at the University of Virginia. He married a Boston girl and moved to Boston in 2007 after clerking in

New York City for a federal judge and working for a private law firm.

In the US Attorney's Office, Hafer started on the drug task force. In 2009, he headed the prosecution of an international cocaine trafficking ring that resulted in the extradition of thirteen Colombian drug lords who were manufacturing drugs in Colombia and smuggling them into Boston. In 2011, Hafer won a conviction for money laundering against mob lawyer Robert George, who previously represented Frank Salemme and John Martorano. And in 2012, Hafer prosecuted Trevor Watson, a gang member who served time for the 2000 stabbing of Boston Celtic great Paul Pierce, for attempting to kill an informant.

Tall and lean with light brown hair, Hafer was getting to know Boston, and more specifically, its criminal underworld, when he was thrust into the Bulger case. After Bulger was captured, Hafer was recruited to join the prosecution team and started doing much of the pretrial grunt work—reviewing old transcripts and case files, tracking down witnesses, and finding experts and cops who worked on the original murders. The young prosecutor's knowledge of the case came mostly from reading news clips and books and seeing the film *The Departed*, which was part of his curriculum at UVA law school. When he saw the first pictures of Bulger in custody, Hafer knew there would be an identification issue because the aged gangster looked so different than he did on the streets of Southie in the 1970s, '80s, and '90s. So it fell to Hafer to file for a court order mandating that Bulger shave off his gray beard.

"He looked completely different. Some of these witnesses hadn't seen him in thirty-five years," Hafer said. "As we were getting ready to file it, months into the litigation, eventually one day he just showed up and had shaved."

For Hafer, joining the Bulger team was "the opportunity of a lifetime," and he marveled at the rotating cast of characters paraded in and out of Judge Denise Casper's courtroom.

"You had the Italian bookmakers, the Jewish bookmakers, the loan sharks, the Irish bookmakers," Hafer said. "The huge Southie dopers, the victims' families, the victims' children. You'd go from laughing, to being angry, to hearing this really poignant emotional testimony. There was really never a dull moment. It was just incredibly colorful."

The case would be a history lesson of a bygone era when Cadillac-driving gangsters in fedoras and scally caps shook down business owners and bookies, took bets on pay phones, wrote them down on scraps of paper, and paid off cops with paper bags of cash.

"Historically, these kinds of people, you don't really have that as much anymore," Hafer says. "You don't have such a hierarchical criminal organization running a city. It's almost like a relic of a time gone by.

"So much of it had been suppressed for so long, with John Connolly, with the corruption, with Bulger being a fugitive," he added. "It was time to air it all out."

Leading Hafer through the maze of murder, death, and mayhem were veteran federal prosecutors Fred Wyshak and Brian Kelly. The team also included DEA agent Dan Doherty, state trooper Steve Johnson, Department of Justice investigator Jim Marra, and IRS agent Sandy Lemanski. Conspicuously absent from the prosecution team was a member of the FBI. That was by design so as not to give even the slightest appearance of conflict or bias, given the history of corruption.

Wyshak, a veteran prosecutor who joined the Boston office in 1989, grew up in Boston's South End in the 1960s and '70s—the same neighborhood where Stevie Flemmi was raised. His family immigrated to Boston from the Middle East during the Depression. Flemmi, a jailhouse artist, was aware of Wyshak's Middle Eastern heritage and once sent him an oil painting he'd created behind bars of Lebanese poet Kahlil Gibran, author of *The Prophet*. Wyshak had to return the painting, however, due to ethics concerns. Other works by Flemmi are said to be on display at a Bureau of Prisons headquarters in Pennsylvania. It was all just part of the game within the game played by Flemmi and Bulger for decades, and they weren't going to stop now that they were in prison.

Wyshak attended New York University and got his law degree from St. John's University before taking a job in the Brooklyn district attorney's office in 1977. He stayed there until 1986, when he moved to New Jersey and became an assistant United States attorney. He worked mob cases in Jersey and became an expert at prosecuting organized crime, which led him in 1989 to Boston to work on the ever-expanding Bulger case as head of the Organized Crime Strike Force.

"I just started working on a few cases that were directed at the Winter Hill associates, a lot of the bookies and loan sharks and drug dealers, and they sort of coalesced into the 1995 indictment of Bulger, Flemmi, Salemme," Wyshak recalled.

Like many who had pursued Bulger, Wyshak was eager to see Bulger in person in handcuffs. He was underwhelmed by what he saw in Courtroom 11 upon the start of the case.

"I had never seen him before except in pictures. He certainly didn't look anything like what I expected him to look like," Wyshak said. "He looked like an old man at that point, with a beard. Not the vicious individual that had been described to us by numerous individuals. I guess he had lost a lot of muscle tone. I would say it was a bit disappointing."

Hafer, Wyshak, and Kelly worked under Boston US Attorney Carmen Ortiz, who had been appointed to the post in 2009 by President Obama. She made her presence felt quickly in Boston in 2010 when she locked up crooked State Senator Diane Wilkerson and Boston City Councilor Chuck Turner for taking bribes. It was a sensational sting in which Wilkerson was caught on video stuffing cash into her bra. A year later Ortiz's team convicted corrupt Massachusetts Speaker of the House Salvatore F. DiMasi—arguably the state's most powerful public official—for taking kickbacks from government contracts. Public corruption was her hallmark when the Bulger case landed in her lap.

The prosecutors' expertise in corruption would serve them well as they laid out the Bulger case and exposed in broad detail how cops and government officials crossed over to the dark side and enabled the gangster's bloody reign of terror.

27

O N THE ELEVENTH FLOOR OF the gleaming waterfront courthouse, Judge Denise Casper, a middle-aged African-American
jurist, presided. Casper grew up in New York, got her law degree at Harvard University, and worked for Boston powerhouse law
firm Bingham McCutcheon before being appointed to the federal
bench by President Obama in 2010. Bulger, an unabashed racist, sat
just feet away as Casper oversaw the proceedings. It was karma that
a liberal, black female judge now controlled the fate of the preju-
diced Irish gangster, who fought integration and busing in Southie
in the 1970s and would later support the right-wing politics of President Donald J. Trump.

Just weeks before the trial, Casper decimated Bulger's defense in
a landmark ruling. Bulger's lawyers wanted to argue that Whitey
was under an immunity agreement with a former US attorney
named Jeremiah O'Sullivan. According to the attorneys, the gangster was told by O'Sullivan that he could never be charged with
any crime—short of murder—as long as he kept feeding the feds
information, mainly on Boston's La Cosa Nostra. At the time of
the supposed secret deal, O'Sullivan was chief of the New England
Organized Crime Strike Force, a shadowy unit that operated under
the US Attorney's Office. The defense team provided no details
about the deal and no documentation. O'Sullivan wasn't talking
either. He was long dead.

In the 1970s and '80s, O'Sullivan, along with the FBI, was under intense pressure to take down the Italian Mafia at any price. It had been the primary mission of the Bureau since the 1960s and the days of J. Edgar Hoover.

Under O'Sullivan, the heat was turned up high on Boston's Italian mob, which was led by Gennaro "Jerry" Angiulo and his North End crew. The local faction answered to Raymond Patriarca's crime syndicate, which was based in Providence, Rhode Island. It had always been an odd criminal arrangement in New England. Despite Boston being a much larger city than Providence, the Rhode Island capital had a far stronger and more influential Mafia presence that was linked directly to New York. As a result, Boston's mob always answered to Patriarca.

As O'Sullivan built his case against the Boston Mafia, a federal wiretap picked up chatter of a potential hit on him, which left the young prosecutor and father of two spooked. Bulger claimed O'Sullivan cut the immunity deal with him in exchange for protection from mobsters who wanted him dead.

As proof of the deal, Bulger's attorneys filed an eleventh-hour appeal before the trial seeking to have the original jurist, Judge Richard Stearns, removed from the case. The attorneys argued that Stearns was conflicted because he worked in the US Attorney's Office at the time O'Sullivan chaired the Strike Force and knew or should have known about the supposed arrangement.

In the pleading, Bulger's attorneys pointed to a 1978 race-fixing case at Suffolk Downs racetrack in East Boston that led to the indictments of thirteen people—most connected to the Winter Hill Gang—and two unindicted coconspirators. Those two unindicted coconspirators were Bulger and Flemmi. The racket netted millions in winning bets made in Chicago, Philadelphia, New York, and other locales. The crooked gamblers were told who to bet on, in which race, and were instructed not to make bets at Suffolk Downs, nearby Wonderland Greyhound Park, or any other Massachusetts racetrack.

In 2002, O'Sullivan testified before a congressional hearing probing FBI corruption in the Bulger case and acknowledged dropping Bulger and Flemmi from the race-fixing indictment, but claimed it was because evidence against the others was stronger. During that same hearing, O'Sullivan, who died in 2009 at age sixty-six, testified under oath that he never gave Bulger or Flemmi immunity.

But that didn't stop Bulger's legal team. J. W. Carney, the lead defense attorney, also wrote in the pleading that he planned to call as a witness former FBI director Robert Mueller, who worked in the US Attorney's Office with O'Sullivan and Stearns and was a close friend of the latter.

The strategy worked as Stearns was removed from the case, but no ruling was ever made on Bulger's immunity deal. After Whitey was caught in Santa Monica in 2011, one of the questions he asked FBI agents Phil Torsney and Rich Teahan on the flight back to Boston was whether O'Sullivan was still the US attorney.

After Stearns's removal, Casper was assigned the case and her first order of business was to rule on Bulger's immunity claim with O'Sullivan.

"Because O'Sullivan is deceased, there's obviously no evidence of that agreement," Hafer explains. "We scoured all the files. There's no affirmative evidence of that agreement anywhere."

While Carney claimed it was a secret deal, the government fought it aggressively, arguing that even if Carney's unsubstantiated claims were true, it wouldn't have held up bureaucratically or legally.

"Under no circumstances would someone in Jerry O'Sullivan's position ever have been authorized to make such a deal," Hafer said. "No sentient human being would have made that agreement . . . There is no such thing as an agreement to allow someone to commit undefined future acts, including acts of violence . . . It was like grasping at smoke. There was no detail provided."

Judge Casper agreed and tossed out Carney's claim, delivering the first of many legal blows to Bulger. Carney was resolute, though, and vowed that his client would take the stand and blow the lid off the corruption in the FBI. It made for sensational headlines and exhilarating pretrial theatrics, but prosecutors were not impressed.

"He insinuated, he wrote in a pleading, unsworn, not under oath, not by a witness with personal knowledge," Hafer said. "But he never backed it up with anything."

The trial was slated to start on June 10, 2013, but Carney filed a last-minute motion to delay after it was revealed that a state trooper interfered with a probe into the criminal activity by Bulger hit man—and government star witness—John Martorano. Casper dismissed Carney's motion, the jury was seated, and the runway was cleared for Boston's trial of the century.

On June 12, 2013, Whitey arrived at the Moakley Courthouse with great fanfare. He walked slowly in shackles along the Boston waterfront, clad in an orange prison jumpsuit and wearing noise-canceling headphones, escorted from a helicopter by heavily armed US marshals to a waiting prison van. The image of the aged gangster's perp walk dominated the news cycle and was broadcast across the globe.

As the trial got underway, Boston Harbor was partially shut down. The US Coast Guard and Boston Police patrolled the waters surrounding the courthouse. Armed officers guarded a nearby marina. Bomb-sniffing dogs scoured the city blocks around the courthouse. Just down the street in Southie, where Bulger plied his trade for decades, the coffee shops and dark barrooms were abuzz.

In his opening statement, Kelly began the prosecution's case by painting a chilling portrait of Bulger as a bloodthirsty, Machiavellian killer. In methodical and dramatic fashion, the prosecutor described how Bulger murdered at least nineteen people while running a criminal enterprise that destroyed families, corrupted law enforcement, and flooded Boston with drugs and despair for three-plus decades.

"It's a case about organized crime, public corruption, and all sorts of illegal activities ranging from extortion to drug dealing, to money laundering to possession of machine guns to murder, nineteen murders," Kelly told the hushed courtroom. "It's about a criminal enterprise, which is a group of criminals who ran amok in the City of Boston for almost thirty years . . . At the center of all this murder and mayhem is one man, the defendant in this case, James Bulger.

"He was no ordinary leader," Kelly continued. "He did the dirty work himself because he was a hands-on killer."

Wearing a green sweater tucked into jeans and white sneakers, Bulger, then eighty-three, sat at the defense table listening intently, sandwiched between his attorneys, J. W. Carney and Hank Brennan. His brother Jackie, a disgraced court clerk, sat behind him, but Billy, mysteriously, was not in the courtroom. Hard-nosed beat reporters and columnists who had covered the Bulger gang for decades sat attentive while dozens of reporters from across the country and the world were herded into an overflow room with closed-circuit TVs to watch the trial unfold.

Kelly laid out the case, showing organizational charts of the Winter Hill Gang through the decades, illustrating Bulger's rise in the organization. And then he started laying out the murders. It was a shocking and macabre journey through Boston's darkest criminal era.

Kelly said Bulger made "a fortune" shaking down bookies and drug dealers, loan-sharking, and trafficking drugs in his hometown—a sharp jab at Bulger, who built his legend on the fabricated claim that he kept drugs out of Southie.

"Bulger liked to promote the myth that he had nothing to do with drugs," Kelly argued. "But you will hear from these drug dealers that in the 1980s, Bulger was deeply involved in the distribution of drugs in the South Boston area, especially cocaine. And he and his gang made millions at it."

The prosecutor laid out the charges: twenty-three counts of money laundering, two racketeering counts, five weapons charges, two extortion counts, and of course, nineteen murders.

He detailed how Bulger and his cohorts paid off cops "so they could get tipped off to investigations and stay one step ahead of the honest cops who were actually trying to make a case against them.

"It was part of a strategy they had, and it worked," Kelly said.

Kelly piled on the Southie crime lord and hit him where it hurt: he called him a *rat* in open court.

"Even though Bulger told people he didn't like rats, the evidence will be that Bulger was one of the biggest informants in Boston," Kelly said.

"Bulger routinely met with FBI agent John Connolly and gave him information, some true, some false, but all designed to protect himself and mislead other investigators, or get the competitive edge that he wanted," Kelly said.

Bulger's double dealing was one of the case's "grotesque ironies," because he regularly executed others suspected of being informants, the prosecutor added.

There was no better example of Bulger's informant executions than the case of Brian Halloran and Michael Donahue, the two men who were gunned down in 1982 as they left a waterfront bar. Halloran knew about Oklahoma businessman Roger Wheeler's murder and was giving information to the feds. His death warrant, and unfortunately the innocent Donahue's as well, were signed when Bulger found out Halloran was talking.

"Bulger learned from his own corrupt FBI connections that Halloran was trying to give information to law enforcement," Kelly said. "This offended him . . . Bulger took action because he did not want the FBI to learn the truth about Roger Wheeler."

Wheeler, CEO of the lucrative Florida gambling business World Jai Alai, was shot right between the eyes in Oklahoma by John Martorano outside his country club in Tulsa after finishing a round of golf. Bulger and his crew had their sights set on taking over World Jai Alai with the help of the business's crooked accountant, John Callahan, who was skimming cash from the gaming operation and paying off Bulger's gang.

After Martorano gunned down Wheeler in Oklahoma, he killed Callahan in Florida.

"By the time this 1982 murder of Halloran and Donahue had occurred, Bulger and his coconspirators had already killed another thirteen people, because this little murder spree had been going on since the early '70s," Kelly told the court. "All of these murders were committed to promote or protect Bulger's criminal enterprise."

Kelly went into detail about the earliest murders, including the slayings of six men in the 1970s during the Southie gang wars. Bulger's role was often to drive the "crash car" behind the shooters, which required him to slam his car into another vehicle to cause chaos for arriving cops.

He told the tale of Eddie Connors, a Bulger henchman whose fatal mistake was bragging about helping Bulger's gang. Flemmi and Bulger executed him in cold blood at a pay phone, spraying the booth with bullets. A stomach-churning picture of Connors slumped down, covered in blood and broken glass, was shown to jurors on a massive wide screen.

Kelly also prepared the jury for the parade of killers they would soon be hearing from, including Martorano and Flemmi. The gangsters had already cut controversial deals with prosecutors by pleading guilty to racketeering charges. Both, Kelly said, would implicate Bulger as a murderer and the mastermind behind the gang's reign of terror.

"You'll hear that Martorano ultimately got a sentence of fourteen years—not enough," Kelly conceded. "He did confess and he did cooperate and he did help solve crimes that had been unsolved for three decades."

He called Flemmi "a vicious killer" who was not only Bulger's partner in crime and murder, but also "in the informant business." The two mobsters fed John Connolly information about "criminal rivals" and together they "paid thousands" to corrupt agents and crooked cops.

He told the sordid stories of Flemmi's girlfriend, a beautiful blonde named Debbie Davis, and Flemmi's stepdaughter Deborah Hussey, both of whom had been strangled to death. He then slowly read off the names of all nineteen murder victims.

"That, ladies and gentlemen, is what this case is about," he said. "A defendant, James Bulger, who was part of a criminal gang which extorted people, paid off cops, earned a fortune dealing drugs, laundered money, possessed all sorts of guns, and murdered people. Nineteen people."

Kelly let that number—nineteen—hang in the air inside the courtroom.

Carney countered with the only card he had to play: government corruption. He wove an elaborate tale about how the FBI used Bulger, and others, as part of a decades-long mission to topple La Cosa Nostra.

"What happened was, beginning with Robert Kennedy, when he was the Attorney General, and J. Edgar Hoover, when he was the head of the FBI, was that a commitment was made, a focus was made by federal prosecutors to smash the organization known as the Mafia," Carney said. "This became a nationwide crusade on the part of every prosecutor and the majority of the FBI agents working for the federal government."

Carney then claimed that Flemmi was a "top echelon" informant for Connolly, but declared that Bulger was "never an informant for John Connolly."

"There were two reasons for this. Number one, James Bulger is of Irish descent, and the worst thing that an Irish person could consider doing was becoming an informant because of the history of the troubles in Ireland," Carney said. "The second reason was . . . James Bulger was not deeply tied to the Italian Mafia."

He noted that although Bulger had Mafia associates, he never would have gotten inside information on the organization because he wasn't Italian. Instead, Carney claimed Flemmi was the one giving Connolly all the goods. The reports in Bulger's FBI file amounted to "junk tips" that were meaningless, or duplicates of information from other informants. The real FBI relationship with Bulger worked the opposite way, Carney claimed, saying Bulger paid for information to keep himself out of trouble.

Bulger handed Connolly lump sums of cash—$5,000, $10,000, and $50,000—which allowed the rogue agent to lead a "lavish lifestyle." Bulger also paid Connolly's boss, John Morris, $5,000, and greased up other cops and agents.

"He wanted information for when there would be a wiretap set up, a situation where a bug is placed in a room or in a car," Carney told jurors. "And in return for these payments, he was told where the bugs were placed.

"He wanted to know when searches were going to be executed so that he could make sure to clear his stuff out of those locations. And that when the police showed up to execute a search warrant and hopefully find drugs or evidence of illegal gambling or illegal loans, there was nothing there," Carney said. "And, finally, if he ever was going to be indicted, he wanted a heads-up so he could leave town. That's what he was paying for."

Carney also laid the groundwork for jurors to look with disgust upon the government's star witness, John Martorano, portraying him as an opportunist who cut an astonishing deal with prosecutors that allowed him to serve just twelve years in prison for twenty murders in exchange for testifying against Connolly and Bulger. The deal also meant Martorano would not be prosecuted on state charges for the murders of Roger Wheeler in Oklahoma and John Callahan in Florida, where he could have received the death penalty.

Martorano also negotiated immunity for his girlfriend, who harbored him for years, and assurances that he wouldn't have to testify against his brother, Jimmy Martorano, who Carney said "had also been committing murders." In addition, he wouldn't have to testify against fellow Bulger gang member Pat Nee, whom Carney also called "a murderer."

The cherry on top was the $26,500 Martorano received from the feds for his cooperation, as well as being allowed to keep the $250,000 he got for his book deal.

"The federal government was so desperate to have John Martorano testify in a manner that they wanted against John Connolly and James Bulger that they basically put their hands up in the air and said, 'Take anything you want,'" Carney said.

The defense attorney also blasted another key witness, Kevin Weeks, who admitted to his role in five murders but served just five years in prison. He too was allowed to keep money he received for his book and movie rights, the attorney added.

But Carney saved the best for last. Stevie Flemmi, he said, agreed to flip on Bulger to save his own life. The feds took the death penalty off the table for the Wheeler and Callahan murders, and in addition, Flemmi's brother, a crooked Boston cop named Michael Flemmi, was allowed to keep property Flemmi bought with "illegal" gains, Carney said.

He blamed the murders of Davis and Hussey on Flemmi. He said Davis had been cheating on Flemmi and making fun of him for being "old" behind his back. Hussey, meanwhile, was a drug addict and prostitute who was molested by Flemmi for years when she was a teenager. When she revealed the molestation to her mother, who was Flemmi's common-law wife, Flemmi killed her because he feared she would go to the police, Carney claimed.

The crafty defense attorney didn't stop there.

He also incredulously claimed that Bulger had nothing to do with the Wheeler and Callahan murders. Instead, he alleged that Flemmi and Martorano hatched the plan with corrupt FBI agent Paul Rico, who had once busted Bulger and served as Flemmi's handler.

While acknowledging Bulger had "an unbelievably lucrative criminal enterprise in Boston," the Southie crime boss "had nothing, no interest, no motivation, no reason to go out of his comfort zone and ever get involved in anything in Florida, where he knew no one," Carney told the jury.

Carney's true strategy, as the trial unfolded, was to plant the seed with jurors that Bulger had been given immunity by the federal government, hoping that perhaps just one might believe such an outlandish claim and have "reasonable doubt" to deadlock the jury. It was a legal "Hail Mary."

28

O N THE MORNING OF JUNE 14, 2013, most Bostonians were
exhausted from staying up until 1 a.m. to watch the heart-
breaking first game of the Stanley Cup Finals, in which the
Chicago Blackhawks came back to beat the Boston Bruins 4–3 in
triple overtime. Reporters, lawyers, court officers, and trial spectators talked about the crushing defeat, and many looked haggard
at the Moakley Courthouse.

That morning, Bobby Long, a grizzled former Massachusetts
state trooper who had chased Bulger for years, woke up early in his
Norwell home, showered, shaved, and slipped on his favorite court
suit. The retired cop was like a kid on the first day of school. He'd
thought this day would never come, but here he was, about to head
into Boston federal court to take the stand and testify against his
longtime nemesis, Whitey Bulger.

Four months earlier, Long was at his retirement home on Marco
Island, Florida, and fell off the roof of his garage as he was making
some repairs. He suffered several compound fractures and was air-
lifted to a Level 1 trauma center. He nearly died.

He had been using crutches and occasionally a cane to walk ever
since the accident, but on the day of the trial, he was determined to
walk into that courtroom on his own. And he did exactly that when
he took the stand as the first witness in the *United States v James J.
Bulger* trial. Packed with media, relatives of the nineteen victims

killed by Bulger and his crew, fellow cops, and lawyers, Long was
ready to face the man who had terrorized his city for decades.

"Nobody ever thought he'd be brought to justice," Long recalls.
"Our eyes connected once. I wasn't going to take mine off of his.
He eventually looked away."

Long's history with the Winter Hill Gang and Bulger stretched
back to the early 1970s. In 1977, Boston led the nation in truck
hijackings as Winter Hill and other gangsters targeted trailers on a
regular basis to swipe things like razor blades, Polaroid film, appliances, TVs, seafood, or anything else of value. The state was seeing
an average of two hijackings a day. By comparison, California had
two *a year*. Drivers were being threatened, kidnapped, and beaten.
Trucking companies were shutting down because they couldn't get
insurance for their loads in Massachusetts.

Despite interagency mistrust, the state police through Bobby
Long and the FBI through an agent named Dave Brady, who re-
ported to FBI supervisor John Morris in the Boston office, joined
forces to bust up the truck hijacking rings. As it happened, Nick
Gianturco, Charlie's brother who would later be implicated in
Bulger-related corruption, was looking to get back to the Boston FBI office at the time and called his friend John Connolly to
help him get transferred home. Connolly recommended that Nick
Gianturco join "Operation Lobster" with Dave Brady and Long.
Long says Gianturco did a "great job" working undercover as they
broke up several hijacking rings over three years.

"It was a tremendous success. From averaging two hijackings a
day, there was only one in all of 1979," Long recalls.

The honeymoon between the state police and the FBI was short-
lived, however. After Operation Lobster, which made national news,
the agencies agreed they would work informants together and share
information. But the day after the Operation Lobster arrests, two
FBI agents went to Walpole State Prison to try and flip one of the
hijackers arrested in the sweep, without telling state police.

A few months later, the state police stumbled upon the infamous Lancaster Street garage in Boston's old West End, which served as a hideout and meeting spot for all of Boston's top gangsters, including Bulger, Flemmi, Boston mob capo Donato Angiulo, who was Jerry Angiulo's brother, and lieutenants from the Patriarca crime family.

"We knew we had a gold mine there," Long says. "Anybody who was anybody in organized crime was coming to that garage. I was saying to myself, 'How can they operate so openly and no one is doing anything about it. Boston police don't know anything about it? The FBI doesn't do anything about it?'"

Long, despite the interagency rift, went to US Attorney Jeremiah O'Sullivan for funding to pay for surveillance at the garage, telling the young federal prosecutor that he could work the case with Brady, so long as Brady wouldn't have to report back to the FBI.

"I can't do that," O'Sullivan told him.

Long had already suspected that John Connolly was feeding Bulger information and was a major weakness, at the very least, in the Bureau.

"I never liked him [Connolly] from the day I met him," Long says.

He told O'Sullivan that the operation couldn't involve the FBI, but that they'd work with any other federal agency: the Drug Enforcement Administration, US Customs, the Bureau of Alcohol, Tobacco and Firearms, but no FBI.

"I can't do that. It would be political suicide for me," O'Sullivan told him.

O'Sullivan funded the operation jointly anyway and ordered the FBI and state police to work the case, along with the Suffolk County district attorney. Long and Brady set up in a flophouse across the street from the garage, which sat in a then-run-down neighborhood filled with hookers, junkies, and grifters.

Now decades later in the summer of 2013, with Bulger sitting just feet away in the packed courtroom, Bobby Long identified grainy black-and-white photographs of Bulger, Flemmi, and Donato Angiulo at the garage. It was like a gangster history class. He pointed out mobsters and victims, like Bucky Barrett, from video surveillance footage shown to the jury.

He recounted how he and Dave Brady watched a parade of rogues come through the garage chitchatting brazenly about their crimes and both believed they were going to bust the city's underworld wide open. But the flow of gangsters at Lancaster Street came to a sudden stop and Bulger's loose lips on audio bugs tightened. In fact, he stopped talking at all, except to make wisecracks faux-praising the job state police were doing on the Massachusetts Turnpike. The jig was up.

The operation was compromised—by both the state police and the FBI. Turns out, Long testified, corrupt state trooper Richard Schneiderhan met with Flemmi in Braintree and told him he believed the Lancaster Street garage had been bugged. Flemmi went to Connolly, who confirmed the bug with O'Sullivan. Connolly told Bulger and the operation was dead on arrival.

Long, who retired in 1990 and became a licensed private investigator, continued to track down tips on Bulger after he fled in 1995, including once being hired by a Boston TV station to track down a tip that Bulger was hiding in Cuba. The tip proved false.

Like many in the Massachusetts State Police from that era, Long has no love lost for the FBI. In fact, his hope was that the trial would serve two purposes: putting Bulger away for life and exposing corruption at the highest levels of the Bureau. It was, after all, Long's former boss, Colonel Jack O'Donovan, who was the first to sniff out that Bulger was getting tipped off by crooked FBI agents. Long wished the colonel were alive to witness the corruption being exposed once and for all.

29

A S THE TRIAL UNFOLDED, THE prosecutors paraded a wide array of characters in and out of Judge Casper's courtroom, many right out of central casting. Their interactions with Bulger were daily theater. Their casual tones when talking about murder and violence and their colorful language incited everything from gasps to laughs to tears, depending on the day.

One day, Hafer called James Katz, a Dorchester bookie who initially refused to testify before a 1994 grand jury because he was afraid of Bulger and his henchmen. He later flipped after he was offered a reduced sentence and entry into the Witness Protection Program.

"If I were to testify, I felt my safety would . . . It would have been compromised probably," Katz testified.

Katz was in jail at the time of the grand jury and told the court he feared he could be killed in prison if he flipped on the Bulger gang.

"I knew that the people I would testify against . . . they could even reach me in jail," Katz told the court.

"And who were those people you were concerned about?" Hafer asked.

"The Bulger group. Stevie and Whitey," he said.

Katz told of an elaborate network of bookies in and around Boston and reported that you needed to pay "rent" to either the Mafia or Bulger's gang. He said Bulger and Flemmi hiked the "vig"—a fee for making a bet—to ensure the gang made more money from gamblers. He talked about "shylocks," which were described as loan sharks who charged exorbitant interest, clandestine meetings at the Lancaster Street garage, payoffs to Winter Hill mobsters at coffee shops and barrooms, and gangsters with memorable names like William "The Midget" McDonough and Joe "The Barber" Spaziani.

Katz, who was convicted of wire fraud, bookmaking, and money laundering in Massachusetts and South Carolina, went into the Witness Protection Program alone, leaving behind his wife and three daughters. The family reunited in the late 1990s when he dropped out of the program and relocated to "start a new life," he testified.

Hafer asked him about the Bulger gang's reputation for violence.

"You could wind up in the hospital, let's put it that way," he said. "In those days, it was murder and a lot of beatings."

Another bookie who took the stand was Dickie O'Brien, an eighty-four-year-old Korean War veteran from Quincy. O'Brien was feeble and needed an oxygen tank to breathe.

O'Brien testified that, starting in the late 1950s, he took illegal bets on horse racing and sports and ran numbers. The numbers were a black-market lottery based on a number that ran in the newspaper daily, as there was no legal state lottery back then. He worked for Raymond Patriarca and recalled meeting with the mob boss in Providence the day Jimmy Hoffa was arrested.

Patriarca was distracted by the Hoffa arrest, so he directed O'Brien to go work under the Angiulos in Boston.

After the Angiulo mob was broken up by the feds and several top capos went to prison, O'Brien was "independent." He said Bulger summoned him to a Quincy restaurant and strong-armed him into working for Winter Hill. He paid Bulger $2,000 a week, he testified.

"I said I was with the North End," O'Brien testified. "He said,

'Forget the North End. If you want to be in business, you're with us.' And that was put down as law."

Bulger showed his true colors a few times during the trial, including once as O'Brien was grilled by Hafer about the tale of a bookie who owed a large amount of money and was trying to break away from the organization. The bookie, George "Chickie" Labate of Brockton, was ordered to a meeting with O'Brien, Bulger, and Martorano at a hotel in Braintree, Massachusetts.

"Mr. Bulger came over to him and said, 'You're going to go your own way?'" O'Brien testified. "He said, 'You know, we have a business besides bookmaking.' Labate says, 'What's that?' Mr. Bulger said, 'Killing assholes like you.'"

Whitey erupted in laughter at the defense table. Judge Casper shot him a look. Hafer recoiled and looked at Wyshak in disbelief. Carney and Brennan glared at their client. When Bulger's chuckles subsided, he looked at Judge Casper and said, "Excuse me."

O'Brien, who was jailed for lying to a grand jury probing the Bulger gang in 1993, was friends with Martorano and served time with him and Flemmi in the Plymouth House of Correction. The elderly ex-bookie told of a couple of brushes with death of his own, including once in Florida when Flemmi paid him an unexpected visit.

"If I'm not home in twelve hours or so, go to the FBI in Miami," he told his daughter before the meeting. "And don't go home."

It was exactly the type of fear that Hafer, Wyshak, and Kelly needed to get in front of the jury. These witnesses feared Bulger would end their lives for a buck.

As O'Brien left the stand, it was clear that he was one of the lucky ones who got away.

FOR ALL THE GRAVITY OF the proceedings, the trial often had a circus-like atmosphere. Academy Award–winning actor Robert

Duvall, who was in Boston shooting the legal thriller *The Judge*, dropped in to watch the spectacle one day. There was an endless conga line of rogues and plug-uglies brought to the stand that gave the trial a feeling of a *This Is Your Life* TV episode starring Whitey.

Grainy footage of gangsters in track suits, mobsters in Cadillacs, and gruesome autopsy photos were shown daily. Videos of a young and fit Bulger, his muscles bulging from tight T-shirts, stood in stark contrast to the elderly gangster sitting at the defendant's table, although marshals and correctional officers in charge of watching Bulger before and after court said he regularly did push-ups in his cell, in defiance of his advanced age.

Wyshak, tall with short gray hair, carried himself with an air of calm but spoke quite powerfully and with stark authority when pressed. He and his fellow prosecutors had a front-row seat and regularly heard Bulger gruffly barking out orders to his attorneys, muttering under his breath, and chuckling inappropriately at various moments throughout the proceedings.

"The first time he opened his mouth, you could tell he was a vicious guy. Just that voice. He had a voice," Wyshak said. "He was complaining we took all his money from him. It was the way he spoke. You could see he had disdain for everyone and everything."

The only break during the two-month trial, besides weekends, came over the July 4th holiday. The Fourth of July was on a Thursday, so Judge Casper sent the jury home on Wednesday for a long weekend.

On Monday, when court resumed, the prosecutors were preparing at their table opposite Bulger's defense team, attorneys Carney and Brennan. Carney, bald and bespectacled and with a scholarly air about him, was red-faced with an "Irish tan." He had obviously been in the sun all weekend.

Bulger was brought into court by the marshals and plopped into his chair between his lawyers. He had spent the long weekend in isolation in the Plymouth House of Correction and was not in a good mood.

"Morning, Jim. How was the weekend?" Carney said in an affable tone.

Bulger was incensed. He glared at Carney and said, "How the fuck do you think it was, Jay?"

Carney did attempt to keep Whitey's spirits up while he was behind bars, however. As he was awaiting trial, Bulger wrote love letters to Greig on Carney's legal pad. The attorney carried them on visits to Greig in prison, where he allowed her to read them. She wept, as did Bulger when he read her responses, again delivered by Carney. Ethical questions were raised by prosecutors and others about Carney delivering the missives, but the barrister dismissed them, saying, "There is no regulation or law that should prevent two people from expressing love."

Whitey was hands-on with his defense team, and at times seemed to direct them on who to cross-examine and who to leave alone. Drug trafficker Billy Shea, a longtime friend of Bulger, was greeted warmly by the gangster.

"Billy," Bulger said, nodding to Shea as he took the stand.

"Jim." Shea nodded back. It was like two old friends running into each other in a coffee shop. Except it was in a federal courtroom in the biggest criminal case Boston had seen perhaps in its entire history.

Shea testified for an hour and a half about the scope of drug dealing that he and Bulger did together. He told a story of how Bulger, Flemmi, and Weeks once walked him downstairs to an alley in Southie. It was a dramatic tale that had everyone in the courtroom on the edge of their seat. Shea thought his "number was up," but was let go without being harmed.

Bulger seemed as riveted by the story as anyone in the courtroom. As Shea continued his testimony, Bulger wrote a note and slipped it to Carney. Shea had never cooperated against Bulger in the past. His testimony was devastating on the drug charges and Hafer expected he would be torn apart on cross-examination. Instead, Carney read Bulger's note, stood up, and said, "I have no questions."

"We saw that scenario play out several times," Hafer said. "It seemed that if Bulger thought he was a stand-up guy or liked the person, he didn't want his lawyer cross-examining him."

There were many explosive moments throughout the trial, but none as big as when news broke that Stephen "Stippo" Rakes, one of Bulger's extortion victims—and a potential witness in the case— was found murdered. Rakes, whose liquor store was stolen from him by Bulger and his crew, had attended the trial every day.

On July 16, 2013, he left the courthouse. His body was found the next day on a rural roadside in Lincoln, Massachusetts. A state trooper called prosecutor Brian Kelly with news of Rakes's death.

"Are you still planning to use Rakes?" the trooper asked Kelly.

"We're still trying to figure that out," he answered.

"Well you're not using him now. We just found him in Lincoln," the trooper said.

The story sent shock waves through the courthouse and sparked fears that Bulger had somehow reached out from behind the prison walls to kill a witness. Hafer says the news had some jurors "petrified."

"It was 2013, this kind of stuff doesn't happen anymore," he said. "We knew [Bulger] didn't like him."

Prosecutors were concerned about the impact Rakes's death could have on the jury, but were also worried he might have committed suicide because they took him off their witness list. The day he left the courthouse for the last time, Kelly told Rakes they wouldn't be calling him. Rakes, who had a previous perjury conviction, had expressed a burning desire to take the stand to face Bulger in court.

"When he turned up dead and there were no visible signs—he

wasn't stabbed or shot or beaten—we thought he had committed suicide," Wyshak said. "It was almost like this case had become his life. That we didn't want to call him as a witness, we thought he may have harmed himself. We didn't actually think someone killed him for Bulger."

Others, though, wondered if maybe, just maybe, Bulger still had the clout to reach out from prison and have a witness killed. The satirical website *The Onion* had a field day with the news, posting a fake story the next day with the headline "Everyone in Whitey Bulger Trial Found Dead in Woods Outside Dorchester."

Kelly laughed at the *Onion* story but, like Wyshak, was pretty sure there was no conspiracy.

"We doubted there were still Bulger loyalists out there killing witnesses, but we didn't know what was going on," Kelly said.

He and Wyshak had faced death threats in the past from Whitey's crew, including in the early 1990s when they were building the case that became the 1995 indictment. Back then, the US Marshals office was so concerned about the threats against the two prosecutors that they sent agents to their homes to beef up security, including putting alarms on their cars to warn them if a bomb was installed.

Kelly's kids were toddlers at the time. He didn't tell his wife about the threats and assured her it was routine for marshals to protect prosecutors. But he knew otherwise.

"It was concerning," he admits. "It probably would have been more concerning if I had realized at the time how vicious and crazy the Bulger gang really was."

The Rakes mystery was solved quickly, as authorities revealed it was unrelated to the Bulger trial. It turned out he was poisoned by a disgruntled business associate named William Camuti, who laced Rakes's Dunkin' Donuts iced coffee with cyanide. Camuti was convicted of Rakes's murder in 2017 and sentenced to life without parole.

It was yet another stranger-than-fiction tale in the Bulger saga—and it wouldn't be the last.

30

For Wyshak, who had spent a career chasing the mob, getting in bed with a murderous killer like John Martorano was a necessary evil in order to finish off Whitey. A confessed killer of at least twenty people, Martorano was the star witness for Wyshak, Kelly, and Hafer. It was Wyshak who struck the devil's deal with Martorano in 1995 that gave him twelve years in prison in exchange for his testimony against Flemmi, Connolly, and Bulger. The deal was made all the easier for Martorano to cut after he learned that Flemmi and Bulger were lifelong rats.

Wyshak had already used Martorano to put Flemmi and Connolly away, including helping Florida prosecutors convict Connolly of murder for the Callahan slaying. As sweet as those cases were for Wyshak, the real prize was always Bulger, and now it was time for Martorano to finish the job.

An imposing figure with salt-and-pepper receding hair, beefy jowls, and deep lines on his face, the seventy-two-year-old walked into the courtroom through a side door and made a passing glance at Bulger, who sat at the nearby witness table.

The two friends and former partners in murder hadn't seen each other in person since 1982 and both were a far cry from the muscular pair seen in surveillance photos throughout the previous days of the trial. Born in the Winter Hill stronghold of Somerville, Massachusetts, Martorano was the son of a gangster bar owner who hailed from Sicily. His father owned Luigi's, a restaurant on Washington

Street in Boston's South End that was a rowdy after-hours spot for mobsters.

The family moved when Martorano was young to East Milton, where he attended private school and was a football star playing on the same squad as future *60 Minutes* correspondent Ed Bradley. Martorano turned down several athletic scholarships to college and instead got into the family business: bookmaking and strong-arming. He started hanging out in Boston's notorious—and now nonexistent—Combat Zone, where he fell under the tutelage of Flemmi.

On the day of the trial, Martorano walked into court a free man, having served his time and fulfilled all obligations to the court. He drove a silver Mercedes-Benz and lived a quiet, suburban life with his girlfriend in Milford, a leafy suburb about thirty miles outside of Boston.

Wearing a mobster's black power suit, a light blue shirt, and matching pocket square, Martorano filled the witness box with his brawn. He wore glasses but swapped another pair on and off as he needed one to look at the courtroom—and Bulger—and another to read the documents provided by Wyshak that grimly detailed his three-decades-long killing spree.

A father of five, Martorano admitted taking part in twenty murders. His testimony started with Wyshak leading him through a string of slayings stemming from barroom and street-corner disputes between him, his brother, James, and a crew of gangsters from East Boston, Somerville, and Roxbury. He described casually gunning down a Southie boxer named Tony Veranis in a nightclub packed with thirty people. He was never charged.

He talked about stalking rivals to their homes and executing them in cold blood, with zero consequences. He talked about dumping bodies at North Station, near Boston Garden, and Blue Hills, a woodsy state reservation just south of Boston, as calmly as one might discuss the weather.

He regaled the courtroom with gangster tales of after-hours brawls in the Basin Street Club in Boston's South End, and traveling to Providence with Flemmi to meet New England Mafia boss Raymond Patriarca to get protection during the 1960s gang wars. He told stories of paying off jockeys to fix horse races.

He testified that he stabbed a rival named Jack Banno in an alley off Boylston Street while out on a date. He drove Banno to the hospital and planned to drop him off to get treated, but instead finished him off when Banno woke up and continued arguing. Banno was stabbed twenty times.

He recalled going to Montreal with Winter Hill Gang boss Howie Winter and Brian Halloran in the early 1970s to visit Flemmi while Flemmi was a fugitive. He said he gave money to Flemmi's common-law wife, Marion Hussey, to help him remain on the run.

He recalled meeting Bulger in 1972 when Bulger came into Martorano's restaurant, Chandler's, for an infamous meeting where Howie Winter ordered a truce between the feuding Mullins and Killeen gangs. Martorano brokered the meeting where Winter called for peace between Bulger, who was the lone survivor on the Killeen side, and a trio from the Mullins gang: Tommy King, Pat Nee, and Jimmy "The Weasel" Mantville.

"They patched it up," Martorano testified. "Whitey seemed to surface as the leader."

The reconfigured crew, led by Bulger, started working with Martorano to run the gaming, loan-sharking, and strong-arming rackets in Southie. In 1973, the gang was called upon by Jerry Anguilo to kill a bookie named Al Notarangeli, who owed Anguilo and the Boston mob money. Martorano told a chilling tale of how gangsters scoped out neighborhoods in search of Notarangeli in a deadly game of cat-and-mouse.

There were several failed hits. In one, Bulger drove a "crash car" equipped with a police scanner, while Howie Winter and Martorano were in two separate vehicles. All of the vehicles were equipped with walkie-talkies so they could talk to each other. They followed a brown Mercedes leaving a bar called Mother's, believing they were tailing Notarangeli. The crew pulled up beside the sedan and Martorano and Winter peppered it with machine gun spray, killing one of the occupants.

Only it wasn't Notarangeli. It was a bartender named Michael Milano. Milano was killed while passengers Diane Sussman de Tennen and her boyfriend, Louis Lapiana, survived. Lapiana was paralyzed and spent his life in a Veterans Administration hospital before dying in 2001. Sussman de Tennen, who was twenty-three the night of the shooting, recalled the horrific assault, telling teary-eyed jurors that Lapiana was the love of her life.

"All of a sudden there was this noise, this continuing stream of noise, gunfire," Sussman de Tennen testified. "Nonstop. Dozens and dozens of shots. It was a machine gun . . . When I heard the sound, I ducked. That's probably the only reason I am here today."

Eleven days after the March 8, 1973, botched hit, Bulger orchestrated another failed attempt to kill Notarangeli. The gang pulled off another drive-by and blasted another vehicle, killing Al Plummer, a father of six from Andover, Massachusetts, and wounding two organized crime figures, including bookie Frank Capizzi. Notarangeli was not with them.

"I had been hit in the head and felt warm blood running down my neck," Capizzi testified. He said one hundred bullets hit the vehicle and that he sustained more than thirty wounds from gunshots, glass, or shards of metal. After the attack, he fled Boston with his family.

"My wife and children were living in the throat of the dragon for forty years without any help from anyone," Capizzi told the jury. "I never wanted to get killed."

A few days after the Plummer execution, Martorano gunned down Notarangeli's brother, Joe "Indian Joe" Notarangeli, at a pay phone inside a Medford restaurant. The hit man said he wore "a construction yellow hat, a pair of sunglasses, a full beard and a long meat-cutter's coat" as a disguise.

Wyshak guided Martorano through the grim sequence of senseless hits that culminated when the crew finally caught up with Al Notarangeli on February 11, 1974, at a restaurant. Notarangeli had a Bible and $50,000 in cash he hoped to pay Martorano to give to Angiulo as a peace offering. Instead, Martorano shot him point blank in the head inside the car, killing him. He and Bulger put the body in the trunk of a stolen Buick and dumped it in Charlestown, where it was re-stolen by some unknowing teens—with the body in the trunk, Martorano told the jury.

He ran through killing after killing, answering Wyshak's questions methodically as the prosecutor went through a staggering body count and timeline that included fathers, sons, brothers, and husbands. Some were bookies, some were killers, some were informants, and some were innocent.

Martorano provided the first implication in the trial of Bulger's powerful politician brother Billy. The hit man said he met John Connolly in the mid-1970s and was told by Whitey that the G-man was an old friend from Southie. Whitey told him his brother helped Connolly get his FBI job and that Billy, in return, asked Connolly to watch out for Whitey.

"Bulger said that John Connolly is an FBI agent, that he grew up in Southie," Martorano said, recalling the conversation with Bulger. "He just got assigned to Boston, and he went to see his brother Billy and told Billy, 'I owe you for keeping me honest and making me finish this thing and become an FBI agent and stay out of trouble and if there's anything I can do for you, let me know.'"

Billy told him, "If you could keep my brother out of trouble, that would be helpful to me," Martorano testified.

In a 2019 interview with the authors, Billy Bulger drew a sharp line between his brother's criminal life and his own life of public service.

Asked if Whitey ever put pressure on him to help his criminal enterprises, Billy Bulger said, "No, I don't think so. He was very respectful of that. I think that he knew that I had a point of view that was as strong in my sense, as his was in his. So, I could even play back his own words, and say 'Now you don't want me to go awry and I don't want you to.' That sort of thing."

Wyshak laid Martorano's deal out for the jury, pushing him to reveal why he flipped on his friends. The burly gangster said he felt betrayed. It was Flemmi and Bulger who tipped off the feds to his Florida hideout, where he was arrested in 1995 after sixteen years on the run. Martorano was one of the mobsters indicted in the 1978 race-fixing case, but Bulger and Flemmi gave him a heads-up that the bust was coming and he went on the run. Over the years as a fugitive, Martorano continued to work with Bulger and Flemmi, running rackets and executing rivals on command.

"They were my partners in crime, they were my best friends, they were my children's godfathers," Martorano testified. He said his youngest son was named James Steven in tribute to Bulger and Flemmi.

"After I heard that they were informants, it sort of broke my heart," he told the court. "They broke all trust that we had, all loyalties. I was just beside myself with it."

Bulger sat slumped in his chair and seemed disinterested in the proceedings. Martorano, who has a variety of nicknames, including "The Basin Street Butcher" and "The Executioner," had the courtroom riveted as the serial killer held nothing back.

Wyshak asked how he made a living currently and Martorano replied, "Social Security," eliciting snickers from the gallery. The prosecutor read from his lengthy plea agreement and slowly read the names of twenty people murdered by Martorano. The hit man confirmed killing each of them, including Wheeler and Callahan.

Martorano testified that the order came from Bulger and Flemmi to kill Callahan, a close friend and longtime associate of Martorano, because he was going to implicate the crew in Wheeler's May 27, 1981, murder. Callahan was a sharp-dressed accountant by day, but drank and caroused with gangsters by night.

"Did you ever hear the phrase 'Wannabe gangster'?" Wyshak asked.

"That's what he was," Martorano answered.

A millionaire industrialist, Wheeler had sniffed out a skimming operation at World Jai Alai in Florida in which the Winter Hill gang, with Callahan's help, was embezzling from the gambling business. Callahan originally suggested the gang force Wheeler to sell the business to them, but when Wheeler balked, the decision was made to kill him.

Crooked FBI agent H. Paul Rico, who was retired from the Bureau, was Callahan's head of security and set the wheels in motion for Wheeler's slaying.

"Callahan wanted to get Mr. Wheeler killed so he wouldn't get in trouble," Martorano testified. "He said that he discussed it with Paul Rico."

Flemmi and Martorano both pleaded guilty to Wheeler's murder and were going to testify against Rico, but he died before he went to trial on murder charges.

Martorano told the jury it was Rico who provided him Wheeler's golf schedule and description. Flemmi sent him a murder "kit"—a suitcase filled with machine guns, pistols, and masks—which Martorano picked up at a Tulsa bus station. He said he put on a fake beard and sunglasses, approached Wheeler in the parking lot of Southern Hills Country Club in Tulsa, and shot the businessman in the face.

"I saw a guy coming over the hill carrying a briefcase," Martorano said. "It looked like him. He was heading toward that car. So I head toward that car. He opened the door and got in. So I opened the door and shot him. Between the eyes."

The jury was shown a graphic autopsy photo of Wheeler's face with a bullet hole in the middle of his forehead. He said Callahan paid him $50,000 for the slaying, which he split with Flemmi, Bulger, and Joe McDonald, a Winter Hill associate who went with him to Tulsa.

Wyshak walked Martorano through the maze of death, illuminating for the jury how the brazen Wheeler killing touched off a string of murders as the gang desperately scrambled to contain the situation and gain control of World Jai Alai.

Callahan got drunk one night back in Boston and told his pal Brian Halloran about the Wheeler murder and who was behind it. Halloran was facing charges in an unrelated case and sought to trade info about the Wheeler killing and the Winter Hill Gang's role in hopes of getting a lighter sentence.

Bulger ended Halloran's negotiations on a South Boston street when he gunned him down, along with Michael Donahue. Martorano said Connolly—whom he referred to by his nickname "Zip"—signed Halloran's death warrant by telling Bulger that Halloran was talking to the feds.

"He said that Halloran had went to the FBI and told them that I had killed Wheeler," Martorano testified. "Bulger said he learned this from his friend Zip."

Callahan was the next victim in the World Jai Alai bloodbath because Bulger feared he would rat out the gang. The decision to kill Callahan was made in a 1982 meeting he attended in New York with Bulger and Flemmi.

"[Bulger] said that Zip told him that Callahan is going to get so much pressure on him that he is going to fold and we are all going to go to jail for the rest of our life," Martorano testified. "Bulger did all the talking. Stevie just listened. They thought that he wouldn't hold up. They wanted to take him out."

Martorano considered Callahan a "friend" and said he "objected" to the execution but was overruled.

"I didn't want to kill Callahan," he said. "Eventually, they convinced me. It was two against one and it was three of us. And I finally agreed, 'It has got to be done. It has to be done.'"

Martorano was such close pals with Callahan that Callahan gave him money while he was on the run and let him use his condo and car in Plantation, Florida. Still, on August 1, 1982, Martorano picked him up in a van at Fort Lauderdale International Airport, shot him in the head, and dumped his body in the trunk of his own car.

When he and a cohort moved the body from the van to Callahan's car, they heard him "moan," so Martorano shot him again. Then they drove around the Little Havana neighborhood of Miami and tossed his belongings out of the car "to make it appear drug-related." The car was dumped at Miami International Airport, where it was found days later. After the slaying, Martorano and Flemmi met in Florida with Rico, the retired FBI agent, to discuss the future of World Jai Alai. Martorano remained on the run for another thirteen years until he was arrested in 1995 in Delray Beach.

While Martorano coldly detailed the murders he committed, it was all about tying Whitey to each body, which Wyshak did one after the other. The wily prosecutor steered Martorano to the 1975 killing of Tommy King, a Mullins gang member, bank robber, and rugged Southie boxer who famously beat up Bulger at Triple O's in 1975.

"Him and Tommy couldn't get along. They were always butting heads together," Martorano told jurors. "He wanted to get rid of Tommy."

Martorano said Bulger came up with a "ruse" to set up King's murder that involved lying to King about helping them kill a deadbeat bookie named "Suitcase" Fidler. Martorano, Bulger, Howie Winter, and King all met at Carson Beach in Southie, where Flemmi handed out guns, supposedly to use to kill Fidler. King, who was wearing a bulletproof vest, was given a gun with blanks in it.

With Bulger driving, Winter and Martorano got in the backseat and Martorano executed King with a gunshot to the back of the head. The crew drove toward a pre-dug grave at Tenean Beach in Dorchester, a marshy area along the Neponset River, just off Interstate 93 under an MBTA Red Line bridge. Martorano and Winter got out of the vehicle and went back to Somerville to check on a horse race, while Bulger drove on and buried King in a chest-deep hole along the river.

King's wife, Margaret, testified that she went to Triple O's when her husband didn't come home and confronted Bulger.

"Where is my husband?" she asked the mob boss.

"He's probably in Canada robbing banks," Bulger responded.

Over the ensuing years, Bulger was infamously caught on a DEA bug saying to pals as they drove on I-93 past the river, "Tip your hat to Tommy." The comment was a mystery until October 2000, when Weeks led cops to the burial ground. King's body was unearthed on the beach, along with the decaying corpses of Debbie Davis and Paul McGonagle, Catherine's former brother-in-law. Bulger lived for many years in a condominium that overlooked the burial ground.

Martorano's testimony was exhaustive as the jury heard three days of him confessing to murder after murder, including eleven he says he committed with Bulger, as well as a day and a half of Brennan and Carney lambasting him as a liar, a "serial killer," and an opportunist.

"You even lied to your best friend, John Callahan, before you murdered him," Brennan said.

"Correct," Martorano answered. "To me that was a necessity. I couldn't tell him I wanted to shoot him."

Brennan asked him if he was a "serial killer."

"Serial killers kill until they get caught or stopped," Martorano answered. "I didn't. I wasn't a serial killer.

"A serial murderer kills for fun, they like it," he added. "I don't like it. I never did like it."

He was also asked if he was remorseful.

"Yes," he responded flatly.

As Martorano left the court, he smiled at Bulger.

It was a devil's grin.

31

A FTER THREE DAYS OF MARTORANO'S ghoulish testimony, the prosecutors needed the jury to hear from the loved ones of those left behind by the gang's bloody reign. So Wyshak, Hafer, and Kelly brought in a string of tearful relatives of Bulger's murder victims who helped shed light on the wreckage, as well as the depths of the corruption.

Sandra Castucci, wife of murder victim Richard Castucci, took the stand and laid the foundation for prosecutors to start painting a vivid picture of the deadly coordination that went on between Whitey and the FBI. Richard Castucci was a mobbed-up strip club owner and bookie. He was golfing buddies with Sammy Davis Jr. and palled around with the Rat Pack. A photo was shown to the jury of Castucci with Frank Sinatra at Sammy Davis's wedding.

Castucci was in deep to loan sharks and was executed in Somerville in December 1976 by Martorano, with Flemmi and Bulger standing by. The mobsters tossed his body in the trunk of Castucci's Cadillac and dumped it in Revere, a city known for its mob boneyards, where it was discovered during a snowstorm.

Sandra Castucci testified after her husband's murder that she was strong-armed out of his nightclubs by New England mob boss Raymond Patriarca, who told her he was taking them because her husband owed the Mafia money. The real reason Castucci was killed, though, was that word leaked to Whitey and Flemmi that he was an FBI informant. Whitey was an FBI rat at the time of the killing. This marked the first known occasion that he participated in a murder while under the Bureau's watch. In 2009, the Castucci family won a $6 million wrongful death suit against the federal government.

The seventy-six-year-old widow's testimony set the stage for James Marra, a special agent with the Justice Department's Office of the Inspector General, who provided the most damning evidence of Whitey's status as an FBI mole. Marra read from Bulger's seven-hundred-page informant file over four long days, making him one of the longest witnesses of the trial. He revealed that Whitey was known officially to the Bureau as "BS 1544," a secret code number used to protect his status as an informant.

Marra's testimony was visibly uncomfortable for Whitey and his defense team, who made clear from the outset of the trial that they would seek to dismantle claims that he was a protected FBI informant. It meant nothing legally to the charges in the case but was obviously a priority for Bulger, who at that point had nothing left but his street reputation and legacy.

Marra, who spent thirty-five years in the DOJ, was an expert in internal affairs matters in the FBI. He had investigated dozens of federal agents for wrongdoing over the years. He was part of the US attorney's prosecution team in 1994 that won a landmark $58 million settlement against the Teamsters labor union for embezzlement, kickbacks, and bribery. And he was a key witness in Connolly's 2008 murder trial in Florida, which ended with the disgraced G-man being found guilty of second-degree murder and getting forty years in prison.

For Wyshak, Kelly, and Hafer, Marra was a key witness, as Bulger's informant file did much more than shed light on his decades-long relationship with the FBI. It also corroborated many of the killings Whitey was charged with—including several that were chillingly outlined to the jury by Martorano.

As Marra sat in the witness booth, just fifteen feet from Whitey, he read from report after report drafted by several different FBI agents and their supervisors detailing Bulger's status as an informant. The eighty-five-year-old gangster's blood boiled.

"The glares he gave to me on the stand, you could feel and sense the evil in him," Marra told the authors of this book in 2019. "If looks could kill."

As lawyers talked at sidebar with Judge Casper about Bulger's voluminous FBI informant file and how it should be presented to the jury, the disgraced mob boss slouched in his chair, angrily muttering.

"I'm not a fucking informant," he seethed.

It was one of the more intense moments of the trial up to that point and exposed Bulger's nasty side as his lawyers desperately sought to spin the facts and rewrite history.

Wyshak at one point had enough of the defense team's charade, telling Judge Casper, "I understand that for whatever reasons, whether it's the ego of the defendant or attempting to preserve his reputation, he does not want to be called an informant, but I am not going to tailor my questions in a manner that preserves that ridiculous contention."

Marra's testimony was crippling. He said Bulger began working as an FBI informant in 1971, but was shut down because he wasn't providing useful information. He was put back into the program in 1975 and became a "Top Echelon—Organized Crime" informant for the next fifteen years, until Connolly retired. His primary handler was his Southie pal Zip Connolly, but he also provided information to other agents through the years, including Dennis Condon, John Morris, and James Ring, Marra testified.

"He'd be considered to be a very valuable source of information," Marra said, referring to the official FBI status Bulger had for decades.

The reports Marra detailed showed that Bulger met with several FBI agents, not just Connolly, further blunting the defense claim that the informant file was filled with false information crafted by

Connolly to hoodwink his superiors. The records showed Dennis Condon wrote multiple reports about contacts with Bulger in 1971. FBI agent James Scanlon was his supervisor at the time.

Bulger was released as an informant in 1971, but in 1975, he was back on the books under Connolly's purview. Scanlon was also Connolly's supervisor for two years, until 1978 when Morris took over. In November 1980, then–special-agent-in-charge of the Boston office Lawrence Sarhatt wrote a memo saying that he met with Morris, Connolly, and Bulger for "four hours" at an East Boston hotel. Flemmi was conspicuously absent from the meeting, lending more credence to prosecutors' assertions that Bulger himself was feeding information to the FBI and wasn't just along for the ride with Flemmi.

Whitey told Sarhatt at that meeting that the Massachusetts State Police were "aware of his informant role with the FBI."

"However, he is not concerned with his personal safety because no one would dare believe that he is an informant," Sarhatt wrote. "It would be too incredible. Notwithstanding this notoriety, he indicated to me that he wants to continue the relationship with the FBI."

From February 1983 through May 1990, James Ring was Connolly's supervisor and wrote several reports about Bulger and Flemmi. He too noted that he met personally with them, including multiple meetings in 1984.

"I have met with these informants on approximately four occasions," Ring wrote in an October 17, 1984, report.

Marra read through a slew of Connolly's informant reports on Bulger, all littered with information about murders, gun running, drug deals, and bank robberies. Bulger spun elaborate lies to his handlers to deflect the investigative spotlight away from himself.

After the 1982 Brian Halloran/Michael Donahue murders, he was particularly vocal with Connolly as he planted fabricated stories designed to throw agents off his trail. Two days after the murders,

Bulger told Connolly that Halloran might have been killed by the Mafia because he was talking to the feds.

Then he claimed the Mafia put a "hit" on Halloran because Halloran gunned down a rival in a restaurant and was planning to pin the killing on mobster "Cadillac" Frank Salemme's brother Jackie. The mob, Bulger told the agent, wanted Halloran dead because Halloran was a "weak person" who "might make a deal" to implicate Jackie Salemme.

He also claimed Halloran's mind was "blown out on coke" and that he was shaking down drug dealers all over Southie, suggesting his unpredictable street antics could have led to his murder. He suggested Halloran could have been targeted by Jimmy Flynn and Jimmy "The Weasel" Mantville, two Charlestown associates who knew Halloran's brother was a state trooper and suspected he was a rat.

Finally, he gave yet another scenario: that Halloran was killed by Jimmy Flynn because several Irish mobsters were afraid he would tell the feds about a murder in Canada. Bulger told Connolly the crew held a fund-raiser at an Irish civic club in Malden, Massachusetts, to raise money to send Flynn on the run. Halloran knew all about it and was going to squeal to the feds, which is why he was targeted for death, Bulger said, according to Connolly's reports.

Based on the bogus info, Flynn was arrested and charged in the slaying but was acquitted at trial in 1986. He went on to run the Teamsters movie crews in Boston, and appeared in several made-in-Boston films, including playing a judge in a scene with Matt Damon in *Good Will Hunting*. In an ironic twist, Flynn was the Teamsters' transportation supervisor during filming in Boston for *The Departed*.

Marra also outlined a series of damning FBI reports and memos detailing the murders of Wheeler and Callahan, many of which exposed Connolly as being complicit.

The informant files remained sealed for years and were first acknowledged following Bulger's 1995 indictment. But they remained redacted until a landmark 2003 decision by Congress that gave the DOJ's Office of the Inspector General full oversight to investigate all federal agencies, including the FBI, Bureau of Prisons, Bureau of Alcohol, Tobacco and Firearms, DEA, and even the US Attorney's Office. The FBI had fought tooth-and-nail to keep them sealed during the 1995 case and the ruling opened up the floodgates.

"The FBI was happy policing itself," one source said.

The detail Marra outlined in court was stark. Had the legislation not been changed in 2003, the reports never would have seen the light of day. The way they were written made it clear that Connolly and his fellow agents assumed they never would have been made public.

Whitey's lawyers challenged the veracity of the reports, saying there was "missing information" to verify their authenticity. And they pointed the finger at the DOJ for allowing Bulger's reign of terror to go on for decades.

"Certainly the DOJ needs to protect the fact that they let somebody they believe is a killer run loose, kill people throughout the Boston area, and never charge him," Brennan told the court.

Marra was subjected to one of the longest and nastiest cross-examinations of the trial as Brennan pointed out lies in Connolly's reports, challenged Marra's knowledge of the truth behind the reports, and questioned whether the information led to any prosecutions.

"Hank Brennan was ruthless on him, trying to prove Bulger wasn't an informant," Hafer recalled. "I'm sure that was driven by Bulger because it really didn't mean much legally."

The defense was relentless in pushing their narrative of Connolly as a rogue agent who made up information from Bulger, or attributed information to Whitey that actually came from Flemmi.

Wyshak called their claim "fiction" and pointed to volumes of reports not only from Connolly, but from Condon, Ring, Morris, Scanlon, and others.

"Unless it is Mr. Bulger's contention that all of these agents got together to fabricate this file for some reason, his contention that he was not an FBI informant is simply absurd," Wyshak said.

Former FBI supervisor John Morris, who was retired and living in Florida, was called by prosecutors and took the stand for two days. He told a sordid tale of corruption in the Boston FBI office, including fudging reports with Connolly to protect Bulger and Flemmi. The disgraced agent, who was granted immunity and flipped on Connolly, met with Bulger scores of times, took at least $7,000 in bribes, and hosted dinners with the gangsters at his home while in charge of the Boston FBI.

"I knew I was completely trapped," Morris said. "I was in so far I could never get out of it. I didn't know what to do. I felt awful."

Morris admitted he was the agent who anonymously first leaked Bulger's relationship with the FBI to the media in 1988. As he did with Marra, Bulger expressed hostility toward Morris in court, at one point muttering under his breath, "You're a fucking liar."

Brian Kelly was furious at the comment and asked Judge Casper to order the gangster to watch his tongue.

"I know he spent his whole life intimidating people, including fifteen-year-old boys in Southie, but he shouldn't be allowed to do it here," Kelly said.

Judge Casper said she didn't hear the comment but advised him to let his lawyers do the talking.

"Do you understand?" she asked.

"Yes," Bulger responded.

When it came time for Bulger's team to lay out their case, they didn't call any of the agents Marra mentioned who were still alive, including Sarhatt, who did testify at Flemmi's 1998 trial and was still alive in 2013. He died in July 2018.

In fact, there was only one agent who claimed Bulger wasn't an informant—Robert Fitzpatrick, who was the special agent in charge of the Boston office from 1981 to 1986. Fitzpatrick was the only witness at all called by the defense team, but rather than bolster Whitey's claims that he wasn't an informant, he told a series of whopping lies that ultimately landed him a perjury conviction after the Bulger trial.

Fitzpatrick, who wrote a book about the case, testified that Whitey told him he wasn't an informant and claimed he was brought in to clean up the Boston office in 1980. Both turned out to be lies, but they weren't the most fantastical fabrications Fitzpatrick told on the stand.

He told the jury it was he who put the handcuffs on Boston mob boss Jerry Anguilo. He also said he personally recovered the rifle that James Earl Ray used to assassinate Dr. Martin Luther King at the Lorraine Motel in Memphis, Tennessee, in 1968. Both proved to be total fabrications.

Kelly grilled Fitzpatrick on the stand, which visibly angered Bulger. As the prosecutor started tearing into Fitzpatrick, Bulger shot him an angry look that sent chills down Kelly's spine.

"He turned around really quickly and glared at me," Kelly said. "I really went at Fitzpatrick hard. He clearly didn't like it. He turned around really fast and I thought, 'This guy is just a maniac.'

"For an old guy, he was threatening looking," he added. "He had this aura of evil, even as an old man, sitting in the courtroom when he looked at you. I was glad the marshals were there."

Three years after Bulger's trial, Fitzpatrick was convicted of six counts of perjury and six counts of obstruction of justice because of his lies on the stand. He was sentenced to twenty-four months' probation and fined $12,500.

"Fitzpatrick admitted that he lied when he testified at Bulger's trial that he tried to end Bulger's relationship with the FBI and target Bulger for prosecution but was overruled by higher authorities in the FBI," US Attorney Carmen Ortiz said.

The testimony was a disaster for Bulger's defense, but it would only get worse.

32

WHITEY'S POLITICALLY CONNECTED FAMILY WAS largely spared throughout the trial, as Billy Bulger had already been publicly pilloried during his circus-like 2003 congressional testimony, after which he was forced to resign his lofty perch as president of the University of Massachusetts.

But a handful of other relatives were dragged into the case in July 2013 when the jury was played recordings of a series of jailhouse conversations between Whitey and his family. Ken Brady, the investigator and guard at Plymouth, burned all the calls to a disk and handed them over to prosecutors.

In one recording, the mobster was heard telling Billy Bulger's son, William Bulger Jr., and his sister about the 1975 murder of Edward Connors, a Dorchester tavern owner gunned down in a Dorchester phone booth.

"Pa-pa-pa-pa-pow," Bulger whispered in the October 13, 2012, call, mimicking machine gun fire.

Connors was one of the nineteen victims Bulger was charged with killing.

"Somebody threw my name in the mix," Whitey told his nephew and niece, who could be heard laughing on the tape.

"As usual," William Bulger Jr. says.

In another taped conversation with his brother Jackie, a disgraced ex–clerk magistrate for the Boston Juvenile Court, Whitey talked about pointing a shotgun at kids casing out his Southie liquor store.

"They're getting ready to stick the joint up, so I picked up a shotgun and I'm aimin' it at them. And the guy looked up and, 'Oh,'" Whitey says in the December 11, 2012, recording, while breaking into laughter.

"See you later," Jackie chimed in.

"And I put one in the chamber," Whitey said. "One went this way, one went that way. . . . We were lucky they didn't try to do nothing."

While the tape was played, Whitey was smirking at the defendant's table.

BULGER HAD NOTHING TO LAUGH about when his protégé Kevin Weeks strolled into court to testify against his former boss and mentor.

Weeks's name was sprinkled throughout the trial and it was already well established that he'd turned on Whitey. Now it was time for the jury to learn about the six decomposed corpses that he'd led investigators to at two separate makeshift burial grounds in Boston's Dorchester neighborhood.

Like Martorano, Weeks was a free man, despite his admitted role in five murders. He too had cut a sweetheart immunity deal with the government in exchange for his testimony against Bulger and Flemmi, and he was living just down the street from the courthouse in his old Southie neighborhood.

A former bouncer at Whitey's haunt, Triple O's, Weeks earned the nickname "Two Weeks" in 2000 because he flipped on Bulger and Flemmi after just a few weeks in federal prison in Rhode Island.

Whitey didn't show much interest in most witnesses, but when Weeks came in—his surrogate son, whom he hadn't seen in seventeen years—he sat up in his chair and craned his neck to watch the beefy thug take the stand.

"I was with him over twenty years," Weeks told the jury. "Sometimes I'd beat somebody up."

They shook down landlords, businessmen, bookies, and drug dealers. They moved kilos of cocaine across Boston, sometimes up to twenty-six kilos—fifty-seven pounds—at a time. He recalled shaking down a drug dealer named "Red" Shea for $15,000 plus $1,500 monthly payments, using a fake Uzi machine gun given to Whitey by Connolly as a gag gift.

One bookie who wanted out had to pay the gang $500,000. Whitey called it "severance." He recalled shaking down a bookie named Kevin Hayes—the father of National Hockey League players Kevin and Jimmy Hayes—for $25,000 cash plus $1,000 a month in rent during football season. Hayes later testified that he was brought to the basement of The Haunty, where Weeks threatened to shoot him in the head if he didn't pay. There was a plastic tarp on the floor.

Weeks said the gang had gun "hides" all over Southie, including one that had a sliding electronic wall where they stashed machine guns, silencers, masks, and ammo. He said the gang regularly oiled and wiped down firearms to remove fingerprints. After shooting people, they would destroy the guns. He recalled moving stashes of weapons after the indictments came down in 1995. They had handcuffs to restrain people during shakedowns and murders and knives to use for "intimidation."

He testified about paying off Connolly, Morris, Schneiderhan, and other cops and FBI agents. He described Whitey as his "mentor." And he verified infamous surveillance photos showing him, Whitey, and Flemmi having clandestine criminal meetings while casually walking around Southie's Castle Island. He said he made as much as $2 million in the roughly fifteen years he was partnered with Bulger.

For the prosecutors, Weeks, like Martorano, was another key to checking off murders as Weeks was involved in the planning, execution, and cleanup of several of the killings in the indictment.

Weeks had the courtroom on edge as he described the May 1982 killings of Halloran and Donahue on South Boston's waterfront. Halloran was targeted because, he said, "we got word that he was cooperating with the FBI on a couple of murders." The crew didn't even know who Donahue was.

After the drive-by double murder, Whitey had dinner at Teresa Stanley's house. Then they drove back to the murder scene, which by then was surrounded by police tape and mobbed with cops, and they grabbed a hubcap that flew off Whitey's "hit car" after the shooting. Whitey bragged about the shooting later that night to Flemmi and another gangster.

A couple of days after the murders, Whitey, Flemmi, and Weeks brazenly went and marveled at the bullet-riddled Datsun in a South Boston tow lot where the car was being stored by police.

"Let's get out of here before someone spots us," Whitey told the crew after examining his handiwork for a few minutes.

Days later, Weeks got the guns out of the backseat of the Chevy Malibu and removed the stock from a carbine because Bulger "liked that stock." He kept the stock but tossed the guns into the ocean at Marina Bay, an ocean pier in nearby Quincy.

Asked how he felt after the slayings, Weeks told the jury, "I just was involved in a double homicide, so there was no getting out. I knew I was in."

His second day of testimony got more gruesome as Weeks recalled the string of murders at The Haunty. He talked about watching Bulger execute Bucky Barrett and watching Flemmi pull out the victim's teeth. He, Flemmi, and associate Pat Nee buried the body.

He recalled Whitey telling him about the Tommy King and Paulie McGonagle murders and the strangulation of Debbie Davis. He said Bulger told him that Flemmi wrapped the twenty-six-year-old beauty's face in duct tape and told her "you're going to a better place" before she was strangled. Whitey was unclear about who strangled her—him or Flemmi, he testified.

Weeks later led cops to those three bodies at another makeshift burial ground on Tenean Beach, along the shores of the Neponset River in Dorchester.

He admitted making fake IDs for Whitey and delivering them to him in Chicago in 1996 while Bulger was on the lam. He talked with him regularly on pay phones and met with him several times at the New York Public Library.

Defense attorney Jay Carney dragged Weeks through an agonizing and intense cross-examination that went on for hours and exploded when the topic of Whitey being an informant came up. Referencing Weeks's light sentence for his convictions and participation in five murders, the attorney said, "You won against the system."

"What did I win? What did I win? Five people are dead!" Weeks shouted. "We killed people that were rats, and I had the two biggest rats right next to me."

With that, Whitey's anger spilled over once again.

"You suck," Bulger said.

"Fuck you, okay," Weeks shot back.

"Fuck you too," Whitey snarled.

"What do you want to do?" Weeks bellowed. He was ready to fight his former boss in the middle of the courtroom.

Judge Casper was livid.

"Hey, Mr. Bulger," the judge said, her voice rising. "Mr. Bulger, let your attorneys speak in this court for you."

After Weeks's turn wrapped up, he left the stand, glaring at Whitey. The judge called the attorneys to sidebar and admonished Carney and his partner Hank Brennan.

"Is it fair to say that you're going to speak to your client after today's session about this outburst?" Judge Casper said.

"Yes, your honor," Carney replied.

But there was still one final courtroom confrontation to come.

33

HEARING KEVIN WEEKS CALL HIM a rat rattled Whitey enough to scream "fuck you" in Judge Casper's courtroom, but what came next from Bulger's lifelong criminal partner Flemmi brought out perhaps the darkest moments of the two-month trial.

Bulger was dressed sharply in a pressed blue button-down suit the day his former right-hand man took the stand to publicly turn against him. It was a long time coming and the tension was high as Flemmi walked into the courtroom, marking the first time the two gangsters had seen each other in eighteen years. Both men had aged, but Flemmi's longer stretch behind bars made him look more withered than his former friend.

The prosecutors knew Flemmi was key to corroborating most of the murders, the drug dealing, gambling, and racketeering, but the biggest question was whether he would be able to help them nail Whitey for the murders of Debbie Davis and Deborah Hussey. Would the jury believe this lifelong criminal and admitted killer who turned informant to save his own life?

Wearing a green prison jumpsuit and matching green windbreaker, Flemmi took the stand and immediately set the tone by saying emphatically they were both informants since the early 1970s and that Whitey was the boss when it came to their FBI snitching. The pair met with agents "hundreds of times," but it was Bulger who called the shots and "did all the talking" with their notorious handler, John "Zip" Connolly.

"He was the one that was really friendly with Connolly," Flemmi, slumped in the witness chair, testified.

It was another blow to the defense. The two gangsters, once inseparable and united in ruling Boston's underworld, squared off in the courtroom at one point with Flemmi standing defiantly with his hands on his hips, staring at Whitey.

"Fuck him," Bulger grumbled under his breath.

"Really?" Flemmi shot back.

Flemmi, who is serving life but was spared the death penalty in the Oklahoma and Florida murders for agreeing to turn on Whitey, casually ran through the roster of murders as though discussing his breakfast. He repeatedly implicated Bulger, including in the grim strangulations of Flemmi's stepdaughter, Hussey, and his mistress, Debbie Davis.

According to Flemmi, Hussey was killed because Whitey determined she was a junkie who might talk to cops, while Davis was considered to be a "vulnerability" because she knew they were FBI informants.

Recalling Davis's murder, Flemmi said, "She walked in the entrance there, and he [Bulger] grabbed her by the neck. I couldn't do it. He knew it. He told me, 'I'll take care of it.'" Davis's family sobbed in the gallery, as did one juror.

Asked by Wyshak how it made him feel to stand and watch helplessly as Whitey choked the life out of the twenty-six-year-old beauty, he said, "It affected me. It's going to affect me until the day I die."

He added, coldly, "I loved her, but I wasn't in love with her."

Whitey dragged her to the basement, where she was stripped naked and her teeth were yanked out, per the usual routine. Flemmi said Bulger then went upstairs to lie down. Flemmi, Pat Nee, and another associate buried the woman's mutilated body at Tenean Beach.

He told a similar tale about Hussey's killing, but things turned ugly when Bulger's attorney, Hank Brennan, grilled Flemmi about having sex with Hussey, his stepdaughter. The attorney needled Flemmi that the girl, who was seventeen years old when he admitted having oral sex with her, called him "Daddy."

"That was a consensual relationship," Flemmi said, fuming. "On just two occasions. Moments of weakness. And I regretted it all my life."

As Brennan pressed him about discrepancies in his stories about Hussey's murder over the years, the defense attorney suggested that it was Flemmi who killed her because she told her mother— Flemmi's common-law wife, Marion—that he molested her. Enraged, Flemmi blurted out an oft-repeated rumor about Whitey having a penchant for underage girls in his heyday.

"You want to talk about pedophilia, right over there at that table," Flemmi said, pointing to Bulger sitting at the defense table. "He had a young girlfriend, sixteen years old, he took to Mexico."

While Whitey had erupted at far less scandalous accusations during the two-month trial, Flemmi's bombshell barely elicited a sigh from Bulger, who didn't have the energy or strength to defend his own lies anymore.

The final witness to testify for the prosecution was a foe from Bulger's more recent past.

FBI manhunter Scott Garriola flew in from Los Angeles to walk jurors through Whitey's final hours as America's most wanted criminal.

There would be no outbursts from Bulger this time. The Irish mob boss and accused killer respectfully observed Garriola as he took the witness stand and described how he managed to lure Bulger out of the apartment at the Princess Eugenia and also the cache of weapons they found inside apartment 303.

Prosecutor Zach Hafer asked the FBI agent if Whitey had stocked up on all those weapons for an eventual shootout with those coming to arrest him.

"I asked him that question," Garriola told the jury. "He paused. And then he told me, 'No, because a stray bullet may hit someone.'"

AS THE EXHAUSTIVE EIGHT-WEEK TRIAL wrapped up, there was one key figure whose name came up repeatedly in the Moakley Courthouse and who hadn't been heard from: Pat Nee.

The notorious bank robber, gunrunner, and triggerman was supposed to be a star witness for Bulger. Jay Carney was prepared to call him, but Nee told Judge Casper he would refuse to testify by invoking his Fifth Amendment right against self-incrimination. Nee's attorney, a seasoned Southie criminal defense lawyer named Steven Boozang, felt Bulger was using his client for no other reason than courtroom theatrics—and he and Nee weren't going along for the ride.

"It's become readily apparent that this is not a legal defense, but a client-run defense," Boozang said.

An Irish national and loyal gunrunner for the IRA, Nee was a violent bank robber and enforcer who had a long, storied history with Bulger. There were some who believed he too was a protected FBI informant.

Born in Rus Muc, a Gaelic-speaking village in Galway, Ireland, Nee was the oldest of six children. His dad was a laborer and his mom cleaned office buildings. The family immigrated to Boston on an English cruise ship and settled on East Sixth Street in Southie, right around the corner from the Bulger clan.

Young Pat seamlessly fell into a life of crime, stealing Hummel ceramic figures and jewelry during home break-ins.

"I learned how to steal and I liked the adrenaline rushes and the excitement," Nee told the authors of this book.

He joined the Mullen gang at age fourteen and immersed himself in the bloody gang wars that rocked Boston in the 1950s and

'60s. He briefly abandoned his criminal career when he joined the Marines and went to Vietnam, where he became a US citizen while fighting the war. He returned to Southie in 1966 and rejoined the Mullen gang.

Whitey and Nee played a dangerous game of cat-and-mouse during the 1970s as they took turns stalking each other as rival members of the feuding Mullen and Killeen gangs. One night in Charlestown, Nee and Bulger chased each other through a housing project, firing bullets at one another. Bulger carried a German-made submachine gun while Nee brandished a .30-06—"30 odd six"—military rifle outfitted with a scope. At one point, Nee spotted Bulger across a courtyard. He dropped to one knee and tried to get Bulger in his crosshairs, but the Southie gangster escaped.

Their final violent clash came when Whitey ambushed him at the corner of N and Fifth Streets in Southie one night. Nee and another thug were in Nee's brother's car when Whitey and two henchmen pulled up, got out, and opened fire, riddling the sedan with bullets. Nee hid on the floor and was shredded by shattering glass, receiving cuts all over his face and body.

"I saw the flashes of the guns," Nee said. "I have no idea how they missed me."

Nee and Whitey reluctantly joined forces when Bulger took control of the Winter Hill Gang. The former rivals put aside their differences for the good of their criminal careers, but Nee says he "never trusted" Bulger.

The jury heard from Weeks and others how Nee was the one who orchestrated the Valhalla gun-running scheme and helped Weeks lure John McIntyre to the basement of The Haunty. Nee was implicated in several slayings, including the killings of Bucky Barrett, Brian Halloran, and Michael Donahue, but was never prosecuted.

"Pat Nee is a stone-cold killer," Donahue's son, Tommy, told reporters after closing statements in the case. "He has been his whole life. He was involved in my father's murder . . . No charges were brought upon him. He's involved in countless violent crimes."

According to Weeks, Nee helped him and Flemmi exhume the remains of McIntyre, Hussey, and Barrett from the basement of The Haunty when the death house was sold. Flemmi, Weeks, and Bulger reburied the bodies across from Florian Hall, where they were later found, thanks to Weeks. Nee wasn't allowed to help with the second burial because Whitey didn't trust him, Weeks testified.

Nee told the authors of this book that Whitey confessed to him that he was an FBI informant. He said it was him who helped the FBI wire the Mafia's North End hideout.

"He told me at one point, before I took off on the Valhalla case," Nee said. "We were out at Castle Island with Weeks and O'Neil. He pulled me aside and said 'I helped Zip with the bug at Prince Street.'"

Nee went on the run for several years after being charged in the Valhalla case until he was arrested in 1987. He served just two years in federal prison for the gun-running case, which could have landed him a life sentence. Upon his release, he started a crew that robbed armored trucks. He served ten years of a thirty-seven-year sentence for a 1991 armored truck heist in Abington, Massachusetts, that was foiled by authorities, including FBI agent John Gamel.

Nee said that after serving his sentence for Valhalla, he avoided Whitey and hid his criminal endeavors from the Southie crime boss.

"He was an informant. I didn't talk to him at all," Nee said. "He kept us all either in prison or on the run. We were never able to piece it all together."

During the trial, like Martorano and Weeks, Nee was a free man. He still lived in Southie and walked the streets freely. In fact, it was announced during the trial that he'd be starring in a Discovery Channel reality show about bookies called *Saint Hoods*. None of it sat well with jurors and some were scared.

"People looked sick in the beginning," juror Scott Hotyckey said. "I think they were terrified. People asked me, 'What if Pat Nee comes to your house?'"

With Nee bowing out of the courthouse drama, all that was left was for Whitey to take the stand. The crime lord's pretrial pledge to expose government corruption at the highest level had the courthouse buzzing, but ultimately fell flat, as he decided not to testify.

It was disappointing to prosecutors, who were eager to grill the mob boss.

"Carney touted from day one, 'Wait until he takes the witness stand. Wait until he testifies. Wait til you hear what he has to say,'" Fred Wyshak said. "He was essentially threatening the government that he was going to expose all their wrongdoing, saying, 'When everybody hears his side of the story, we're going to have a very different picture.' At the last minute, as usual, he didn't testify."

Zach Hafer added, "There was a real disappointment that Bulger didn't testify. And that was calculated.

"If he had testified, he could have been asked about all this stuff. He knew that. It sort of enabled just this little bit of doubt to be out there. Was he really an informant? Did he meet with Jeremiah O'Sullivan? If he had taken the stand and been confronted with the absurdity of some of the claims, and the lack of any kind of backup, that little bit of residual doubt would be gone . . . We wanted the jury to hear that. That was part of the story."

After the demise of Whitey's much-anticipated final stand, the jury got the case and delivered its verdict after five long days of deliberation. They pored over piles of sickening crime scene photos and mountains of evidence.

On the day of the verdict—August 12, 2013—Bulger was picked up before dawn at the sally port of the Plymouth County Correctional Facility by state police and US marshals with guns drawn. He was transported by motorcade forty miles north to Boston, where along the way he passed the death pits that had hidden his secrets for so long, and his old neighborhood where his notorious legend was constructed over decades. Traffic along the busy highway into the city came to a standstill as motorists craned their necks to catch a glimpse of the former crime boss as he sped by.

The jury of eight men and four women convicted Whitey on thirty-one of thirty-two counts in the racketeering case, with the only not guilty delivered on the extortion of bookie Kevin Hayes.

They also found Bulger guilty of eleven of the nineteen murders, including the strangulation of Deborah Hussey, as well as the killings of Wheeler, Callahan, Halloran, Donahue, Tommy King, Edward Connors, Richard Castucci, Bucky Barrett, and John McIntyre. The jurors deadlocked on the killing of Debra Davis.

Her younger brother Steven Davis, who had been a fixture at the trial, holding court outside the courthouse and always willing to give a colorful quote to reporters, was stunned by the ruling.

"It's hard to digest," he said moments after the verdict came down. "With all the years since '81, I've been looking for answers, searching for answers, and I come out with an NF [No Finding]. It's not good enough . . . I believe I deserve more than an NF. I'm disappointed."

Wyshak, Hafer, and Kelly were also disappointed at the "no finding" on the Davis killing. It was the one small victory for Whitey and a tough loss for the prosecutors, as they hoped to deliver justice to the Davis family while also proving undeniably that Bulger was a heartless killer of women.

Still, the verdict, after four decades, finally held Bulger accountable for his evil reign.

"This day of reckoning for Bulger has been a long time coming," US Attorney Carmen Ortiz told reporters. "So many people's lives were so terribly harmed by the criminal acts of Bulger and his crew . . . We hope they find some degree of comfort in the fact . . . that Bulger is being held accountable for his horrific crimes."

Hafer, who previously worked in public corruption in the US Attorney's Office, said that despite Whitey's refusal to testify, the case did hold several corrupt public officials accountable.

"It's important for the public to have confidence that when assistant US attorneys who prosecute corruption cases are confronted by corruption by police officers or law enforcement, that we're just as offended by it as members of the public and we're going to expose it," he said. "That level of corruption by someone as high in the FBI as John Connolly was, for people who do this job for all the right reasons, is repugnant."

Fred Wyshak, who had worked on Bulger-related cases most of his career, said the verdict affirmed the hard work of a small group of dedicated investigators who refused to cave to political, bureaucratic, or institutional pressure and corruption.

"The group of people who did this case . . . had to fight the department," Wyshak said. "Elements in the FBI didn't like this case from the beginning, didn't want this case to happen, and tried to pull a lot of strings to derail it over the years . . . So what you had was a small group of prosecutors and investigators who basically fought the system to make this case happen."

Jay Carney, for his part, wasn't impressed and said he was "very pleased" with the verdict because he thought it vindicated Whitey on the Davis killing and also exposed deep corruption in the FBI and beyond.

"Mr. Bulger knew as soon as he was arrested that he was going to die behind the walls of a prison . . . or be injected with a chemical that would kill him," Carney said. "This trial was never about Jim Bulger being set free."

Some of the victims' families were relieved with the results but felt bad for the families of the eight victims that did not get a guilty finding.

Donahue's son, Tommy, said of the verdict: "It's a good feeling. But my heart also goes out to those families who were searching for that closure."

For Kelly, the case marked the end of a twenty-plus-year chapter in his life. When he started chasing Bulger's gang, his kids were toddlers. When the verdict was handed down, he had one son in college and two other children in high school.

"It was a case well worth doing," he reflected. "It exposed corruption that had to be exposed. It held accountable murderers and drug dealers who had to be held accountable. As much of a time drain as it was, it was well worth it. I'd gladly do it again."

As Whitey left the courtroom in shackles, he smiled and gave a thumbs-up to his brother Jackie and nieces and nephews. It was a sickening moment for the victims, but they'd soon take solace in knowing that Whitey's reign of terror was truly over and his life in prison would be anything but peaceful.

PART III

THE MURDER

34

I'S NEVER NEWS WHEN AN aging retiree leaves the cold confines of Boston for the dry, warm climate of Arizona, but Whitey Bulger was no ordinary retiree and he was going to no ordinary place.

After the guilty verdict, the now convicted mob killer was shipped from Plymouth to the Metropolitan Detention Center in Brooklyn. Following a quick stay there, he was shipped to the federal transfer center in Oklahoma City before finally being sent to the United States Penitentiary in Tucson, Arizona. He'd never see his beloved Boston or Massachusetts again.

Whitey loved the Southwest and had traveled there extensively while he was on the run. But this time he wouldn't get to visit Tombstone or the Painted Desert. With any luck, he'd never get to see the outside of a prison wall for the rest of his life.

The US Penitentiary in Tucson housed 1,552 inmates in its high-security facility. There were few inmates that were deemed more high security or high profile than Whitey.

But he was eighty-four years old now, and the years he'd spent in jail before and during his sensational trial had taken their toll. The regimen of daily push-ups helped; however, his body and mind were slowing down. Not even the notorious Whitey Bulger could defeat Father Time.

During his first few days as a federal prison inmate, Bulger befriended a young convict named Clement "Chip" Janus.

Janus, a member of the Rosebud Sioux tribe, grew up on the Crow reservation in Pryor, Montana. His mother died from a drug overdose and his father wasn't around, so Chip was raised on the reservation by his grandfather, a US Marine veteran. The grandfather was also an artist and he saw promise in Chip, so instead of giving him toys for Christmas, he put art supplies under the tree. But life on the reservation was particularly bleak, so Chip created his own excitement, drinking, carousing with friends, and boosting cars. He did a short stint in prison but was later sent back on federal gun charges.

"I was mad at the world and ran around with a huge chip on my shoulder thinking somebody owes me," he recalls.

He was incarcerated in Tucson for two years before Whitey Bulger walked into his life. By then, Chip had committed himself to doing his time and pursuing a career as an artist when he got out. The warden was so impressed by his talent that he put Chip in charge of the prison art room, where he taught oil painting and charcoal sketching to other inmates.

One day, while he was putting the finishing brushstrokes on several uncompleted projects, Whitey strolled into the art room with his customary gray sweatpants, white shirt, and a white baseball cap to inspect his work. Chip specialized in Native American art, so there were a number of paintings of tribe members in their traditional dress. Bulger was a huge fan of Native American art also, and he took his time studying each piece quietly without disrupting the artist's concentration.

The next morning, as Chip Janus made his way across the prison yard under the constant surveillance of rifle-toting guards perched atop gun towers, he bumped into a friend who said, "Whitey wants to shake your hand."

Chip didn't break stride, as he had only ten minutes to get from his cell to the art room, where he was scheduled to teach that day.

"It's a very controlled movement inside the yard," he explains. "The guards warn you that they'll shoot you if there are any problems."

He walked swiftly over to Bulger and extended his hand.

"Nice to meet you, but I gotta go."

"Can I come and talk to you?" Whitey asked.

"Alright, yeah," Chip answered. "I'll be in the art room."

Bulger made his way to the art room the next day.

"Wow," he sighed as he took his eyeglasses off and browsed Janus's artwork up close. "You did this?"

The prison art instructor nodded. "Yeah, I did that."

"You have great talent," Whitey told him. "I've been around the world. I saw the *Mona Lisa* in Paris. Do you know who I am? Did you know I was in Alcatraz?"

"Nah, I didn't know any of that stuff," Chip said. "How was it in Alcatraz?"

In truth, Chip Janus was vaguely aware of who Whitey was by now. When Bulger first got to Tucson, prisoners from the east coast marked his arrival with whispers and surrounded him like hungry sharks.

"Oh my God, is that him?" some inmates would ask.

But to convicts from the western United States, the geriatric former crime boss wasn't the most infamous inmate in the yard. Also housed in Tucson was Brian Mitchell, the man who kidnapped and raped Elizabeth Smart; former US Army private Steven Green, who was one of five American soldiers that gang-raped a fourteen-year-old Iraqi girl and then murdered her family; and Colombian cartel boss Diego Montoya Sánchez.

"Some old guy is trying to make friends with me, says he was in Alcatraz," Janus told a guard.

"Yeah, that's Whitey Bulger," the guard replied. "He was the mobster that was on the run."

It didn't appear that Whitey had made any friends in Tucson, so he began hanging around the art room with Chip, and soon their conversations would spill over to the yard.

"There was a big art heist back in Boston at a place called the Isabella Stewart Gardner Museum. Everybody thinks I have the paintings but I never laid my hands on 'em." Whitey laughed.

In 1990, at the height of Whitey's power, two robbers disguised as police officers entered the museum after hours, tied up the security guard, and stole thirteen pieces of priceless art including Vermeer's *The Concert* and Rembrandt's dramatic work *Christ in the Storm on the Sea of Galilee*. It was the richest art theft in the world. As his former protégé Kevin Weeks once said, "When we learned about it, we pulled in every crook we knew and gave them a good beat down for information but we never found them." The FBI maintains a $10 million reward for the safe return of the stolen art.

Whitey also told Chip about the letters and phone calls that his lawyer received from filmmakers that were developing *Black Mass*, a Hollywood biopic eventually released in 2015 about Bulger's life of crime starring Johnny Depp in the lead role.

"He's a good person [Depp]. But I don't understand why he took the role," Bulger said. "Even Johnny doesn't believe I was an informant. My lawyer is talking to Depp's agent. I'm gonna decline because I can't stand the *Boston Globe* guys that wrote it. If I was out, they wouldn't be writing that shit about me."

Whitey bragged to Janus that he'd once shot up a *Boston Globe* printing press with a machine gun. He told the prison art teacher that if he were to ever sit down for an interview, he'd speak only to Barbara Walters. The legendary television journalist had interviewed world leaders like Fidel Castro and countless Hollywood stars. Bulger felt that he was deserving of the same celebrity treatment.

He also schooled Chip about his life at Alcatraz and Joe "The Animal" Barboza, another notorious Boston mobster turned government rat.

"Barboza was killed for being an informant," Bulger said in mock disgust. "They reached out and touched him in San Francisco for being a rat. He was a big player in the game and lots of stuff happened with him. He was a hit man who turned informant and was blown off his feet because of it."

"How'd you manage to stay on the run all those years?" Chip asked him.

"They thought I was outta the country when I left." Whitey shook his head and laughed. "There were sightings of me overseas but that never happened. I was right there in front of 'em the whole fucking time."

He also explained that it was his and Catherine's love of pets that led to their capture.

"We'd go outside our apartments for walks in Santa Monica and every morning we'd feed this cat. That cat was gonna be the death of me. Some days I didn't want to go out there but Catherine would wanna feed the cat. I told her to just leave the fucking thing alone, but she had this thing for this stray animal. If she didn't feed that cat, we wouldn't have gotten to know all those people. I didn't wanna build any relationships. I never wanted to spend any money either because I didn't want to attract any attention."

THEIR CONVERSATIONS ALSO CENTERED ON Bulger's friendship with Joe Carnes. Whitey commissioned Janus to paint some portraits of Carnes wearing a traditional Choctaw headdress that he could send as a gift to his brother Billy back home in Southie.

"I can't pay you any money, but I can write you some stories and send you some signed photos. Trust me, they're worth something."

As the two men sat on a bench in the prison yard, Bulger's menacing stare constantly shifted, watching every prisoner who passed by. He'd count how many times they'd walk by and then get up to confront them.

"Hey, what're you doing?" the eighty-four-year-old gangster would ask in a stern voice. "I'm trying to have a conversation here, you walked by a few times. What're you doin'? You wanna ask me something?"

Bulger understood that he was a high-level target for any prisoners looking to make a name for themselves and expected that someone would take a run at him sooner or later.

"When they give it to me, I hope they give it to me quick, because I gave it quick," he told Janus.

One prisoner that Bulger kept a close eye on was Louis Eppolito, a former New York City police detective turned hired Mafia killer for the Lucchese and Gambino crime families. Eppolito was serving life in prison for several gangland slayings and also had been contracted for failed hits on John "Junior" Gotti and notorious mob rat Sammy "The Bull" Gravano. Like most people with deep knowledge of the underworld, Eppolito didn't buy Bulger's story that he was never an informant for the FBI.

During one controlled movement in the prison yard, Eppolito stood directly behind Whitey and shouted, "Fucking rat!"

Bulger pretended not to hear the insult, as he didn't want to draw the attention of some trigger-happy prison guard standing in the gun towers above. But Eppolito never tried to exact mob justice on Whitey. Instead, Bulger was nearly killed in an attack he didn't see coming.

Four months after he had arrived in Tucson, Whitey's luck almost ran out when he was jumped by another prisoner who went by the nickname "Retro."

Whitey was bringing photos of Joe Carnes to Janus's art room when Retro, a well-known heroin addict, rushed him and stabbed him in the skull and neck with a homemade knife. The wounds were nearly fatal. Bulger was rushed to the prison infirmary, where doctors worked desperately to stop the bleeding. Somehow, even at the advanced age of eighty-four, Whitey was strong enough to survive the assault.

He stayed in the prison infirmary for more than a month while Retro was tossed into solitary confinement, which had been his goal. The attacker owed drug money to some prisoners in the yard and had no way to pay them. By trying to kill Bulger, he saved himself from a similar fate at the hands of the inmates he'd welched on.

"It's called a check-in move," Janus explained. "Retro attacked Bulger to get taken out of the yard, thrown into solitary, and out of his debt. He also knew that if he killed Whitey, he'd go down in history."

While Bulger was recovering from his stab wounds, he sent photos of Carnes to Chip Janus for reproduction.

"Somebody put them in my art teacher's locker," Janus recalls. "He also sent me a note telling me that he would be fine and for me to say hello to everyone. I laughed because he didn't have any friends—just me. But he was showing that he had the prison wired and that he could get things to me."

While in the infirmary, Bulger sought counseling from a female prison psychologist. He was falling into a deep depression as he longed for his girlfriend, who was still in prison thousands of miles away. Following her guilty plea, Catherine was sent to the Waseca Federal Correctional Institution, a low-security facility with 660 female inmates in Minnesota.

The young psychologist became intrigued by the aging, lovelorn gangster. The two spent hours together, according to Janus.

"I get to write to Catherine," Bulger told his friend after he was released from the prison hospital. "The psychologist came up with some brilliant story so I'd get to write to Catherine. I know the woman's grandmother. She was from South Boston."

Soon, someone at the Tucson prison complained about the relationship between Bulger and the staff member. Officials began investigating whether the psychologist slipped Whitey a cell phone that he used in prison and if she sold autographed photos that Bulger had given her.

"He was the master at charming people," Chip Janus recalled.

Prosecutor Brian Kelly agreed. "It's no surprise that he's been breaking the rules and trying to manipulate the system," Kelly said. "He's been doing that his whole life."

In Southie, Bulger was revered like some kind of god. He maintained that cult of personality while incarcerated in Arizona, where he regaled younger inmates like Chip with stories about Alcatraz and sweet-talked staffers into giving him special treatment. But Whitey could not rely on his fearsome reputation any longer. He needed to allow his advancing age to work in his favor. For prisoners and prison workers alike, any attention bestowed on them by a celebrated, old-school gangster such as Bulger was considered an honor.

He carried himself with an air of invincibility and his reputation preceded him, but he was also old and frail. The combination of his gangster cred, jailhouse celebrity, and frailty gave him some protection in Tucson, but what really kept him safe was that he was in a prison specifically designated by the Bureau of Prisons as a safe haven for high-profile informants. At Tucson he was far away from hard-core mobsters who would want to kill a rat like him. But before he could really grow his power behind the Arizona prison walls, officials shipped him off again, this time to a federal lockup in central Florida.

35

BULGER'S HEALTH STEADILY DETERIORATED SHORTLY after he was placed into the humid confines of the Coleman Federal Correctional Complex, a massive 555,000-square-foot facility about fifty miles northwest of Disney World in central Florida. The prison sits about ten miles outside the town of Coleman, which is known as the "Cabbage Capital of the World."

As in Tucson, Whitey was just one of several high-profile prisoners that now called Coleman home including Leonard Peltier, the Native American activist serving life in prison for murdering two FBI agents during a shootout in 1975, and Amine El Khalifi, an Al Qaeda supporter convicted of plotting to attack the US Capitol building by suicide bombing in 2012.

Bulger was housed in an adjacent complex known as Coleman II, which, like USP Tucson, was deemed safe for informants and gang members. Alone and isolated, he began to write his friend Chip Janus right away. The night terrors induced by LSD experiments he'd been subjected to in the 1960s were creeping back, making it impossible for him to get a good night's rest. At 12:18 a.m. on December 2, 2014, he picked up a pencil and crafted a letter to the prison art teacher in Tucson:

> *I prefer Tucson because of the yard time I enjoyed there and because it had the best art department of any place I've been. I have to give credit to the Native American artists. Marilyn Monroe seems to be their fa-*

vorite American icon. If I was an artist, I'd be doing pictures of American gangster[s] like N.Y Mobster + Bank Robber "Legs Diamond."

Whitey then got more serious about his physical condition and his legal battle, as he appeared confident that he'd one day get back in front of a jury to plead his case:

My health is going down hill—I'm now in a wheel chair and in intense pain—finally got x ray, [and was]told "you have arthritis." Fell down using walker, knocked out and cut head—took anti-biotics to knock out infection but pain is back . . . headaches . . . Hope to get to hospital sooner or later.

I'll receive new trial, my 2 [second] lawyer fighting for me via appeal—did not receive fair trial and not allowed to bring facts to jury plus witnesses against me who were facing the electric chair and death by lethal injection in O.K and Florida received big deal by Gov. [presumably Flemmi and Martorano before they agreed to testify against Bulger]. *All witnesses against me* [except for Flemmi] *are free + wealthy. Gov. let them keep their assets.*

Bulger promised to keep Janus up to date on his case.

At 85 years now, don't have too much more time—especially as every time I turn around something else is wrong with my health. Come what may, I consider I had a good life—a great family—and many adventures along the way.

I remain your friend always,

> *James Bulger (1428 AZ my lucky number those were the Good Old Days) Keep Smiling!*

Now wheelchair bound, Whitey could do nothing but reflect on his life of crime. His mind remained sharp, but his brittle body had robbed him of vitality and strength. While continuing to deny that he was a killer of women and an FBI informant, he never apologized for the path he chose. He was at peace with the idea that he could not outrun impending death, but was saddened with knowing that his version of events would never be fully told.

Bulger had been working on a manuscript about his life when he was captured in Santa Monica. The unfinished book was taken into evidence and its whereabouts are still unknown.

Instead, he continued to share his sordid tales with prisoners he paid to push him around the prison yard and fetch his breakfast and lunch.

"When I first saw Whitey, I didn't realize he was Whitey," former Coleman inmate Nate Lindell recalled. "He looked like a pale, white-haired geezer in a wheelchair. Probably a chomo [child molester], I thought. [I] Couldn't see him robbing a bank, killing people, or any other respectable crime."

According to Lindell, Bulger looked frail but always wore a scowl on his face as a repellent against those who might do him harm. The attack he survived in Tucson was still fresh in his mind, and his increasing headaches were most likely the result of the knife wound to his skull.

While his prison bodyguards managed successfully to shield Bulger, there were times that the crippled gangster was left alone.

One day while Whitey was napping in the prison yard, an inmate known for selling used shoes tried to steal his sneakers while they were still on his feet.

"Hey stop that," Nate Lindell shouted. "He ain't dead yet!"

The prisoners all laughed and Bulger went back to sleep.

Whitey was an easy mark at Coleman, and although he wasn't beaten up by the sneaker thief, the incident hurt his pride. Had the prisoner tried that even ten years earlier, he'd surely be dead. But Bulger was defenseless now. Even worse, he was a joke.

Bulger daydreamed about his former life as the most feared

gangster in Boston and as a young inmate at Alcatraz, a place where real criminals were treated with respect. He began corresponding with a writer named Michael Esslinger, who was working on a book chronicling the history of the Rock. Whitey was all too eager to chat about his "alma mater." But he also wrote Esslinger about his affection for Catherine.

"He deeply loved her. He wrote about her every time," said Esslinger. "He always communicated to me that he loved his life there [in Santa Monica] with Catherine . . . He looked back at it as the best days of his life."

Whitey also shared his feelings about Catherine in other letters to his friend Chip Janus, where he even stated that he was willing to die for her:

My woman—wife of 40 years met her when she was 23, I was 45—poor girl she has had a rough go of it. She's in prison in Waseca (MN)—she is an instructor for the "Paws Program" training dogs to be service dogs for the Handicapped and Autistic Children— one of the more worthwhile projects in prison—great utilization of prison man hours (womans—woman hours) She has moved up in the program—we write daily so she fills me in on how they train the dogs . . . Took 2 years and 11 months before we could write each other—tried to be considered common law husband + wife— Rejected in a country that recognizes "Same Sex Marriages!" . . . Don't know when ordeal ends for her . . . Will do the best I can to settle down. [I] want to live to see Catherine free when I am ready for the next and final stage.

Catherine had $100,000 for her reward and capture. Catherine + I on the run for 16 years that flew by too fast. We were together night + day and never had an argument or cross word. But years of our lives were taken from us after capture and both put in isolation. Her, no bail and had no police record . . . I offered if they would free

her that I'd plead guilty to all charges and will accept execution and
no appeal. I will opt for fast track for execution in one year (to save
them $$$ + time). She has never hurt anyone—her only crime was
loving me. They (prosecutors) refused.

By this time, Hollywood was gearing up for the anticipated re-
lease of the feature film *Black Mass*, a project that the real Whitey
Bulger wanted nothing to do with. The Warner Bros. movie
about the gangster's rise to power was filmed in the Boston area
in 2014. Director Scott Cooper chose to shoot in neighborhoods
like Dorchester and Cambridge, but never Southie out of respect
for victims' families. It wasn't that Whitey was completely against
the idea of a movie about his life, he just wanted it told his way: his
well-crafted story of a gentleman gangster who became a Robin
Hood–type figure for needy families in his beloved South Boston.
This image had been shattered at his trial as all of his dark truths
were revealed in court. Bulger had even invited Mark Wahlberg,
who'd costarred in *The Departed*, to visit him while he was behind
bars in Plymouth in the hope that the Dorchester-bred actor might
share his biased vision.

"He wants me to come down and visit him," Wahlberg said
during an interview with a Boston radio station at the time. "Maybe
he'll give me the exclusive rights to tell his story, 'cause ya know, we
do it better than anybody else."

But Wahlberg never pursued it, and another homegrown project
led by Ben Affleck and Matt Damon failed to get off the ground.
Bulger did allow recorded conversations with his lawyer Jay Carney
to be used in a documentary that was heavily slanted in his favor, as
it continued to float the balloon that he was never an FBI informant.

After *Black Mass* was released in theaters and then on DVD,
Bulger wrote Chip Janus once again to express his feelings about
the movie and its star:

(Depp) played John Dillinger in "Public Enemies," saw it and en-
joyed it—never saw "Black Mass"—have no desire—not at all
accurate—wish I had accepted (Depp's) offer to meet, felt I couldn't
or I'd look like I endorsed the picture—Hollywood and John Morris.
Will explain some day—too weary to begin. A Long Healthy Life
and Lots of Happiness.

Your friend—Jim Bulger 1428 AZ

Inside Coleman, far from the glitz and glamour of Hollywood, Whitey was subjected to humiliation after humiliation. First, an inmate had tried to steal his sneakers; next, he was placed in solitary confinement for allegedly masturbating in his cell. He was caught by a guard making his rounds at 3 a.m. Sexual activity of any kind was forbidden at the prison. Bulger claimed that he was innocent of the lewd offense. He told prison officials that he was applying medicated powder to his genitals to soothe an itch he was too embarrassed to report to the medical staff.

"I never had any charges like that in my whole life," Bulger stated in his disciplinary report. "I'm 85 years old. My sex life is over. I volunteer to take a polygraph test to prove my answer to this charge." As he wrote to Janus:

Frustrating to think I'm in a place where anyone can make an accu-
sation against you and it sticks. Never had this feeling before in any
prison—can't shake feeling that I'm somebody's target. Kind of a
mystery to me—Why? Revenge?

Prison officials didn't buy Whitey's excuse and placed him in solitary for thirty days, revoked his commissary privileges, and confiscated his personal property from his jail cell.

By early 2018, Bulger's health was getting worse. He was sitting each day in his cell trapped in a cage within a cage, slumped in a wheelchair, experiencing blackouts and dependent on nitroglycerin pills to keep his weak, damaged heart from exploding in his chest. Back in Tucson, Whitey had told his friend Chip Janus that he'd never allow himself to be in such condition and that he'd attack a guard and get himself shot instead of just fading slowly away.

THE BEGINNING OF THE END of Whitey's time in Coleman actually was in late February 2018. He had been living in a special housing unit there since April 19, 2017.

On February 23, 2018, he was living in a first-floor cell in special housing and paid regular visits to the prison's assistant health services administrator, Shanna Mezyk. At 8:45 a.m. that day, he was taken to the medical office complaining of chest pains. Mezyk checked his vital signs and performed a cardiac test. It was clear to her that Whitey was experiencing severe cardiac complications.

"We need to bring you to the prison emergency room," the nurse told him.

But for some unknown reason, Bulger refused to go.

"You're treating me like a dog," he complained. "You'll have your day of reckoning and you will pay for this. I know people and my word is good!"

Mezyk reported the threat to Coleman warden Charles Lockett, who was not only her boss, but also a close friend.

Whitey was charged with a "299"—making an implied threat to an employee. It was a less severe charge than a "203," which is when an inmate makes a direct threat to harm or kill a staffer.

Bulger claimed that Mezyk was lying. He told Coleman officials that he asked the nurse to supply him with a long-sleeved shirt for the visit to the ER and that Mezyk started harassing him over it. He argued that the "day of reckoning" comment meant that she was inducing him to have a massive heart attack because she was yelling at him so much.

"It was all blown out of proportion," Whitey argued. "I didn't threaten her."

Bulger was found guilty of the violation on March 16, 2018, and sentenced to thirty days in "DS"—disciplinary segregation. The punishment was pretty standard, but what wasn't standard was what happened next.

After the thirty days were up, Lockett kept Bulger in the disciplinary segregation unit for the rest of his stay at Coleman. On April 10, 2018, the warden tried to have Whitey transferred out of Coleman, but the request was denied by the Bureau of Prisons central office in Washington, DC.

At the time, Bulger was classified as a "high-risk" inmate—the highest possible classification—while his medical classification was "Care Level 3," which is the second highest. According to the Bureau of Prisons, Care Level 3 inmates are "fragile outpatients who require frequent clinical contacts, and/or who may require some assistance with activities of daily living . . . (and) may require periodic hospitalization." Bulger, then eighty-eight, had suffered several heart attacks, was in a wheelchair, used a respirator to breathe, and required almost daily visits from medical staff.

Still, on October 8, 2018, a month after his eighty-ninth birthday, Whitey was mysteriously switched to the lower "Medical Care Level 2." The BOP defines this class as "those who are stable outpatients, requiring at least quarterly clinician evaluation. Examples of such conditions are medication-controlled diabetes, epilepsy, and emphysema."

Warden Lockett claimed that Bulger's health had "dramatically improved" despite his suffering from aortic stenosis, prostate bladder issues, and high blood pressure. After his medical care level was lowered, his transfer to US Penitentiary Hazelton, located 911 miles away in Bruceton Mills, West Virginia, was approved. Joe Rojas, president of the union that represents USP Coleman correctional officers, said there was no valid reason for the transfer since Coleman has all the medical facilities Bulger required.

Furthermore, if Whitey was going to be transferred, he should have gone to the United States Medical Center for Federal Prisoners in Springfield, Missouri, or USP Terre Haute in Indiana—not Hazelton.

In the federal prison system, child predators and rats are generally restricted to three prisons known in the BOP as "The Triangle": USP Coleman, USP Tucson, and USP Terre Haute. Whitey had already been to two of those.

Inmates who have problems at one of the prisons in "The Triangle" are normally moved to one of the other two. For example, convicted child molester Larry Nassar, who systematically molested Olympic and college gymnasts for decades, was the target of threats and assaults at Tucson, so he was moved to Coleman.

"Those inmates can only go in certain institutions," says Rojas, president of the American Federation of Government Employees Local 506 at Coleman. "Hazelton is one of the most violent prisons in our agency. And at Hazelton, you have a lot of mob guys there."

Regardless, on October 23, 2018, Whitey was moved to the Oklahoma City Federal Transfer Center, where he was held for six days in the special segregation unit. Six days later, on October 29, 2018, he was transferred to Hazelton, a prison so riddled with violence that it earned the name "Misery Mountain."

36

WHILE WHITEY WAS PREPARING FOR the transfer to West
Virginia, notorious Springfield, Massachusetts, Mafia enforcer Fotios "Freddy" Geas was spending his days at
Hazelton, calling shots in the prison yard as one of the most feared
gangsters in a penitentiary filled with killers.

Freddy never really operated in Whitey's world of Southie,
Charlestown, and Boston's North End because there are clear juris-
dictional lines in the organized crime underworld between Boston
and Springfield. In the Mafia hierarchy, Springfield falls under the
jurisdiction of the Genovese crime family out of New York City,
unlike Boston, which answers to the Patriarca mob or what's left
of it in Providence, Rhode Island. It's an odd setup, as Springfield
is a much smaller and more rural city, but it has historically had far
more Mafia clout than Boston.

With 150,000 residents, Springfield is the fourth largest city in
New England behind Boston, Worcester, and Providence. It has
a rich history, as it was the birthplace of basketball, the American dictionary, the motorcycle, and the gun. The first American
musket and rifle were manufactured in Springfield, and today the
city is home to the headquarters of global firearms maker Smith &
Wesson.

Like so many troubled cities in the Northeast, economic down-
turns and the defection of industry overseas hit post–World War II
Springfield particularly hard. Massive manufacturing buildings were

abandoned, leaving behind blocks and blocks of vacant buildings and urban blight. In the shadows of these crumbling edifices, a ruthless black market run by the Mafia thrived in the 1970s, '80s, and '90s. Bookmaking, prostitution, drug dealing, strong-arming, loan-sharking, political corruption, violence, and murder became big business, all controlled by the New York mob.

Freddy Geas and his younger brother Ty seized upon this opportunity. Despite their Greek heritage, the brothers became feared hit men for the Italian mob. The brothers could never be made men as they weren't Sicilian, but the Genovese capos needed muscle in Springfield to enforce their rackets and no one was better suited for the job than the feared Geas brothers.

Born in Springfield, Freddy was the oldest of three brothers. He moved to Huntington Beach, California, with his father when he was in seventh grade. A couple of months later, they were joined by Freddy's mother and his two brothers, Ty and Tom. Freddy had long, blond hair as a kid and fit right in with the surfing culture in Huntington Beach. He skateboarded and surfed, wore Vans slip-ons, loved fishing, and raved about the burgers on the boardwalk. Later, the family moved back to Springfield and Freddy's parents split up. Their mother abandoned the family and they never heard from her again.

Freddy's father ran a family diamond importing business, which Freddy helped run. Once back in Springfield and with their mom gone, Freddy and Ty immersed themselves in the seedy underbelly of the Mafia-infested western Massachusetts city. Their brother, Tom, joined the Marines.

"My uncle and aunt had a jewelry store," Freddy told the authors in an October 2019 letter. "We had a few wiseguys that shopped at the store and were also friends with my family so I got into moving football parlay cards and knock off merchandise at school.

"The money was easy," he continued. "The guys were serious

and I liked the lifestyle . . . Life was pretty easy. On the one hand
you're dealing with lowlifes and [on the other] all the other normal
people. [It was] very easy to separate the two."

Freddy and Ty built rap sheets that were impressive from a young
age. Ty was sentenced to a year in jail after shooting a weapon into
the air during a brawl at a high school hockey game. He was just
seventeen. Freddy too picked up a felony conviction for that brawl,
for threatening to kill a witness to the mayhem. He was twenty-
two years old at the time.

That same year, Freddy picked up another assault conviction for
destroying an antique car during a melee at a Springfield nightclub
called Sh-Booms. Freddy was charged with beating a cop in 1990,
was nabbed in a 1996 truck heist, and went to jail for a pair of brutal
baseball bat beatings. Ty got a year in jail in 2006 for bludgeoning
a man at Mardi Gras, a sketchy strip club in a run-down section of
downtown Springfield that served as the crew's headquarters.

Between the two brothers, they racked up more than seventy-
five criminal arraignments and had been in and out of jail most of
their adult lives.

Much like Whitey Bulger's stranglehold on Southie, the Geas
brothers lorded over the Springfield underworld of pimps, drug
dealers, triggermen, and thieves. You crossed the brothers at your
own peril and with the knowledge that they were feared enforcers
for the Genovese crime family, serving at the pleasure of Springfield
capo Anthony Arillotta and New York mob boss Artie "The Little
Guy" Nigro.

Freddy's ranking with the Genovese family was well-known
among thugs and cops and his toughness went unchallenged. One
night at Mardi Gras, he was holding court with a room filled with
members of the Latin Kings gang. It was well past closing time—
around 3 a.m.—yet the drinks continued to flow and the nude
women continued to dance. A bouncer named Leo discreetly ap-

proached Freddy, and whispered to him, "Hey Freddy, man, I hate to break this up, but I have a baseball game with my son at 8 a.m. tomorrow. Think we could wrap it up so I can get home?"

Freddy looked at the bouncer and nodded.

"Not a problem, Leo," he said.

Freddy stood up from his seat, put his hands up, and announced to the group of gangbangers that the party was over.

"Time to go, guys. I gotta get Leo out of here. He's got an early Little League game with his son. Let's go. Out," Freddy said.

And just like that, the gangbangers dispersed. The room was cleared. That was the kind of respect that Freddy had in Springfield. He had the reputation of being a gentleman's gangster. He was a criminal to the core, but he respected civilians—like Leo—and honored those who were outside of their world trying to provide for their families.

To the outside world, Freddy is a bloodthirsty mob killer and career criminal doing life for two slayings, including the November 23, 2003, execution of Springfield mob boss Alfredo "Big Al" Bruno. Bruno was gunned down outside a Springfield social club on the orders of Nigro, which were carried out by Freddy, Ty, Arillotta, and Springfield mob capo Felix Tranghese. With the New York mob's blessing, the brothers hired the gunman, a low-level mobster named Frankie Roche, to execute Bruno so Arillotta and the Geas brothers could take over the Springfield mob.

In between all the brutality and murders, Freddy fought for a semblance of life balance.

He met his wife, Tracy, on a blind date. They married and had a son, Alex, and daughter, Taylor, but, as his criminal record grew and he was behind bars more and more, the relationship fell apart. They divorced in 2003, when Taylor was ten.

"My parents had the funniest divorce of all divorces," Taylor Geas tells the authors in an exclusive interview. "They drove to the courthouse together, and then went to grab breakfast afterward."

The couple remained friendly and continued to have breakfast together regularly to catch up on the kids, in between Freddy's jail stretches.

"They loved us, and so nothing else really mattered," Taylor says. "We were their common ground. They put their differences aside because they both agreed that Al and I were the best things to ever happen to them."

Taylor and Alex grew up in Connecticut with their mother, who remarried in 2006. Both graduated from college and Taylor credits their dad—despite his dark side—with keeping them on the right path.

"The reason Al and I are the way we are is because although many people don't believe my dad is a good man, there's no denying that he's always been a good father," she said. "And that's why, plain and simple, my brother and I turned out the way we did."

She has fond memories of him taking them to the North End in Boston as kids to get pastries and to her first Red Sox game, where he transformed Taylor—then a Connecticut-raised Yankees fan— into a Red Sox fan. He even got her to partake in an obligatory "Yankees Suck" Fenway Park chant. They sat near Boston's famed "Pesky Pole," named for Red Sox Hall-of-Famer Johnny Pesky, and caught a foul ball.

"It was always about the little things with my dad. It never took much to make him happy," she recalls. "We had our routines together, but even the ordinary and everyday things were better with him."

Taylor didn't know about her father's mob connections, though. To her, he was just a doting dad who was at every one of her softball games and loved taking them out for impromptu junk-food sprees at Burger King. While he was in and out of jail for most of her life, she was always told as a kid that he wasn't around because he was in the army. There were, though, occasional hints of her dad's violent streak.

At one of her softball games when she was in her early teens, there was a loudmouthed third-base coach for the opposing team. Taylor was pitching and the coach kept taunting her. Freddy was in the stands and had had enough. Stocky and in tip-top physical condition, Freddy stormed across the field to the third-base box and stood right behind the coach. The coach had no idea who Freddy was but knew he was in a pickle.

Freddy leaned toward him and said, loudly, "I'm gonna put you in a fucking coma if you don't shut the fuck up."

The game stopped. The opposing team had no idea what was going on. The stands were silent. The coach stood still, having no clue how close he had come to hospitalization or worse. Freddy walked back to the stands, sat down, and play resumed. No one said a word.

In 2008, the Geas brothers along with Arillotta were charged with extortion for shaking down mobbed-up nightclub owners' lucrative illegal poker machines. The case was an appetizer to squeeze witnesses as prosecutors built a murder indictment for the hit on Big Al Bruno.

In 2009, the Bruno murder and a laundry list of other violent crimes were bundled into a sweeping federal RICO racketeering indictment by the US attorney in the Southern District of New York. In all, nine Springfield mobsters and members of the Genovese family, including Freddy and Ty, were charged in a spectacular case that blew open Mafia secrets.

In addition to Bruno's killing, the brothers were charged with executing Arillotta's drug pusher brother-in-law, Gary D. Westerman, because they believed he was talking to the feds. It was Freddy who pumped two bullets into Westerman's head in November 2003 and the gang buried him in an eight-foot grave in the woods. Arillotta, who flipped on the Geas brothers during the 2011 federal trial in New York, testified that Freddy dug the grave weeks earlier in preparation for the inevitable burial of an unspecified rival, but no one knew who it was going to be until Westerman's corpse was tossed in.

The night after the killing, Freddy, Ty, and Arillotta went to Morton's Steakhouse in Hartford to celebrate. After dinner, they drove back by the burial site and Freddy laughed, joked, and sang mockingly about the murder.

"Freddy started singing 'On top of Old Smokey . . . all covered in blood,'" Arillotta testified.

Westerman's remains were not recovered for seven years until Arillotta led law enforcement to the rural burial site.

Taylor Geas recalls learning about the federal RICO indictment and her father's arrest in Florida the night she was set to emcee her high school senior variety show. She was now wise to the fact that her father wasn't in the army, but instead was a soldier for the mob.

"I thought it was going to be totally fine," she said. "He'd been in and out all the time when I was a kid."

But it wasn't fine. Freddy, Ty, and Nigro were convicted in 2011 on the RICO case, including both murders and the attempted murder of a mobbed-up union boss, largely based on the testimony of Arillotta. All three were sentenced to life without parole. Arillotta cut a deal and served just eight years, while Tranghese, who also flipped on the Geas brothers, served just four. Roche, the gunman who executed Bruno, also testified against the brothers, and Nigro and was sentenced to fourteen years.

Prosecutors said Arillotta wrestled with flipping on the brothers and tried to tell them to turn informant to spare themselves from life in prison.

"Arillotta appeared to take no pleasure from cooperating against people he claimed as some of his closest friends," prosecutors wrote in court filings. "Arillotta thereafter repeatedly expressed disappointment at the fact that his former friends—the Geases in particular—were not pleading guilty because he did not want to see them spend the rest of their lives in jail."

The Geas brothers' New York attorney, Frederick Cohn, re-called some "tense" fighting between Freddy and Ty during the trial.

"Freddy was very pleasant to me. His brother was very diffi-cult," Cohn said. "And he was difficult for Freddy to control. I think Freddy tried to keep him under control in Springfield but was not totally successful.

"Freddy never expected much from the trial. We knew it was severely uphill," Cohn, who retired shortly after the case, contin-ued. "Really, once [prosecutors] decided they weren't going to go for the death penalty for him, it was pretty much written in the sky that he was going to go away forever. I can't say he was alright with it, but it was part of the game. That whole old school mafia thing . . . These guys expected to die in the street or in jail."

Freddy shook Cohn's hand at the end of the trial that sealed his fate. He still occasionally sends Cohn Christmas cards.

"He was always respectful," Cohn said. "I don't recall that we ever had a disagreement. I had generally a good feeling about him. I wouldn't want to stand between him and a big profit, though, if he had a weapon."

Just like Kevin Weeks, Pat Nee, and John Martorano, Arillotta is a free man after being released from prison in 2017. He was of-fered the Witness Protection Program but declined and moved back to Springfield, where he hasn't exactly kept a low profile. In July 2019, while still on federal probation, Arillotta was charged with making threats and assault and battery with a dangerous weapon for allegedly throwing a carton of lemonade at a female relative, striking her in the leg, during a dispute over a dog.

For Taylor Geas, the conviction was devastating. She was just twenty-three years old and her dad was going away forever. A few days after her dad's conviction was splashed across the front page of the Springfield newspaper, she wrote an emotional piece portraying a different side of him.

"When I'm sitting across the table from him during our visits I don't see a monster, I see a flawed man that's paying for the choices he made," she wrote. "The person I know is the father that would tuck me in at night, and tell me funny stories until I fell asleep. He was the person that taught me how to throw a baseball, and got me my first pair of soccer cleats."

Taylor believes her father refused to flip on his codefendants to protect her and her brother Alex from possible retribution from mobsters.

"When the government offered him the option to become an informant, he didn't because of us," she says. "The hardest thing he's ever had to do was make the decision to not be in our lives anymore. And people think he did this because he's a thug who swears by the code, but his loyalty lies with us before anybody else. And so he made the decision to spend the rest of his life in federal prison so that Al and I could lead normal lives. Because of him, we don't have to live looking over our shoulders."

The brothers headed off to the catacombs inside the federal prison system. But Freddy Geas's greatest mob hit was still to come.

FREDDY AND TY GEAS WERE originally sent to a federal prison together in Kentucky, but their shared incarceration didn't last long. In 2012, they were split up after they brutally attacked and bludgeoned a child molester. Taylor recalls that she didn't hear from her dad for six months after the incident because he was in solitary. While Ty stayed in Kentucky, Freddy was moved to Hazelton.

Because of his Mafia status and brutal reputation, Freddy became a shot-caller at Hazelton, meaning he was a top gang leader in a unit filled with killers and gangsters. While the Springfield and Boston mobsters worked separately on the outside, inside the walls of Hazelton, mobsters from both territories stuck together. And there were plenty of Massachusetts gangsters on Freddy's unit for him to join forces with, including several who had been betrayed by Bulger.

One was New England Mafia boss "Cadillac Frank" Salemme, who was sent to Hazelton briefly following his 2018 conviction in the unsolved 1993 murder of Steven DiSarro, owner of The Channel rock club in South Boston.

Salemme and his son, Francis P. Salemme Jr., were silent partners in the club and DiSarro was killed because Salemme believed he was talking to the FBI. Flemmi had also testified at Salemme's 2018 trial that he walked into Salemme's home in Sharon, Massachusetts, and saw the younger Salemme and another Boston mobster, Paul Weadick, strangling DiSarro. DiSarro's body was buried behind a Providence mill, where it was unearthed in 2016 thanks to an FBI tip.

Weadick was also convicted of the slaying and served time in Hazelton with Freddy. The younger Salemme died in 1995. Weadick has said he and Freddy were friends at Hazelton.

Another mobster Freddy befriended was Frederick Weichel, a South Boston man who was framed by Bulger for the murder of Robert LaMonica, who was gunned down in a parking lot outside his apartment in Braintree, Massachusetts, in 1980. Weichel believed that Whitey had set him up for a fall by giving his name to authorities.

Freddy Geas and Weichel became close in prison in Massachusetts and the Springfield mobster couldn't stomach the idea that his friend had spent thirty-six years locked up for a crime he didn't commit.

"We were at (Massachusetts Correctional Institution) Shirley together, talked every day," Freddy told the authors of this book in a January 26, 2020, letter from USP Hazelton. "Nice guy."

Freddy said Weichel would have him "grab friends" in the Massachusetts prison to stand watch while Weichel worked out in the prison yard in the "sub-arctic" weather.

He said he has lost touch with Weichel but was glad to hear he was exonerated.

"The last time I was with him he was in court so I hope he has made it home," Freddy wrote.

Freddy's longtime attorney and friend, Daniel Kelly, said Freddy spoke to him of the injustice of Weichel's conviction.

"He referenced that [Weichel] was framed," Kelly said. "Freddy was a stand-up guy, the last of the Mohicans."

A friend of Weichel's even wrote Whitey a letter in prison, begging him to do the right thing and provide an affidavit or sworn testimony that Weichel was innocent. Bulger flat-out refused and denied that he was the one who fingered Weichel for the 1980 murder:

I have never testified against any man, have never caused any man to be put in prison. I too have been falsely accused.

Whitey did reveal that he knew the identity of the real killer but wouldn't give up any other information:

I won't name him—or force him, just as I choose not to tell the truth in my own trial about certain incidents even though the guilty lied— Strange perhaps but that's what I felt the thing to do—Keep Silent in a Corrupt Trial. No Regets, JB (James Bulger).

Despite a lack of cooperation from Whitey, a judge later overturned Frederick Weichel's conviction and granted his freedom in April 2017.

Despite his friend's freedom, Freddy Geas wanted Bulger to pay for his betrayal, but he never thought he'd get the opportunity to exact his own brand of justice on the notorious gangster turned FBI informant.

Instead, Geas had to manage the tribal politics inside "Misery

Mountain," where inmates are classified by race and gang affilia-
tion. Top-echelon gangsters like Freddy helped to organize crime
within the prison walls and negotiate disputes between bloodthirsty
gangs such as MS-13, the Bloods, the Crips, and the Latin Kings.

The daily routine and dangers of Hazelton wore heavily on
Freddy, but somehow he always remained upbeat when talking
with his daughter, Taylor. He called and wrote his kids often and
they visited him a few times a year.

The regular contact would soon be disrupted as Freddy Geas,
the relatively unknown enforcer from western Massachusetts,
would soon become a key figure in the history of organized crime
in America.

37

Whook Whitey Bulger was transferred to Hazelton, he was wheeled into a powder keg of bureaucratic dysfunction and violence.

The notorious penitentiary already had two murders in 2018 and was in the midst of a staffing crisis that pitted the correctional officers' union in a nasty battle against Warden Joseph Coakley. The prison's problems were national news as the dispute made its way all the way to the White House.

Opened in 2004 in Bruceton Mills, West Virginia, a tiny rural town of just eighty-five residents in the northeast corner of the state, Hazelton came with a $129 million price tag and is the second largest federal prison in the country. With 1,300 hardened criminals prowling its six buildings and sprawling yards, it's got a long history of violence that led to its nickname, "Misery Mountain."

Within the federal prison system, Hazelton is well-known as a place not safe for two types of inmates: pedophiles and informants. Violent attacks are a daily occurrence, and murders don't raise many eyebrows.

In October 2007, an inmate named Jesse Harris was stabbed to death by two inmates serving life sentences. In December 2009, Jimmy Lee Wilson, a twenty-five-year-old serving eleven years for armed robbery, was killed during a race-fueled brawl involving at least five other inmates. In 2017, the year before Whitey arrived, there were 275 reported violent incidents, which was up 15 percent from the previous year.

Besides the hiring freeze, the Trump administration ordered the federal Bureau of Prisons to eliminate six thousand unfilled positions. The cuts slashed more than 1,800 correctional officers' positions nationwide, including 127 at Hazelton.

The result at Hazelton was that Warden Coakley started shifting regular prison employees from their normal duties to work behind the walls in units. The practice, known as "augmentation," only added more stress to an already stressful and dangerous environment. The situation was at a breaking point in early 2018 as the officers' union took their complaints to Washington.

"With less corrections officers in the prisons, BOP has turned to augmentation . . . which means that cooks, foremen, secretaries, electricians, teachers, accountants, or counselors are augmented to replace officers inside the prison," David Cox, president of the American Federation of Government Employees, which represents federal correctional officers, said in February 2018. "Augmentation can result in one correctional worker supervising hundreds of dangerous prisoners, including terrorists, gangs, and murderers inside each facility with no backup."

As the staffing and overtime crisis took root, Coakley began putting only one officer on duty in units, in defiance of congressional mandates, angering the officers' union. Besides endangering the officers, single-staffed units meant fewer inmate shakedowns and searches and more opportunity for prisoners to hide weapons and cause chaos.

There was incentive for Warden Coakley to keep overtime costs down: he and other federal wardens and BOP administrators were raking in hefty bonuses for controlling costs. The Bureau of Prisons shelled out $1.6 million in bonuses to executives and wardens in 2017 and 2018, and Coakley himself raked in more than $50,000 in bonuses from 2015 through 2018.

On February 25, 2018, Representative David McKinley, a West Virginia Republican whose district includes Hazelton, led a bipartisan effort that sought to force the Trump administration to hire more correctional officers. McKinley and fifty other members of Congress fired off a letter to Trump's then–attorney general Jeff Sessions to reinstate the six thousand positions that were on the chopping block.

"We must address the staffing crisis our corrections officers face before the safety in our prisons deteriorates further. Inadequate staffing creates dangerous conditions for our officers and our communities," McKinley wrote. "Our prison guards have never failed us when we've called them to duty. They risk their lives every day they enter these dangerous prisons to protect our communities from hardened criminals."

Regardless, the troubled prison's officer ranks were severely depleted as the hiring freeze wasn't lifted. Down more than ninety officers, COs at Hazelton were being forced to work overtime shifts, sometimes as many as three in a row. It wasn't uncommon for correctional officers to work double shifts with no sleep.

The troubles would only worsen. The prison was locked down nine times in 2018 for violence and weapons incidents. Five officers were attacked. Already overburdened officers were reaching their breaking point when a pair of inmate killings escalated tensions. On April 2, 2018, Ian Thorne, a forty-eight-year-old Washington, DC, heroin dealer serving twenty years for orchestrating a prison murder, was killed by two shank-wielding inmates. A few months later, on September 17, 2018, Demario Porter, a twenty-seven-year-old who was serving a two-year sentence for probation violations, was killed by another inmate. Porter, who was charged at age sixteen in the 2007 slaying of an elderly barber in Washington, DC, had been at Hazelton for only two weeks.

In a letter to Congress sent on October 10, 2018—just two weeks before Whitey was sent to Misery Mountain—the Hazelton correctional officers' union pleaded for more resources and expressed fears that cuts were going to lead to bloodshed. Justin Tarovisky, a former college football player who headed the Hazelton correctional officers' union, warned Congress that Coakley's cost-cutting moves posed "significant danger," especially the decision to single-staff units. The move, the union argued, directly violated Congress's 2016 funding bill, which stated: "All BOP high security institutions would have at least two correctional officers on duty in each housing unit for all three shifts."

"The staff at FCC Hazelton can no longer afford to stand by and let this particular administration place them in perilous situations," Tarovisky wrote. "The administration at FCC Hazelton has cultivated an atmosphere amongst all supervisors that places miniscule [sic] savings (what they believe to be cost-saving measures) over the safety and well-being of all staff working at this complex."

Just five days before Whitey arrived, five lawmakers responded swiftly to the union's call. US Senators Pat Toomey and Robert P. Casey Jr. of Pennsylvania and Joe Manchin III and Shelley Moore Capito of West Virginia, along with US Representative Bill Shuster, a Republican from Pennsylvania, wrote a letter to Sessions urging him to address "dangerous staffing issues" at federal prisons in both states.

The letter referenced the Thorne and Porter murders, as well as the brutal 2013 murder of Correctional Officer Eric Williams at USP Canaan in Pennsylvania. Williams, thirty-four, was just two hours away from the end of his shift and was working a unit at Canaan alone when he was ruthlessly set upon by a Mexican Mafia member named Jessie Con-ui. Williams was savagely shoved down a set of stairs by Con-ui, who pulled out two homemade shanks and stabbed the officer more than two hundred times. Dozens of inmates did nothing as they watched the sickening eleven-minute attack, which was caught on video.

Congress boosted the BOP's $7 billion federal prison budget by

$106 million in 2018 to address "dangerous continual understaffing," but the agency was still not increasing full-time hires, the lawmakers said.

"We are writing to express our deep concerns about the Bureau of Prisons' (BOP) staffing practices . . . and the failure to follow clear congressional directives to hire more full-time correctional officers," the October 25, 2018, letter states.

In September 2018, Taylor Geas, her mother, and brother traveled to Hazelton to visit Freddy. He normally didn't talk much about his case or his appeals, but on this visit, he was upbeat and chatty about the potential of his appeal because another inmate he knew had just beat a case for which he was serving 140 years.

They talked about Taylor's new job, and Freddy talked about the model airplane-building class he was teaching at Hazelton.

"He looked really good, looked like he was in good shape," Taylor remembers. "He had looked old and tired and stressed in the past. Every time we go, we talk like he's coming home, for his own sanity. He was telling us not to lose hope."

In June 2018, just a few months before Bulger was transferred to Hazelton from Coleman, he told author Michael Esslinger that he missed being at the Tucson prison and preferred it to Coleman.

"He seemed to be at odds with the conditions there [at Coleman]," Esslinger recalled.

It was one of the last known missives from Whitey, and the frail ex–crime lord said he hoped that he'd one day be reunited with Catherine.

"He talked about Catherine and his hopes that when she got out, that he'd be able to see her again, that she could come visit him," Esslinger said. "He said she was the love of his life for sure."

Whitey wouldn't get his wish, as his fate would soon be sealed at Misery Mountain.

38

WHEN WHITEY BULGER ENTERED HAZELTON, he was a far cry from the muscled and menacing gangster who controlled Southie for decades. He wasn't even the fit-for-his-age old man who groused and was combative during his trial. He was now an invalid, and the Bureau of Prisons higher-ups, including Warden Coakley, threw him to the lions.

At 9:17 a.m. on October 29, 2018, Bulger was transported from the Oklahoma City federal prison transfer center. Even though he was there for only a short period of time, he was kept in a segregated unit during his stay.

At 6:45 p.m., he arrived at Hazelton. He was wheeled off a prison bus and brought into "intake," where his case file was reviewed and he was assigned a cell in general population, despite the fact that the unit was filled with Italian Mafia members and associates, including several from Massachusetts.

"They sent him to the worst open yard," said Joe Rojas, head of the USP Coleman correctional officers' union. "This is an open yard with a lot of mobsters walking around, from Boston, Philly, and New York. Of course, Whitey Bulger walks in, they must have been drooling."

After dusk, at 8:35 p.m., Whitey was assigned to unit 229L—on the second tier of the unit—in a cell with Paul J. "Little Paulie" DeCologero, a Boston mobster serving twenty-five years for racketeering and conspiring to kill a nineteen-year-old woman named

Aislin Silva. The DeCologero crew made its money selling drugs and kidnapping and robbing dealers, among other rackets. They were based in Burlington, Massachusetts, a toney suburb north of Boston, and the crew was run by DeCologero's uncle, Paul A. "Big Paulie" DeCologero, who ran drugs briefly for Whitey and Flemmi in the 1980s.

The gang answered to Providence's Patriarca mob and was involved in a beef in the 1990s between Whitey's rival, "Cadillac Frank" Salemme, and another Italian crew trying to muscle in on Salemme's Boston rackets. The elder DeCologero stopped running drugs for the Winter Hill Gang after he got out of prison in 1992, which "irked the mob leaders." The dispute led Whitey to put out a contract on "Big Paulie."

"Little Paulie" was among several members of the crew rounded up in 2001 in a racketeering case that included the infamous—and gruesome—Silva killing. It was "Big Paulie" who made the call to kill the attractive blonde in November 1996 because they feared she'd rat out the gang after a cache of guns was found in the apartment she shared with one of the mobsters. First, they planned to give her a fatal "hotshot" of heroin by telling her it was "good cocaine." When that failed, she was taken to an apartment by three gang members who broke her neck, chopped her up with hacksaws, and dumped her remains behind an elementary school. Her remains weren't found for ten years.

"Little Paulie" had a cell at Hazelton just a few doors down from Freddy Geas, who was in number 219L. But because Bulger was in a wheelchair, he couldn't be housed on the second tier, so "Little Paulie" and Freddy wouldn't have their chance to meet the notorious crime lord that night. At 9:53 p.m., Whitey was sent to cell 132L on the first level of the 120-man unit.

Normally, inmates are segregated by race, but Bulger, an avowed racist, was assigned to bunk with a black inmate named Felix Wilson. A mentally ill, thirty-five-year-old Buffalo man, Wilson was serving a thirty-month sentence for a gun rap. He had a history of violence and was stabbed in the neck in Buffalo in May 2011. That same month, he was convicted of attempted robbery, which prohibited him from carrying a firearm. On August 22, 2013, he was riding his bike on a Buffalo street when he was stopped by police and arrested for being a felon illegally carrying a .22-caliber handgun.

As Whitey was wheeled into the unit, the tiers were abuzz with news of the latest celebrity inmate. Word spread fast among the criminals and convicted killers.

"The minute they saw Bulger, I'm sure they couldn't believe it. He's known as a snitch," Rojas said.

"Hazelton is a yard where they don't accept that," added Justin Tarovisky, head of the Hazelton correctional officers' union. "There's a code. If they think you're a child predator or you've cooperated with law enforcement, they'll put a hit on you.

"They're gonna get you. That's the code of the yard. It's a city of criminals. It's hard to prevent that," he said.

Whitey entered the cell and would never leave again. He and Wilson went to sleep for the night. The cell doors opened automatically at 5 a.m. for the start of the prison day, as they do every day. Shortly thereafter, Wilson left the cell. Sometime around 6 a.m., Freddy Geas and "Little Paulie" were seen on video going into Bulger's cell.

At some point before Wilson returned to his cell, Whitey was beaten to death with padlocks stuffed into tube socks. The "lock in a sock" was a common Hazelton killing tool.

The killers swung their makeshift weapons against Bulger's head as he lay in his bunk.

Whitey Bulger must have sensed trouble. He must have shown fear. As he gazed up at his attackers, the look in his pale blue eyes must have been similar to the startled gazes of his many victims when they realized they were staring into the face of the reaper.

The killers continued their attack as they beat Bulger without mercy across his body and head. Whitey's face was bashed in and his eyes were swollen shut. The weighted socks were smeared with his blood.

The tough-guy gangster who executed at will, strangled women, ordered hits like he was ordering lunch, strong-armed bookies, and pumped his beloved South Boston full of drugs that ended lives and destroyed families died helplessly and without putting up any fight. He wanted it quick—and he got it quick.

Bulger's killers slipped out of his cell as quietly as they had come.

There were reports that the killers tried to gouge out his eyes and cut out his tongue—a ruthless tactic used to send a message to rats. But according to a prison source who viewed the corpse, Whitey's body was not mutilated in any way, though Bulger's eyes were so swollen shut that it looked as if he had no eyes at all.

Felix Wilson returned to his cell after the murder and found Whitey covered with a blanket in his bed. He cleaned up the cell and threw several items into the garbage, which was put out with the morning trash. The trash from the cell was taken away and thrown into the prison's incinerator, destroying any potential physical evidence of the killing.

Wilson didn't alert the guards to his cellmate's violent demise and Whitey lay dead in his prison bed until around 8:21 a.m., when an officer walking around the unit called in to the cell and got no response. He went in and discovered the mobster's brutally beaten and lifeless body in the bed. Medical staff was called to the cell and Whitey Bulger was pronounced dead at 9:04 a.m.

He was wheeled out and taken to a triage unit while the coroner was called. The prison's internal special investigations unit was called in. The former public enemy number one, who made global headlines when his sixteen-year flight from justice ended at Princess Eugenia Apartments in Santa Monica seven years earlier, lay deceased on a slab, clad only in his prison-issued boxers.

He had welts from the beating on his chest and his face was unrecognizable. There was a little blood trickling from his left eye, but no other blood. The medical staff tried to open his eyes to check his pupils but were unable due to the swelling.

A year before the murder, Whitey had written a letter to his old Alcatraz pal Charlie Hopkins and said he was tired of hospitals. He said he hoped he would die peacefully at Coleman.

"I prefer to stay here and hope to get a peaceful death," he wrote. "One of those he Died in his Sleep kind."

His death certificate listed his cause of death as "blunt force injuries of the head" as a result of "assault by other(s)."

News of Bulger's murder broke quickly, and the media began scrambling to report the details of how Boston's most infamous crime figure was killed. It didn't take long before Freddy Geas and "Little Paulie" DeCologero were named as suspects.

Both were dyed-in-the-wool mobsters convicted of crimes connected to La Cosa Nostra. Both lived by the gangster's code. Freddy Geas hated rats more than anything. This was personal for him. He knew that Whitey was the cold-blooded liar who put an innocent man—Fred Weichel—in prison for most of his life. Both Geas and DeCologero hailed from the brutal criminal underworld of Massachusetts and were lifers at Hazelton. What both understood more than anything else was that if they killed Whitey Bulger, they would be heroes to the Mafia and gangster legends inside and outside prison walls. When their names were mentioned anywhere, they would be known as the ones who killed Whitey Bulger.

In the end, it wasn't the FBI or Flemmi or Weeks or Martorano or Pat Nee or anyone else who was responsible for Whitey's death. He was responsible for his death. It was gangster karma, payback for a lifetime of deception and lying that cost countless people their lives. There has perhaps never been a starker example in the annals of American criminal history of the mantra "live by the sword, die by the sword."

Whitey Bulger got what was coming to him, and Geas and De-

Cologero were moved into disciplinary segregation at Hazelton immediately after the killing. So was Felix Wilson. The prison went into lockdown for the tenth time in 2018. Also moved into solitary with them was Geas's cellmate, Sean McKinnon, a thirty-two-year-old thief and drug dealer from Montpelier, Vermont. McKinnon was doing eight years for stealing a cache of weapons from a gun store in Barre, Vermont, in March 2016. He traded five handguns for bags of heroin in Hartford, Connecticut, and was nabbed with forty-five bags of dope, pry bars, a shotgun, and ammo.

As Whitey Bulger's battered corpse was shuttled off to the coroner's office, the Bureau of Prisons began investigating the killing along with the FBI, the US Attorney's Office in West Virginia, and the BOP's Office of the Inspector General.

"Regarding the recent incidence of violence at FCC Hazelton, the BOP has sent a team of subject-matter experts to the complex to assess operational activities and correctional security practices and measures to determine any relevant facts that may have contributed to the incident," Bureau of Prisons officials said in a statement. "The team will make recommendations to the BOP's senior leadership to assist in mitigating any identified risks."

The questions over the circumstances surrounding Whitey's transfer to Hazelton were only just beginning. Bulger's attorneys, Jay Carney and Hank Brennan, would be leading the charge to find out what happened.

"[Bulger] was sentenced to prison," Carney said, "but as a result of decisions by the Federal Bureau of Prisons, that sentence has been changed to the death penalty."

Even Freddy Geas's attorney, Fred Cohn, questioned the decision to put Whitey in the mob-infested prison with his former client and echoed Carney's sentiments.

"I would wonder about the decision to put Whitey Bulger particularly there, and in general population, which I think was tantamount to a death sentence," Cohn said.

The violence of Whitey's death was the latest illustration of jailhouse justice for a high-profile inmate. It echoed the violent demises of Jeffrey Dahmer, who was beaten to death with a mop wringer by a fellow inmate in a Wisconsin prison in 1994, and the 2003 murder of pedophile Boston priest Father John Geoghan, who was stomped to death in his cell at a Massachusetts maximum security prison by Joseph Druce. The Geoghan murder, like Bulger's, raised questions about jailhouse security as well as accusations of incompetence and corruption by prison officials.

But for the families of Whitey's victims, the killing was the ultimate justice.

"I was happy as hell when that happened," said Tommy Donahue, who was raised without a father after Bulger killed his dad, Michael, in 1982. "I chugged a beer."

For members of law enforcement who had chased Bulger for sixteen years, feelings were mixed.

"I was shocked when he was killed," Neil Sullivan said. "I thought he was going to Springfield, Missouri, the biggest federal medical facility in the country. A lot of old-time mob guys went there to die of old age. But Bulger wasn't allowed to go quietly."

Rich Teahan didn't like the smell of it either. "I'd put a lot of people in WITSEC [Witness Protection]. When you have a high threat prisoner, you have to do a threat assessment on the facility to ensure it is safe. Somebody fucked up. I don't wish that on anyone—not even Whitey Bulger."

Charlie Gianturco strongly disagreed with his fellow FBI agents' assessment. He relished Bulger's bloody end.

"You live by the sword, you die by the sword," he told the authors of this book before quickly correcting himself. "No, scratch that. It makes Whitey sound valiant, like a fucking knight. He was a slug. He was a killer of women. There's nothing valiant or romantic about that. He got the death he deserved, brutal and painful."

39

FALLOUT FROM WHITEY'S KILLING AT Hazelton happened immediately, with ripple effects in Washington, DC, and Boston. The startling news had a karmic element, and raised simmering questions about whether Bulger was set up to be murdered, which ratcheted up the media frenzy to levels not seen since his 2011 capture made global headlines.

Zach Hafer got a call the morning of Bulger's slaying from a Bureau of Prisons official in West Virginia.

"I just want to let you know Bulger is dead," the official said.

"Thank you for letting me know," Hafer responded. The young prosecutor figured that Whitey had finally succumbed to one of the litany of health issues plaguing the elderly gangster.

"Sir, he was murdered," the voice added.

Hafer was stunned.

"It was shocking. I cannot believe that happened," Hafer reflected. "I cannot believe someone got access to him. But it's also amazing that it didn't happen to him sooner, with the number of dangerous people he crossed over the years."

Margaret McCusker said she spoke to her twin sister, Catherine Greig, by phone from prison shortly after news of the murder broke.

"She was very upset, understandably. It was a very difficult conversation," McCusker said. "I couldn't console her really . . . I felt really bad. I felt bad for my sister and for him. He was a good guy . . . I've read about [his crimes] but he wasn't like that with us."

The sensational jailhouse killing thrust Hazelton into the national spotlight and the crime was immediately used by the officers' union as proof that the BOP's policies were failing.

"Am I surprised there's been another murder? No," Hazelton correctional officers' union president Richard Heldreth said the day after the killing. "It wouldn't surprise me if there was another one tomorrow. We are severely understaffed."

As the investigation unfolded, Freddy Geas and "Little Paulie" DeCologero remained in solitary confinement for months without being charged. While Geas has admitted he attacked Bulger, he claims he acted alone; officials have not commented on whether De-Cologero admits or denies his alleged role in the murder. Whitey's cellmate Felix Wilson was released from prison on April 5, 2019, while Sean McKinnon, whose alleged role is unclear, remained at Hazelton.

In June 2019, Freddy Geas wrote the authors a letter from solitary at Hazelton, which was scrawled with a rubber pencil:

I'm in solitary as of now as the BOP . . . likes to play games with guys in my situation. [They] have us sit back here for years while they decide if they are going to charge us or handle it in the prison.

In July 2019, Geas wrote another letter to the authors, saying, "I'm in the process of being transferred along with Paulie [DeCologero]." That transfer hasn't happened as of the publication of this book.

Geas expressed sympathy in the letter toward Francis "Cadillac Frank" Salemme, who was convicted in 2018 of the 1993 murder of Boston nightclub owner Steven DiSarro, based largely on testimony from Stephen Flemmi.

"Shame about Salemme," Geas wrote. "All the stuff the guy went through and then to go bad at the end."

Salemme was put in jail for eight years in 1995 for racketeering, thanks primarily to information provided to the FBI by Bulger and Flemmi. The North End mob boss was released early from prison in 2003 in exchange for testifying against John Connolly in the disgraced federal agent's 2002 racketeering trial. During that trial, and a subsequent congressional hearing, Salemme said Connolly gave him, Flemmi, and Bulger a heads-up that they were about to be arrested on the 1995 RICO case, allowing him and Bulger to go on the run.

While Freddy never met Salemme, the fact that he expressed sympathy toward Salemme's ultimate fate is a clear statement on just which side Freddy was on in the war between Whitey and the mob.

For Taylor Geas, news that her father was a suspect in the gangster's prison murder was another devastating blow. She didn't speak to her father for months after the killing as he sat in solitary. In January 2018, he wrote her a letter asking her to set up a GoFundMe page for him. Taylor was angry, as her dad had never asked her for money. He didn't need money for an appeal because there wasn't even a case, so Taylor couldn't figure out why he wanted a crowd-sourcing page.

She wrote back to him and told him she was furious with the request and wouldn't do it. When he wrote back to her, he still didn't tell her why he wanted the page put up, but said only: *Just start the page kid.*

Taylor didn't do it, but believes he wanted it because he was afraid he would be sent into the catacombs of another facility—likely the federal "Supermax" penitentiary in Florence, Colorado—and disappear forever.

"He doesn't want to be forgotten," she said.

Geas's restrictions on both phone calls and visitors were lifted in summer 2019 but he still remained in solitary, virtually isolated from the outside world. He could make one phone call per month and get one visitor. During a September 2019 call to Taylor, he again said he thought he was getting transferred.

"He was looking forward to [leaving Hazelton]," she said. "He sounded OK, but he definitely sounded beaten down."

Taylor walks a fine line between love for her father and embracing the man she knows, while also staring the cold reality of his criminal career in the face.

"He's not a monster," she contends. "I'd like to believe that there was a much bigger thing going on . . . that there was a lot going on behind the scenes. Like, my dad was given a job and he had to do it."

She added, "If he did do this, then I really don't know anybody. Because I've never seen him like that."

Bulger's killing further exposed problems at Hazelton and the federal prison system and forced change. In the months after the murder, a wave of new officers was hired at Hazelton. The irony was not lost on prison officials.

"There's a saying among the guards now: Whitey Bulger is still helping out law enforcement from the grave," Justin Tarovisky, senior officer specialist at Hazelton, told the authors. "It took Whitey Bulger getting killed to bring light to the BOP and everything they were doing to us. It's really ironic that he was the straw that broke the camel's back here. It was a perfect storm of events that had to happen."

The union, as well as lawmakers and Bulger's family, have questioned the decisions that led to his demise. Tarovisky says Bulger should have been sent to "SHU"—a special housing unit—and that Warden Coakley should have made that call.

"We've had high-profile inmates here before and we've had more competent wardens who've sent them to SHU," he said. "This warden was not an officer. He obviously didn't understand the gravity of the situation. You're getting paid $180,000 to make these decisions. If you don't, look what happens."

In December 2019, Coleman's warden, Charles Lockett, retired in Florida. Three months later, in March 2019, Warden Coakley retired from Misery Mountain.

"It has been my great honor to serve as your warden," Coakley wrote in a letter to staffers. "I have had a full and rewarding career and I cannot think of a better duty station for which to close it out. I want to thank each and every one of you for the hard work and dedication you display every day! Stay safe!"

In April 2019, Charles Lockett went on national television and defended the decisions to move Bulger, claiming he believed the gangster "wanted to die."

"It's a tragedy, but I don't think anyone was deficient in their duty," he said.

Fred Wyshak, the man who chased Whitey for years and led his prosecution in Boston, was also among those looking for some answers.

"Whatever possessed the BOP to transfer him to a facility and put him in general population where there were Boston mobsters also in general population, is just astounding," he said. "The fact that this occurred within 24 hours of his arrival there is also something that is just mind-boggling."

Whitey's family had its own questions and once again demanded money. Members of the Bulger family, represented by Hank Brennan, the lawyer who cochaired Whitey's defense, filed a $200 million wrongful death lawsuit against the federal government for his prison murder. The announcement was made just days after the death of Whitey's sister Jean Holland, who had unsuccessfully fought for his lottery winnings decades before.

"You almost have to go back to the people who made that fateful decision to place him in this place where he was killed," his brother Billy Bulger told the authors. "It's in the bureaucracy, isn't it? Of the system. It's very hard to find where the responsibility lies. But people frequently bring it up to me. It raised a big question in the minds of many people."

Sitting in the kitchen of their modest East Third Street home in South Boston, Billy Bulger and his wife, Mary, were somber as they reflected on Whitey's death. He was a serial killer, an extortionist, a drug dealer, and a crime boss to the world, but to them, he was family. And much like Taylor Geas, they say they didn't know that side of him.

"He got life, but they gave him death," Mary Bulger said.

"It seems in retrospect to have been a clear case of putting him into harm's way," Billy added softly. "I'm sorry that it happened. I'm sorry that it happened . . . I think in that case they were definitely wrong and it was a foreseeable event. But after that I don't know what to say."

A valuable source in Washington, DC, told the authors that members of Congress were pursuing justice not only for the killers, but also those whose decisions put Whitey into the belly of the Hazelton beast.

"Certainly, the fact that there's something bad that happened at Hazelton was not a surprise," the source said. "The combination— short staff and the mismanagement under the previous warden— probably contributed to this. Clearly the fact he was transferred there is problematic. Some of this is attributed to BOP overall and the decisions being made . . . and some of it to local management per the local warden. It all kind of came to a head."

CATHERINE GREIG WAS TRANSFERRED FROM the federal women's prison in Waseca, Minnesota, to a halfway house on bucolic Cape Cod in spring 2019, where she was forced to wear an electronic monitoring bracelet. The decision to trim Greig's sentence was part of the government's First Step act, which is designed to give deserving prisoners an opportunity for shortened sentences and job training.

The sixty-eight-year-old former fugitive was released in September 2019 and moved in with Whitey Bulger's niece—Billy's daughter Mary—in Hingham, Massachusetts. Her probation ends in July 2020.

"I am pleased to see that Catherine is moving on with her life," her attorney, Kevin Reddington, told the authors. "She is an incredibly strong woman whose only 'crime' was falling in love with Jim Bulger. She had sixteen happy years and those memories give her the strength to live day to day, realizing that she was fortunate to have such a relationship. I wish her the best."

Whitey Bulger's body was flown to Massachusetts and a private Catholic funeral mass was held for him on November 8, 2018, at St. Monica's Parish, in the heart of the Southie neighborhood he had controlled and terrorized for decades. Whitey's brothers, Billy and Jackie, attended, along with some of the gangster's nieces and nephews, his attorney Hank Brennan, and Margaret McCusker.

The Reverend James Flavin, a well-known Southie priest, presided.

"Out of respect for the family and those who were hurt, it was a private service just for the immediate family," he said. "The Church is certainly aware of the deep pain that innocent victims of crime and violence live with every day."

After a traditional service, he told the small congregation: "It is finished."

Whitey was laid to rest at a private burial in sprawling St. Joseph Cemetery in the West Roxbury neighborhood of Boston. The atmosphere was serene and a far cry from the makeshift death pits that were dug under the cover of night for his many victims.

He is buried with his parents, James and Jean Bulger.

Whitey's name is not on the family grave.

Epilogue

APRIL 2019

WE HAD NO PLAN. WE had set up no interviews. But we just knew that we had to see the place for ourselves. Escaping the biting cold of Boston, where winter refused to submit to an early spring, we landed in Los Angeles, California, grabbed a rental car, and drove eleven miles from LAX to Santa Monica.

The weather was sunny and breezy, so we rolled down the car windows to let in the warm California air. We couldn't taste the smog as we'd feared, but traffic along Santa Monica Boulevard was heavy and we hit every red light along the way.

It gave us time to talk.

"Whitey and Catherine probably took this same stretch of road," my coauthor, Dave Wedge, said to me.

I nodded from behind the steering wheel.

"They didn't have a car during most of their time, so they probably took a bus or grabbed a cab," I theorized. "Of course they paid in cash."

We continued the drive to Santa Monica and we eventually found our way to Third Street. I parked our rented silver Nissan and we stepped out across the street toward a white three-story apartment building with the Victorian name—Princess Eugenia. There was no sign out front. It had been taken down long ago to discourage gawkers from taking selfies at the notorious address. We walked up the front steps and entered the vestibule, where Dave pressed the button for the building manager.

"I'm Dave Wedge and I'm here with my coauthor, Casey Sherman," he said. "We're writers from Boston and we're working on a new project about Whitey Bulger. Can you talk?"

"No, I don't wanna talk," said the voice on the intercom. "I'm all done talking."

"Well, can you at least let us in the building?" I asked.

There was no reply and the front door remained locked.

Seconds later, a young resident fresh from his morning run entered the vestibule. He asked us if we needed to get inside. We nodded. He then put his key in the door lock, pushed it open, and we followed him inside.

The interior hallway smelled of fresh paint, with yellow candy stripes covering each wall from floor to ceiling. A small portrait of Queen Elizabeth I hung in the lobby in an attempt to project a regal flair to the building. The queen's eyes followed us as we began knocking on door after door with no answer. We then stepped into the small elevator to the third floor and made our way to apartment 303. I rapped my knuckles on the front door, but again—silence.

We continued to gumshoe and spoke with a couple of residents who had heard about the story we were chasing, but weren't living in the building at the time.

"It's crazy that it happened here," one man said as he bounced a toddler on his shoulder.

We returned to the first floor and knocked on the apartment closest to the front entrance. An elderly woman named Catalina Schlank opened her door and welcomed us inside her home.

We stepped through a narrow hallway that was cluttered with a lifetime of memories and we both sat down on the couch.

"I was more friendly with her because she was helpful to me," Schlank offered with a smile. Her accent sounded European, but the old woman told us that she had emigrated from Argentina decades before. "I have lived here for forty-six years. They were very good neighbors."

Schlank then stood up and walked gingerly across her living room and pulled out a bag.

"Would you like to see the letters?" she asked before fanning a dozen or so cards out on her couch.

We examined the first one. It was a holiday card with an illustration of a red covered bridge in a field of snow. It was a beautiful New England scene. We opened the card and read the inscription.

Dear Catalina,
    May the special gifts of health, peace, joy and happiness be yours throughout the year.

                          Merry Christmas,
                        Carol & Charlie Gasko

I handed the card to Catalina and she stared at it for a moment and then sighed.

"You would never believe they were Mafiosi. He had a nice face, a sweet face."

After spending twenty minutes interviewing the elderly neighbor, we left the complex and were headed toward our car when suddenly we were confronted by the building's maintenance man, who was waving his thick arms in our direction.

"Don't worry, we're leaving," I said, trying to quell his concerns.

"You're here to write a story about Bulger, right?" he asked.

"Yup," Dave replied. "We think we got everything we need. We don't mean to bother you."

"Would you like to see where they caught him?" the maintenance man asked excitedly.

We said yes, and he led us into the basement garage to the exact grease-stained spot where Whitey Bulger's more-than-half-century-long criminal odyssey had come to an abrupt and dramatic end in 2011. Dave took some photos with his phone as I chatted with the worker.

"We knocked on apartment 303, which was Bulger's apartment, but got no answer. Does anyone live there?"

The worker explained that the place was being renovated and that it would be available for rent in another month or so.

"Do you have the key?" I asked. "Can you take us inside?"

The maintenance man smiled and showed us to the elevator, where the three of us squeezed inside. Seconds later, we found ourselves back on the third floor and headed toward apartment 303.

Dave and I took deep breaths. To our knowledge, no reporter had ever been inside the apartment where Whitey Bulger and his girlfriend Catherine Greig had lived as America's most wanted fugitive couple for more than a decade under the names Charles and Carol Gasko.

We stepped into the apartment, which had the rugs ripped up and had just been painted bleach white. There was a brick fireplace in the center of the living room and a screened balcony off to the side. The kitchen was quite small and led to two bedrooms in the back, where the couple had slept separately since the day they moved in.

Bulger was long gone, but you could still feel his ominous presence here. We toured the small apartment, going from room to room, trying to imagine what it had been like for both Whitey and Catherine while living in this space. While they must have felt some sense of relief that they were free, unlike Bulger's closest criminal partner and the crooked FBI agent who covered up many of their crimes, there was also likely a sense of dread that accompanied them each day.

It was the fear of getting caught.

We wonder if Whitey Bulger expressed fear moments before his murder in 2018. As he gazed up at the killers, the look in his pale blue eyes must have been similar to that of his victims, including two innocent women, before he snuffed out their lives. Whitey had survived for decades on the streets and years as a fugitive, but in the end, he could not outrun his own fate. In the words of William Shakespeare: "Time is the old justice that examines all offenders."

Acknowledgments

OUR GOAL IN WRITING THIS book was to deconstruct the mythology surrounding James "Whitey" Bulger and to apply
greater focus on the men and women who banded together
over a span of decades to bring this monster to justice.

The memories of his innocent victims such as Roger Wheeler,
Michael Donahue, Debbie Davis, and Deborah Hussey clung to us
during the course of this project.

I'd like to thank my soon-to-be wife, Kristin York, for her un-
wavering love and support.

This book could not have been written if not for the guidance
of our editor, Matt Harper, and our super agent, Peter Steinberg.
Thank you for trusting us to tell this story the right way.

I am indebted to former and current agents of the FBI for your
honesty, transparency, and valuable insight. A special thanks to
Kristen Setera, John Gamel, Charlie Gianturco, Roberta Hastings,
Noreen Gleason, Scott Garriola, Phil Torsney, Tommy MacDon-
ald, Rich Teahan, Mike Carazza, and former director Andrew Mc-
Cabe for your countless hours answering my questions.

Thanks also to my fellow Barnstable High alums, Neil Sullivan
and Rich Eaton, for taking us deep inside your pursuit of Bulger.
You both make our Cape Cod community proud.

I also appreciated the openness and support of Chip Janus and his wife, Dorcas, who provided us with a treasure trove of Bulger's letters and photos that allowed us to re-create Whitey's life in prison.

A special thanks also to Glenn Gautreaux Jr., Catalina Schlank, Dr. Matthias Donelan, and Ken Brady for your time and kindness. I'd like to give a big shout-out as well to Mike McDonough for providing us some writing space at Work.local in Marshfield and story connections, and to Brian Rogers and John DiPietro for assisting with key interviews.

I'd also like to thank our television partners Jenette Kahn and Adam Richman at Double Nickel Entertainment as well as our Hollywood reps Ellen Goldsmith-Vein and Tony Gil at Gotham Group, and our Fort Point Media partners Andrew Braverman and Parker Knight.

On the home front, of course I am always thankful for my incredible daughters, Bella and Mia Sherman. I'm also grateful to my mum, Diane Dodd, my hero in many ways, as well as my brother Todd Forrest Sherman and our uncle Jim Sherman.

I'd also like to thank the Goldsmith-York family, especially Martha Goldsmith for dissecting the Bulger letters for us.

A final thanks to my writing partner, Dave Wedge, for another incredible journey. Until we ride again.

—Casey Sherman

As a young reporter in my second year at the *Boston Herald* in 2000, I was in awe of the cloak-and-dagger exploits of the tabloid's I-Team, especially their work on the Bulger case. When I got the call to go cover the unearthing of Bulger's victims at Florian Hall and Tenean Beach in Dorchester, I was more than happy to take on the grim task. It was a baptism by fire, as I was thrust into the biggest crime story in Boston, and I was proud to take part. I'll always remember standing there in the snow, gazing at the lighted tents erected around the macabre burial ground, as cops worked shovels and sifted through dirt to unearth the remains that ultimately held Bulger accountable once and for all. The pain and suffering he brought into Boston, and especially South Boston, is unfathomable. I've always felt sorry for the many families whose loved ones were killed or otherwise destroyed by Whitey's crimes.

There are so many people who helped us immensely to tell this story, and I'd like to thank, in no particular order: Taylor Geas, Christina Sterling and Elizabeth McCarthy in the US Attorney's Office, Fred Wyshak, Brian Kelly, Zachary Hafer, James Marra, Steve Boozang, retired Massachusetts state troopers Bobby Long and Thomas Murphy, *Springfield Republican* mob reporter Stephanie Barry, Attorney Dan Kelly, author Michael Esslinger, Justin Tarovisky and Joe Rojas of the correctional officers' unions at Hazelton and Coleman, journalist and friend Jonathan Wells, and Rebecca Mesple.

I would also like to thank our editor Matt Harper and the team at HarperCollins, our agent at Foundry Literary & Media Peter Steinberg, our team at Gotham Group, especially Tony Gill and Ellen Goldsmith-Vein, and our TV partners at Double Nickel. Also, thank you to my wife, Jessica, for supporting me and helping me manage my chaotic life while writing this book; my kids, Danielle and Jackson, for making me smile every day; my good friend Kris Meyer for all the inspiring conversation and hikes in the woods to clear my head, my friend and counsel Attorney Keith Davidson, and of course, my dad, Roger, who may have taught me a few things about bookies over the years, but more importantly, instilled in me the importance of reading the news and understanding the world around us.

—*Dave Wedge*

Notes

Prologue

  2 *continues on his way*: Authors interview with Clement Janus, 2019

Chapter 1

  6 *"have him caught and move on"*: "Statements from the Bureau Over the Years," Maria Cramer, *Boston Globe*, June 21, 2011

 10 *"their weak links"*: Authors interview with Noreen Gleason, 2019

 12 *"find Whitey Bulger"*: Authors interview with Tommy MacDonald, 2019

 13 *"You gotta go"*: Ibid.

Chapter 2

 15 *"trying to catch him?"*: Ibid.

 17 *"coming down in a week"*: Steven Flemmi Testimony, *United States v James J. Bulger*, 3rd superseding indictment, 1999

 19 *looked on in shock*: Authors interview with Phil Torsney, 2019

Chapter 3

 21 *"guy that stands out"*: Authors interview with Clement Janus, 2019

 23 *"streaming down Jimmy's face"*: "Whitey Bulger Was His Dad: The Never Told Story of the Gangster and His Little Son," Stephen Kurkjian and Shelley Murphy, *Boston Globe*, April 3, 2012

 23 *beat up on the street*: Authors interview with Jonathan Wells per his interview with Teresa Stanley, 2019

 24 *"our father was an alcoholic"*: Authors interview with Margaret McCusker, 2019

 24 *soon-to-be ex-husband*: *Whitey Bulger*, Kevin Cullen and Shelley Murphy, page 159, W.W. Norton & Company, 2013

 24 *"Everybody knows who he is around here"*: Authors interview with Margaret McCusker, 2019

25 *"Something bad is going on"*: *Whitey Bulger,* Kevin Cullen and Shelley Murphy, page 307, W.W. Norton & Company, 2013

26 *out the door*: Authors interview with Phil Torsney, 2019

26 *"in touch when I can"*: Authors interview with Margaret McCusker, 2019

26 *"Do you even know?"*: Margaret McCusker Federal Grand Jury Interview, February 9, 2012

27 *Whitey said, "See ya."*: *Whitey Bulger,* Kevin Cullen and Shelley Murphy, page 321, W.W. Norton & Company, 2013

28 *from* Casablanca: Brutal, Kevin Weeks and Phyllis Karas, page 244, William Morrow, 2007

Chapter 4

29 *"Tell him to stay free."*: Brutal, Kevin Weeks and Phyllis Karas, page 247, William Morrow, 2007

31 *"You've got the wrong man"*: *Hitman: The Untold Story of John Martorano*, John Martorano and Howie Carr, page 394, Forge Books, 2012

32 *$535.29 in total*: *United States v James J. Bulger*, Exhibit 14

33 *"put some money in it"*: Authors interview with Clement Janus, 2019

34 *get it upon release. Etc.*: Letter from James "Whitey" Bulger to Clement Janus, 2014

34 *Daisy, Oklahoma*: Authors interview with Mike Carazza, 2019

34 *first months on the run*: Authors interview with Charles Gianturco, 2019

Chapter 5

37 *"never wanted anything to do with him"*: Authors interview with John Gamel, 2019

38 *"think about it"*: Ibid.

41 *wearing a mask*: Patick Nee's lawyer denies slayings, Laurel J. Sweet, *Boston Herald,* July 31, 2013

41 *bounced off the ground*: Kevin Weeks Testimony in James Bulger Murder Trial, July 7, 2013

42 *"but he's not stupid"*: Authors interview with John Gamel, 2019

44 *in Gamel's ear*: Ibid.

44 *"charting his own course"*: Authors interview with William Bulger, 2019

45 *"no one else would do it"*: Ibid.

45 *"the way to go"*: Ibid.

46 *AKA "Whitey"*: Letter from James "Whitey" Bulger to Clement Janus, 2014

49 *"Dillinger did"*: *Hammond Times*, November 24, 1955

50 *"all the marbles"*: "Kevin White: A Reporter Remembers," David Boeri, WBUR.org, January 12, 2012

Chapter 6

52 *"keep the winnings"*: "Hitting Pay Dirt in Southie: A Tale of the $14 Million Split," Christopher B. Daly, *Washington Post*, August 7, 1991

52 *Malone said at the time*: "Reputed Mobster Wins Lottery: State Treasurer Says No Way Was It Fixed," Eve Epstein, Associated Press, July 31, 1991

Chapter 7

56 *"he was very smart"*: Authors interview with Charles Gianturco, 2019

58 *"He was someone else"*: Ibid.

Chapter 8

59 *prescription eyeglasses*: *United States v James J. Bulger*, Exhibit 15

59 *"Aunt Helen"*: Authors interview with Glenn Gautreaux Jr., 2019

60 *"can't bear to see it"*: Ibid.

61 *$40,000 on the family*: *Brutal*, Kevin Weeks and Phyllis Karas, page 254, William Morrow, 2007

61 *he was her nephew*: *United States v James J. Bulger*, Exhibit 15

61 *"sure I have enough contacts"*: Ibid.

61 *not a wife*: Authors interview with Michael Carazza, 2019

Chapter 9

69 *"the name Tom Baxter"*: *Brutal*, Kevin Weeks and Phyllis Karas, page 250, William Morrow, 2007

70 *"I'll call you back"*: *Brutal*, Kevin Weeks and Phyllis Karas, page 253, William Morrow, 2007

71 *thought to himself*: Authors interview with Glenn Gautreaux Jr., 2019

71 *"ordered her to cooperate"*: Authors interview with Mike Carazza

72 *"on Day One!"*: Authors interview with Charles Gianturco, 2019

73 *"anything short of murder"*: "Testimony Cites Soft Spot for Bulger," Patricia Nealon, *Boston Globe*, August 11, 1998

Chapter 10

75 *Mark and Carol Shapeton*: *United States v James Bulger*, Exhibit 16

76 *"put it on me"*: *Brutal*, Kevin Weeks and Phyllis Karas, page 254, William Morrow, 2007

76 *blood could be spilled*: *Whitey Bulger*, Kevin Cullen and Shelley Murphy, page 331, W.W. Norton & Company, 2013

76 *"can't take away from me"*: *Brutal*, Kevin Weeks and Phyllis Karas, page 255, William Morrow, 2007

77 *"don't stand out there"*: *Brutal*, Kevin Weeks and Phyllis Karas, page 257, William Morrow, 2007

78 *John Joseph O'Brien*: *The Brothers Bulger*, Howie Carr, page 35, Grand Central Publishing, 2006

78 *before going on his way*: Authors interview with Phil Torsney, 2019
80 *next stop was Venice Beach*: Ibid.

Chapter 11

82 *"a real good spot for him"*: "Ex-Mass State Police Chief Rips FBI Over Bulger," Scott Croteau, *Worcester Telegram & Gazette*, May 5, 2012

83 *national historic site*: "Records: Ex-officer Admitted to Tipping Mobster to Probe," Shelley Murphy, *Boston Globe*, April 20, 2001

83 *"were informants themselves"*: *Brutal*, Kevin Weeks and Phyllis Karas, page 267, William Morrow, 2007

84 *"went against them"*: *Brutal*, Kevin Weeks and Phyllis Karas, page 269, William Morrow, 2007

86 *"ditches will be for you"*: Author Casey Sherman interview with Kevin Weeks at Curry College, 2008

88 *the safecracker's heart*: Kevin Weeks Testimony in James "Whitey" Bulger Trial, 2013

89 *"criminal associates, friends and others"*: "Two Boston Brothers, One Did Good, the Other Didn't," Elizabeth Mehren, *Los Angeles Times*, September 30, 2000

Chapter 12

91 *"people that were poor"*: "Most Wanted Listing Adds to Lore of South Boston Mob Boss," Elizabeth Mehren, *Los Angeles Times*, September 21, 1999

92 *"Not a bad guy"*: "Mike Barnicle: The Best Friend a Gangster Could Have," Steve Kornacki, Salon.com, June 23, 2011

92 *"confidence in him"*: William Bulger, testimony before federal grand jury in Boston, April 5, 2001

93 *Oriental figurine*: "Gangsters as FBI Partners," Edmund H. Mahoney, *Hartford Courant*, October 22,2008

93 *"should not have done"*: "Gangsters as FBI Partners," Edmund H. Mahoney, *Hartford Courant*, October 22, 2008

94 *"friends in the Bureau"*: Authors interview with Charles Gianturco, 2019

Chapter 13

96 *in exchange for the money*: Authors interview with Phil Torsney, 2019

97 *guided tours of Alcatraz*: Authors interview with Michael Esslinger, 2019

97 *"another $50"*: FBI Witness Interview, February 18, 2011

99 *"mellowed out now"*: Massachusetts State Police Interview with Wendy Farnetti, July 18, 2011

99 *"pick it up for you"*: Authors interview with Catalina Schlank, 2019

100 on the balcony!!!: Card from Catherine Greig to Catalina Schlank, obtained by Authors 2019

101 *calls to his family*: Authors interview with Clement Janus, 2019

101 *"always been very kind"*: Authors interview with Margaret McCusker, 2019

Chapter 14

104 *"the Bulger investigation"*: Author interview with former US Attorney Michael Sullivan, May 10, 2019

105 *with their car idling*: "Mob Suspect May Have Been Spotted in O.C.," Meg James, *Los Angeles Times*, April 5, 2000

105 I will murder you: "Was James 'Whitey' Bulger an Active Senior in Orange County Before His Capture?", Matt Coker, *OC Weekly*, June 23, 2011

106 *"was all Irish"*: Authors interview with John Wells, 2019

Chapter 15

109 *"never know who's listening"*: FBI Agent Mike Carazza Testimony in Catherine Greig Hearing, July 11, 2011

109 *"an example of that"*: Authors interview with Mike Carazza, 2019

110 *"brotherly concern"*: "Mobster's Brother Sentenced to Six Months in Federal Prison," Matt Pratt, Associated Press, September 4, 2003

112 *"official in Massachusetts"*: Hearing before the Committee on Government Reform, 108th Congress, June 19, 2003

112 *"honest answer is no!"*: Ibid.

113 *"in the files"*: Authors interview with John Gamel, 2019

114 *"over eight years"*: "Ex-FBI Agent Contradicts UMass President," Fox Butterfield, *New York Times*, June 30, 2003

114 *Romney told the press*: "Romney Turns Up Pressure to Oust Bulger," Jennifer Peter, Associated Press, June 21, 2003

Chapter 16

115 *"go check it out"*: Authors interview with Richard Eaton, 2019

116 *"very real to me"*: Ibid.

119 *"when you wouldn't have"*: Authors interview with Danny Simmons, 2019

119 *"would have believed it"*: Authors interview with unnamed FBI agent, 2019

Chapter 17

121 *"diminished over time"*: "Whitey Bounty Hits $2M," Laurel Sweet, *Boston Herald*, September 4, 2008

122 *trysts with underage girls*: "Eyewitness to Evil; Gang videotaped sex acts in secret room at gym," *Boston Herald*, April 9, 2001

122 *"so many levels"*: Authors interview with Noreen Gleason, 2019

122 *"being a pedophile"*: Ibid.

122 *"come after me"*: Ibid.

124 *"I loved the work"*: Authors interview with Phil Torsney, 2019

125 *"wasn't the case at all"*: Ibid.

125 *"tracking phone calls"*: Ibid.

126 *"lied to me"*: Ibid.

Chapter 18

129 *"retired studio executive"*: Authors interview with Joe Hipp, 2019

130 *"it was alright"*: Ibid.

131 *"all the nightmares"*: Authors interview with Phil Torsney, 2019

Chapter 19

133 *"from the East Coast"*: Birgitta Farinelli Grand Jury Testimony, August 4, 2011

134 *"he has emphysema"*: Ibid.

135 *get back inside*: Federal Grand Jury Interview with Birgitta Farinelli, August 4, 2011

135 *"John R." and "Mary R."*: Catherine E. Greig's Statement of Facts, March 5, 2012

135 *"I'll tough it out"*: Birgitta Farinelli Grand Jury Testimony, August 4, 2011

135 *"I'm scared of needles"*: FBI interview of Dr. Reza Ray Ehsan, July 19, 2011

135 "Love always, Cxxxxoooo": Catherine E. Greig Government Exhibit, 2011

137 *to get work*: Ibid.

138 *never drove again*: Authors interview with Phil Torsney, 2019

138 *"thought that was strange"*: FBI interview with Joshua Bond, July 12, 2011

139 *"treated me like a son"*: Ibid.

139 *"pair of binoculars"*: FBI interview with Joshua Bond, July 12, 2011

Chapter 20

141 *"close the case"*: Authors interview with Tommy MacDonald, 2019

142 *"find James Bulger"*: Ibid.

143 *"circle of his life"*: Authors interview with Roberta Hastings, 2019

147 *in front of the home*: "Bulger Linked to '70's Antibusing Attacks," Shelley Murphy, *Boston Globe*, April 22, 2001

147 *"not gonna break through"*: Authors interview with Rich Teahan, 2019

Chapter 21

149 *"ridiculous to even think about"*: Authors interview with Noreen Gleason, 2019

150 *"soul a little bit"*: Authors interview with Rich Teahan, 2019

150 *"choking her to death"*: Authors interview with Tommy MacDonald, 2019

152 *"meet with you in person"*: Authors interview with Dr. Matthias Donelan, 2019

152 *"eyelid patients"*: Ibid.

153 *"in fifteen minutes"*: Authors interview with Tommy MacDonald, 2019

154 *"chasing out of Boston"*: Authors interview with Phil Torsney, 2019

Chapter 22

155 *"influence over this region"*: Authors interview with Noreen Gleason, 2019

156 *"followed their lead"*: Authors interview with Neil Sullivan, 2019

157 *"said yes immediately"*: Ibid.

159 *"nothing to show for it"*: Authors interview with Richard Teahan, 2019

Chapter 23

161 *"I'll drink to that!"*: "Santa Monica Reacts to bin Laden's Death," Jason Islas, *The Lookout News*, May 3, 2011

162 *pistol at his bedside*: Inventory of Evidence in Bulger–Greig case, FBI, November 21, 2011

165 *"convinced we had them"*: Authors interview with Neil Sullivan, 2019

166 *"got to work"*: Authors interview with Scott Garriola, 2019

167 *"200 percent sure it's them!"*: Ibid.

168 *"100 percent it's them"*: Joshua Bond Federal Grand Jury Interview, July 28, 2011

172 bullet in the back: Letter from James J. Bulger to author Michael Esslinger, March 22, 2012

175 *"highly significant event"*: Authors interview with Andrew McCabe, 2019

Chapter 24

177 *"I'm James J. Bulger"*: Authors interview with Scott Garriola, 2019

177 *"in a long time"*: Authors interview with Phil Torsney, 2019

178 *"a helluva fight"*: Authors interview with Scott Garriola, 2019

179 *"be his style"*: Authors interview with Neil Sullivan, 2019

179 *"for molesting a child"*: Authors interview with Phil Torsney, 2019

180 *"they're actually consenting"*: Ibid.

181 *"doesn't deserve any of this"*: Ibid.

181 *"would I tell you?"*: Authors interview with Rich Teahan, 2019

182 *"admit his involvement"*: Authors interview with Neil Sullivan, 2019

Chapter 25

185 *"[for Capone] wouldn't you?"*: "Bulger and Girlfriend Appear in Boston Federal Court," WBUR Radio, June 24, 2011

185 *"it doesn't surprise me"*: "Crime Lord Returns to Boston to Face Raft of Charges," Abby Goodnough, *New York Times*, June 24, 2011

186 *"on Santa Monica Boulevard"*: Ibid.

188 *"your clothes anyway!"*: Authors interview with Ken Brady, 2019

189 "best place we ever visited": Authors interview with Glenn Gautreux Jr., 2019

190 *"this gentleman [Bulger]"*: "Whitey Bulger's Girlfriend Offers Glimpse of Her Defense," Associated Press, July 14, 2011

190 *"defiant, and loyal in court"*: Authors interview with Mike Carazza, 2019

192 *"she has no regrets"*: "Catherine Greig Gets Eight Years for Helping Whitey Bulger," Denise Lavoie, Associated Press, June 12, 2012

Chapter 26

193 *"sick to my stomach"*: "Boston mob boss trial underway," ABC News, June 13, 2013

193 *"who was killed"*: "LOL doesn't surprise Donahue," John Zaremba, *Boston Herald*, June 15, 2013

194 *Judge Denise Casper's courtroom*: Authors interview with Zachary Hafer, August 5, 2019

196 *"Bulger, Flemmi, Salemme"*: Authors interview with Fred Wyshak, June 12, 2019

Chapter 27

201 *"that agreement anywhere"*: Authors interview with Zach Hafer, 2019

202 *"backed it up with anything"*: Ibid.

203 *"a hands-on killer"*: *USA v. James J. Bulger*, trial transcripts, June 12, 2013

208 *"Take anything you want"*: Ibid.

Chapter 28

212 *"eventually looked away"*: Authors interview with Robert Long, June 18, 2019

214 *dead on arrival*: Ibid.

Chapter 29

215 *"would have been compromised probably"*: *USA v. James J. Bulger*, trial transcripts, June 14, 2013

216 *"a lot of beatings"*: Ibid.

217 *"put down as law"*: Ibid.

219 *"think it was, Jay?"*: Ibid.

219 *"from expressing love"*: "With sobs, Bulger and Greig Traded Jailhouse Love Letters," J.M. Lawrence, *Boston Globe*, January 10, 2014

221 *"Bulger gang really was"*: Author interview with Brian Kelly, October 3, 2019

Chapter 30

225 *"surface as the leader"*: *USA v. Bulger* trial transcripts, June 17, 2013

226 *"reason I am here today"*: *USA v. Bulger* trial transcripts, June 19, 2013

226 *"wanted to get killed"*: *USA v. Bulger* trial transcripts, June 20, 2013

227 *"helpful to me"*: *USA v. Bulger* trial transcripts, June 17, 2013

228 *"That sort of thing"*: Authors interview with Billy Bulger, June 24, 2019

228 *"beside myself with it"*: Ibid.

229 *"That's what he was"*: Ibid.

230 *"wanted to take him out"*: Ibid.

231 *"It has to be done"*: Ibid.

232 *"in Canada robbing banks"*: *USA v. Bulger* trial transcripts, June 24, 2013

232 *"I wanted to shoot him"*: *USA v. Bulger* trial transcripts, June 19, 2013

Chapter 31

237   *"If looks could kill"*: Authors interview with James Marra, September 5, 2019

237   *"I'm not a fucking informant"*: "'Whitey' Bulger says he's not a snitch, but FBI file tells a different story," CNN, June 25, 2013

237   *"that ridiculous contention"*: USA v. Bulger trial transcripts, June 21, 2013

237   *Bulger had for decades*: Ibid.

238   *"relationship with the FBI"*: USA v. Bulger trial transcripts, June 24, 2013

238   *October 17, 1984, report*: USA v. Bulger trial transcripts, June 21, 2013

239   *to implicate Jackie Salemme*: Ibid.

240   *"and never charge him"*: Ibid.

240   *"didn't mean much legally"*: Author interview with Zach Hafer, August 5, 2019

241   *"is simply absurd"*: USA v. Bulger trial transcripts, June 21, 2013

241   *"I felt awful"*: "'You're a F—cking Liar': Whitey Bulger and the FBI's Sordid History," The Daily Beast, July 1, 2013

241   *"Yes," Bulger responded*: Ibid.

242   *"glad the marshals were there"*: Author interview with Brian Kelly, October 3, 2019

242   *"higher authorities in the FBI"*: Department of Justice, US Attorney's Office, District of Boston press release, August 5, 2016

Chapter 32

244   *"didn't try to do nothing"*: US v. Bulger trial transcript, July 2, 2013

245   *"beat somebody up"*: US v. Bulger trial transcripts, July 8, 2013

247   *"this court for you"*: Ibid.

Chapter 33

250   *"really friendly with Connolly"*: US v. Bulger trial transcript, July 18, 2013

250   *Flemmi shot back*: "'Rifleman' gets a rise out of former partner in crime," Boston Herald, July 19, 2013

250   *"wasn't in love with her"*: US v. Bulger trial transcript July 19, 2013

251   *"regretted it all my life"*: US v. Bulger trial transcript, July 21, 2013

251   *"he took to Mexico"*: "Henchman accuses Boston mob boss 'Whitey' Bulger of pedophilia," Reuters, July 23, 2013

252   *"may hit someone"*: US v. Bulger trial transcript, July 26, 2013

252   *"a client-run defense"*: "Bulger team tries to build its defense in trial's final days," Boston Globe, August 1, 2013

252   *"and the excitement"*: Authors interview with Pat Nee, July 15, 2019

253   *Southie gangster escaped*: Ibid.

253   *"they missed me"*: Ibid.

254   *"countless violent crimes"*: "Pat Nee Testimony a Point of Contention in Bulger Trial," WGBH, July 25, 2013

255   *"comes to your house?"*: "Crime-steeped witnesses raised jurors' ire, suspicions," Boston Globe, August 14, 2013

255 *"he didn't testify"*: Authors interview with Fred Wyshak, June 12, 2019

255 *"part of the story"*: Authors interview with Zach Hafer, August 5, 2019

256 *"I'm disappointed"*: "High Life Brought Low: Jury Finds Whitey Bulger Guilty in Killings, Racketeering," Deborah Feherick, CNN, July 13, 2013

257 *"his horrific crimes"*: "'Whitey' Bulger found guilty of racketeering, murders," *Boston Globe*, August 13, 2013

257 *"is repugnant"*: Authors interview with Zach Hafer, June 12, 2019

257 *"make this case happen"*: Authors interview with Fred Wyshak, June 12, 2009

257 *"being set free"*: "'Whitey' Bulger found guilty of racketeering, murders," *Boston Globe*, August 13, 2013

258 *"searching for that closure"*: "Range of emotions among victims' families," *Boston Globe*, August 13, 2013

258 *"gladly do it again"*: Author interview with Brian Kelly, October 3, 2019

264 *"There was a big art heist"*: Authors interview with Chip Janus, 2019

264 *"We pulled in every crook"*: Author Casey Sherman interview with Kevin Weeks at Curry College, 2008

264 *"He's a good person"*: Authors interview with Clement Janus, 2019

268 *"It's no surprise"*: "Even in Prison, Whitey Bulger Is Pushing Boundaries," Shelley Murphy, *Boston Globe*, February 7, 2015

Chapter 35

270 "sooner or later": Letter obtained by authors from Bulger to Janus, December 2, 2014

271 *"other respectable crime"*: "My Memories of Being in Prison with Whitey Bulger," Nate A. Lindell, The Marshall Project, March 17, 2016

271 *"went back to sleep"*: Ibid.

272 *"best days of his life"*: Authors interview with Michael Essinger, 2019

272 next and final stage: Letter obtained by authors from Bulger to Janus, July 25, 2015

273 They (prosecutors) refused: Letter obtained by authors from Bulger to Janus (undated)

273 *"better than anybody else"*: "Mark Wahlberg: Whitey Wants Me to Visit," WAAF FM Radio, January 2012

274 Jim Bulger 1428 AZ: Letter obtained by authors from Bulger to Janus, January 12, 2017

274 *"answer to this charge"*: Internal Disciplinary Data, James J. Bulger, Coleman II, October 31, 2018

274 "Why? Revenge?": Letter obtained by authors from Bulger to Janus (undated)

275 *"my word is good!"*: "After Whitey Bulger Killing, Warden of 'Misery Mountain' Faces Removal," Danielle Ivory, *New York Times*, November 30, 2018

276 office in Washington, DC: Internal Disciplinary Data, James J. Bulger, Coleman II, October 31, 2018

277　*"facilities Bulger required"*: Authors interview with Joe Rojas, 2019

277　*"lot of mob guys there"*: Ibid.

Chapter 36

280　*never heard from her again*: Letter to authors from Taylor Geas, June 7, 2019

281　*most of their adult lives*: "Murder plots, truck heists and brawls: The backstory of Freddy Geas, suspect in 'Whitey' Bulger death," Masslive.com, November 3, 2018

283　*"to ever happen to them"*: Ibid.

285　*"all covered in blood"*: Ibid.

285　*"when I was a kid"*: Author interview with Taylor Geas, September 10, 2019

285　*"their lives in jail"*: "Audacious homecoming," *The Republican* (Springfield, Mass.), May 8, 2017

286　*"in the street or in jail"*: Author interview with Frederick Cohn, June 12, 2019

287　*"first pair of soccer cleats"*: "Freddy Geas case viewed with a daughter's eye: Reader viewpoint," *The Republican* (Springfield, Mass.), Jan. 21, 2016

288　*club in South Boston*: "This man may have waited 38 years for his revenge on Whitey Bulger," *New York Post*, November 1, 2018

288　*friends at Hazelton*: "The mystery deepens: Why was Bulger left in harm's way?", *Boston Globe*, November 1, 2018

289　*"last of the Mohicans"*: Ibid.

289　JB (James Bulger): "Whitey Bulger Won't Help Man Claiming Wrongful Conviction," Shelley Murphy, *Boston Globe*, October 16, 2016

Chapter 37

292　*from the previous year*: "'Misery Mountain': The jail where 'Whitey' Bulger was slain has history of murder and violence," *Washington Examiner*, October 30, 2018

292　*"with no backup"*: "Exclusive: As federal prisons run low on guards, nurses and cooks are filling in," *USA Today*, February 13, 2018

292　*from 2015 through 2018*: "Federal prison officials get bonuses as staffing shortages, management problems persist," *USA Today*, July 16, 2019

293　*"from hardened criminals"*: McKinley Fights for Corrections Employees; Bipartisan Effort to Stop Bureau of Prisons Staffing Cuts, Rep. David McKinley (R-WV) News Release, February 22, 2018

293　*two shank-wielding inmates*: "Lorton Slaying Catches Up With Inmate," *Washington Post*, October 21, 2000; "James 'Whitey' Bulger's killing is just the latest in a string of troubling violence for W.Va. prison," *Boston Globe*, October 30, 2018

293　*for only two weeks*: "Officials: Inmate killed in fight at federal prison," Associated Press, September 19, 2018; "Barber Slain in Apparent Robbery," *Washington Post*, June 16, 2007

294 *"working at this complex"*: Letter from AFGE Local 420 executive vice-president Justin Tarovisky to members of Congress, October 10, 2018

295 *"more full-time correctional officers"*: Congressional letter to Attorney General Jeff Sessions, October 25, 2018

295 *"not to lose hope"*: Author interview with Taylor Geas, September 10, 2019

295 *"love of his life for sure"*: Author interview with Michael Esslinger, May 20, 2019

Chapter 38

297 *"must have been drooling"*: Author interview with Joe Rojas, executive vice-president of the American Federation of Government Employees Local 506 at USP Coleman, September 25, 2019

298 *Whitey and Flemmi in the 1980s*: US v. Paul A. DeCologero, John P. DeCologero, Jr., Paul J. DeCologero and Joseph F. Pavone; United States Court of Appeals, First Circuit decision, June 23, 2008

298 *"irked the mob leaders"*: Ibid.

298 *a contract on "Big Paulie"*: "Bulger suspect's brother says families had bad blood," *Boston Globe*, November 3, 2018

298 *weren't found for ten years*: US v. Paul A. DeCologero, John P. DeCologero, Jr., Paul J. DeCologero and Joseph F. Pavone; United States Court of Appeals, First Circuit decision, June 23, 2008

299 *a .22-caliber handgun*: New Hampshire Man Pleads Guilty to Gun Charge, Department of Justice press release, November 28, 2016

299 *"hard to prevent that"*: Author interview with Justin Tarovisky, executive vice-president of the American Federation of Government Employees Local 420 at USP Hazelton, August 25, 2019

301 *"Died in his Sleep kind"*: "In letters from prison, Bulger wished for 'peaceful death,'" *Boston Globe*, November 29, 2018

301 *"assault by other(s)"*: James J. Bulger death certificate

302 *a shotgun, and ammo*: "Montpelier man among prisoners isolated over Whitey Bulger killing," *VT Digger*, November 20, 2018

302 *"changed to the death penalty"*: "'Whitey' Bulger, One of the Most Feared Men in Boston's History, Has Been Killed in Prison," WBUR, October 30, 2018

302 *"tantamount to a death sentence"*: Author interview with Attorney Fred Cohn, 2019

303 *"I chugged a beer"*: Authors interview with Tommy Donahue, 2019

303 *"to go quietly"*: Authors interview with Neil Sullivan, 2019

303 *"not even Whitey Bulger"*: Authors interview with Rich Teahan, 2019

303 *"brutal and painful"*: Authors interview with Charlie Gianturco, 2019

Chapter 39

305 *"crossed over the years"*: Authors interview with Zachary Hafer, 2019

305 *"wasn't like that with us"*: Authors interview with Margaret McCusker, 2019

306 *"severely understaffed"*: "Mafia hit man is suspected in former mob boss 'Whitey' Bulger's beating death in prison," *Los Angeles Times*, October 31, 2018

306 *remained at Hazelton*: Federal Bureau of Prisons inmate locator

306 handle it in the prison: Letter to authors from Freddy Geas, 2019

307 *"doesn't want to be forgotten"*: Authors interview with Taylor Geas, 2019

308 *"sounded beaten down"*: Ibid.

308 *"had to happen"*: Author interview with Justin Tarovisky, executive vice-president of the American Federation of Government Employees Local 420 at USP Hazelton, August 25, 2019

309 *"Stay safe!"*: "Hazelton federal prison warden to retire March 31," *MetroNews of West Virginia*, February 6, 2019

309 *"deficient in their duty"*: "Whitey Bulger's prison warden: 'I think he wanted to die,'" NBC News, April 29, 2019

309 *"just mind-boggling"*: Authors interview with Fred Wyshak, 2019

309 *"minds of many people"*: Authors interview with Billy Bulger, 2019

310 *"they gave him death"*: Authors interview with Mary Bulger, 2019

311 *"wish her the best"*: Author interview with Kevin Reddington, October 2019

311 *"It is finished"*: "At Whitey Bulger's funeral, a coda: 'it's finished,'" *Boston Globe*, November 8, 2018

Epilogue
315 Carol & Charlie Gasko: New Year Card from Catherine Greig to Catalina Schlank obtained by Authors 2019

References

Author Interviews
William Bulger, former Massachusetts Senate president
Andrew McCabe, former FBI director
Noreen Gleason, former FBI ASAC, Boston Office
Charlie Gianturco, former FBI agent, Boston Office
John Gamel, former FBI supervisor, Boston Office
Rich Teahan, former FBI supervisor, Boston Office
Roberta Hastings, former FBI analyst, Boston Office
Tommy MacDonald, FBI agent, Boston & New York Office
Phil Torsney, FBI agent, Boston & Cleveland Office
Mike Carazza, FBI agent, Boston Office
Scott Garriola, FBI agent, Los Angeles Office
Neil Sullivan, US Marshals Service
Richard Eaton, former detective, San Diego Sheriff's Office
Danny Simmons, DEA Agent
Robert Long, former Massachusetts State Police detective
Brian Kelly, United States Attorneys Office
Zach Hafer, United States Attorneys Office
Fred Wyshak, United States Attorneys Office
James Marra, United States Department of Justice investigator
Mary Bulger, wife of William Bulger
Catalina Schlank, Bulger neighbor
Joe Hipp, Bulger neighbor
Glenn Gautreaux Jr., Bulger neighbor
Margaret McCusker, Grieg's sister
Taylor Geas, Freddy Geas's daughter
Frederick Cohn, Freddy Geas's attorney
Ken Brady, Plymouth County correctional officer
Pat Nee, Bulger associate
Kevin Weeks, Bulger associate

Clement "Chip" Janus, Bulger friend
Michael Esslinger, Bulger friend and author
John Wells, journalist
Dr. Matthias Donelan, plastic surgeon
Joe Rojas, president, USP Coleman Correctional Officers Union
Justin Tarovisky, Senior Officer Special at USP Hazelton
Tommy Donahue, Bulger victim's son
Michael Sullivan, former United States attorney
Thomas Murphy, retired Massachusetts State Police detective

Correspondence
Fotios "Freddy" Geas

Documents and Books
Whitey Bulger Letters to Clement "Chip" Janus (2014–2018)
New Year Card from Catherine Greig to Catalina Schlank
Steven Flemmi Testimony, *United States v James J. Bulger*, 3rd superseding indict-
    ment, 1999
United States v James J. Bulger, Exhibit 14
United States v James J. Bulger, Exhibit 15
United States v James J. Bulger, Exhibit 16
United States v James J. Bulger, trial transcripts, 2013
Catherine E. Greig's Statement of Facts, March 5, 2012
Catherine E. Greig Government Exhibit, 2011
Hearing before the Committee on Government Reform, 108th Congress, June 19,
    2003
Massachusetts State Police interview with Wendy Farnetti, July 18, 2011
Inventory of Evidence in Bulger-Greig case, FBI, November 21, 2011
FBI interview with Joshua Bond, July 12, 2011
William Bulger, testimony before federal grand jury in Boston, April 5, 2001
Internal Disciplinary Data, James J. Bulger, Coleman II USP, October 2018
Letter from AFGE Local 420 executive vice president Justin Tarovisky to mem-
    bers of Congress, October 10, 2018
Congressional letter to Attorney General Jeff Sessions, October 25, 2018
Whitey Bulger, Kevin Cullen and Shelley Murphy, W.W. Norton & Company,
    2013
Brutal, Kevin Weeks and Phyllis Karas, William Morrow, 2007
Hitman: The Untold Story of John Martorano, John Martorano and Howie Carr,
    Forge Books, 2012

About the Authors

Casey Sherman is a multiple *New York Times* bestselling author of *The Finest Hours* (now a major motion picture), *12: The Inside Story of Tom Brady's Fight for Redemption*, and eight other books including *Above & Beyond, Boston Strong*, cowritten by Dave Wedge and the inspiration for the feature film *Patriots Day*; *The Ice Bucket Challenge*, also coauthored by Wedge and now in development for a major motion picture; and *Animal: The Rise and Fall of the Mob's Most Feared Assassin* (now in development for a major motion picture).

Sherman is also an award-winning journalist and recipient of the Edward R. Murrow award for Journalistic Excellence, the prestigious Truth & Justice Award given by the Cold Case Research Institute, and has been nominated for an EMMY award. He is also a contributing writer for *Time, The Washington Post, Esquire, Huffington Post*, and *Boston* magazine. Sherman is a featured weekly columnist for the *Boston Herald* and has appeared on more than one hundred television programs including *The Today Show, Unsolved Mysteries, ABC World News Tonight, The CBS Evening News*, and *The View*, and on the networks CNN, FOX News, C-SPAN, The History Channel, The Travel Channel, and Discovery. He is the founding partner of Fort Point Media.

He is also a sought-after public speaker and is represented by APB Speakers Bureau. Sherman can be reached on Facebook and on Twitter at *caseysherman123*.

He is a proud graduate of Barnstable High School, Fryeburg
Academy, and Boston University. He lives in Massachusetts.

Dave Wedge is a *New York Times* bestselling author and writer
based in Boston. He has cowritten three books with acclaimed
author Casey Sherman, including *Boston Strong: A City's Triumph
Over Tragedy,* a nonfiction drama about the 2013 Boston Marathon
Bombings adapted for the 2017 movie *Patriots Day*; *The Ice Bucket
Challenge: Pete Frates and the Fight Against ALS*, which was released
in October 2017 and is in development as a feature film; and *12:
The Inside Story of Tom Brady's Fight for Redemption*, which was released in 2018 and was on the *New York Times* bestseller list for eight
weeks. He cofounded Fort Point Media, a content development and
production company, with Sherman.

Dave has also written for *VICE, Esquire, Newsweek*, and *Boston*
magazine and was an award-winning investigative journalist for
the *Boston Herald* for fourteen years. He has also been a radio host
on WRKO in Boston and has appeared on CNN, MSNBC, FOX
News Channel, *Good Morning America,* CBC (Canada), CNBC, E!
Entertainment Network, CBS, and many other local and national
networks.

Follow him on Twitter @DaveWedge and Instagram @davidm
wedge